SOPORIFIC
SERMONS

SOPORIFIC SERMONS

James R. Shott

Copyright © 2003 by James R. Shott.

ISBN :		Softcover		1-4010-9094-X

All rights reserved. No part of this book may be reproduced or transmitted in any form or by any means, electronic or mechanical, including photocopying, recording, or by any information storage and retrieval system, without permission in writing from the copyright owner.

This book was printed in the United States of America.

To order additional copies of this book, contact:
Xlibris Corporation
1-888-795-4274
www.Xlibris.com
Orders@Xlibris.com
17106

CONTENTS

FOREWORD 13

FIRSTLY: SEASONAL SERMONS
These sermons are for Christmas, Thanksgiving, Easter...whatever.

BAH! HUMBUG! AND OTHER JOYFUL CHRISTMAS
    EXPRESSIONS 17
    This is a fun sermon. Enjoy!

BAH! HUMBUG! TO NEW YEAR'S EVE, TOO 25
    On the brevity of life

BAH! HUMBUG! TO BIRTHDAYS, TOO 32
    How to survive them

THE PURSUIT OF HAPPINESS 37
    Independence Day

LETTERS TO OUR PILGRIM FATHERS 44
    Thanksgiving

THE BEAUTIFUL—AND TRAGIC—
    STORY OF A MOTHER 54
    Mother's Day

HEAVEN AND HELL—AND CHRISTMAS 60
    Christmas

A SIGN UNTO YOU 66
    Christmas

DO YOU BELIEVE IN THE VIRGIN BIRTH?......................72
   Christmas...well, sort of.

WHEN THEY BEGIN THE BEGATS 86
   Christmas again. Ho! Hum!

LOOKING FORWARD TO EASTER 92
   Ash Wednesday or First Sunday in Lent

JESUS IS UNIQUE...98
   Easter, preferably Easter Sunrise

DO YOU BELIEVE IN THE RESURRECTION?............. 104
   Easter

THE EMMAUS STRANGER................................. 109
   Still Easter...perhaps the Sunday after

SECONDLY: FICTIONAL SERMONS
   These sermons have the flavor and odor of fiction. Well, what did you expect? The author is A fiction writer.

A VISIT TO FIRST CENTURY JERUSALEM 116
   A look at the first Communion in the Upper Room

THE SHEPHERD 123
   The parable of the Lost Sheep, fictionalized

WHO THE DEVIL IS THE DEVIL? 129
   Let Ol' Scratch speak for himself

THE VIEW FROM THE TOWER........................ 137
   Habakkuk on a bird's eye view of history

LEAH, THE GIRL WITH LOVELY EYES 143
   Jacob's wife—the ugly one

MARY'S HARD QUESTION 149
What were Jesus' mother's thoughts at the crucifixion?

THIRDLY: THEOLOGICAL SERMONS
These sermons are taken from the Gospel According to Saint James the Shott.

EVERYTHING YOU ALWAYS WANTED
  TO KNOW ABOUT SIN 157
Although classed as a theological sermon, this is not profound and stuffy

MY FAVORITE DOCTRINE 165
The Grace of God…but not that old theological stuffiness

BEHOLD, THE FACE OF GOD! 173
The Doctrine of the Trinity…and it's not stuffy theology either

HEAVEN (EVERYONE IS JUST DYING TO
  FIND OUT WHAT IT'S LIKE) 179
You don't know what heaven is like? Well, neither do I. But that doesn't stop me telling you.

GOD'S NAME 186
*Do you know who **Yahweh** is? Neither do I, but I'll tell you anyway.*

GOD IS OUR FATHER 192
Just a simple, pretty sermon with a good illustration

THE JOY OF IGNORANCE:
  DO WE HAVE TO KNOW EVERYTHING? 197
The title says it all. With a little irony.

INFINITY 204
Once again, I'll explain to you something I don't understand

THE FLEECE TEST 210
   Finding a way to prove God really is with us.

FOURTHLY: MISCELLANEOUS SERMONS
   "Miscellaneous" covers a lot of territory. I don't know what else to call it, because it covers all the sermons left over.

THE OTHER MARY 216
   Of the seven Mary's in the Bible, this one is lost in the crowd.

WHO REALLY IS MY NEIGHBOR? 223
   The Parable of the Good Samaritan updated.

TOLERATING INTOLERANCE 229
   Preached at a Unitarian Church

THE GAMALIEL PRINCIPLE 236
   How to handle troublesome heretics.

THE GOSPEL ACCORDING TO
SAINT VINCENT OF LOMBARDI 242
   On winning and losing.

THE MEANING IS MORE IMPORTANT THAN
THE METHOD 249
   Communion and Baptism, with a funny story from my personal experience.

CONFESSION: I STOLE A GIDEON BIBLE 255
   A sort-of book review of the Bible.

HOW GOD SPEAKS 262
   Text: In many and various ways....

ISAAC'S NAME 270
   In Hebrew: "He laughed."

THE WORLD'S GREATEST PRAYER 276
   Offered by Jesus in Gethsemane.

DOWN TO EARTH PRAYERS 283
   Examples of natural, not pietistic, prayers.

THE HARP ON THE WILLOW TREE 289
   Singing the Lord's song in a foreign land.

KING DAVID'S SWEETEST SONG 296
   Was the familiar Shepherd Psalm written when David was young or old?

GRASSHOPPER BURDENS 301
   From the Book of Ecclesiastes

LASTLY—THAT NATIONAL PRIZE WINNER

OLD HUNDREDTH 309
   Psalm 100—the way it ought to be sung.

Dedication

1. To ministers—poor working stiffs—who have to create at least one new sermon every week. Feel free to use any or all of the material in this book. That's not plagiarism or any other form of larceny. It is rather my gift to you.

2. To anyone who has a problem falling asleep at night. These sermons are soporific. Take one and call me in the morning.

FOREWORD

I have always wanted to be a ghostwriter and write sermons for some personality preacher. I love the preparation, but not the delivery. That's why I took early retirement to change my profession (or ministry, if you prefer) from the pastoral ministry to a writer.

During my thirty years in the parish ministry, I estimate that I have preached more than 15,000 sermons. That's a lot of suffering to inflict on my congregations. During that time I served five parishes, and you can bet your social security that I preached the same sermons at every one of them.

Each time, however, I revised, redacted and rewrote them, refining and polishing each one. Maybe the suffering inflicted on my last congregation was not as great as on my first.

I have chosen for this book what I consider my 45 best sermons. My judgment for a good sermon is the audience reaction. If they sleepily shook my hand at the door and muttered, "Enjoyed your sermon," that told me something. If they were bright-eyed and enthusiastic in their comments, then I knew I had pressed a few buttons.

One of my sermons won a national contest. "Old Hundredth" was judged best in the expository category and was included in the book entitled *Best Sermons* (Harper & Rowe, 1988). I don't know why. Maybe the judges (professors and stuffy theologians, most likely) thought it was homiletically correct. I included it in this book, even though I don't think it belongs in my top forty-five sermons.

BAH! HUMBUG! AND OTHER JOYOUS CHRISTMAS EXPRESSIONS

Scripture: Luke 2:8-20 . . . The most familiar part of the Nativity story.

The Preacher's Notes:

Christmas is a joyous time, and this sermon takes a fun look at the history of some of our Christmas traditions. The sermon eventually gets around to the difference between happiness and joy at Christmas time.

BAH! HUMBUG! AND OTHER JOYFUL CHRISTMAS EXPRESSIONS

"Merry Christmas!" is something we will be hearing a lot during the next few weeks. It's a shade better than "Have a good day!"—but not much. To both of these, the proper response is, "Bah! Humbug!"

In spite of this, we are in a season of the year that everybody seems to appreciate, because there is a lot of bliss, cheer, contentment, delight, ecstasy, enchantment, gaity, happiness, joy, jubilation, mirth, merriment, pleasure and rapture going around, according to Roget's *Thesaurus*. And the reason? It's Christmas!

The writers of the Bible did not have the benefit of Roget's *Thesaurus* when they wrote their books. They seemed to be stuck on one word, which they used over and over again. The Bible's three-letter word for merriment is "Joy." You will find this word or some form of it in just about every book of the Bible.

This is particularly true in the Nativity story. First you have a quiet peaceful picture: shepherds guarding their flocks in the night near Bethlehem. The serenity of this scene was suddenly shattered by a joyful explosion as an angel appeared and shouted, *"Behold! I bring you tidings of great joy which shall be to all the people; for to you is born this day in the city of David a Savior, who is Christ the Lord!"*

That was the prelude. The crescendo followed: *And suddenly there was with the angel a multitude of the heavenly host, praising God and saying, "Glory to God in the highest, and on earth peace among men, with whom he is pleased!"*

The bewildered shepherds hurried to Bethlehem to see the

child that the angels sang about. The simple story continues: *And the shepherds returned, glorifying and praising God for all they had seen and heard.* Something joyful had happened, and they celebrated.

Joy is something that sings and dances across all the pages of Scripture in a rich variety. Take a look at the Psalmist's description of going to church: *"I went with the throng to the house of God, with joyful shouts and songs of thanksgiving, a multitude keeping festival."* And another Psalmist tells us to *"sing praises to the Lord, and make a joyful noise to him with songs!"*

Joy! If we really want to express this joy in the extreme, we need to turn to I Peter who says, *"Believe in God and rejoice with unutterable and exalted joy!"* The Apostle Paul says it simplest and best in Philippians when he wrote: *"Rejoice! And again I say, Rejoice!"* Paul could have benefited with a copy of Roget's *Thesaurus.*

Joy is not only a Biblical word, but it is a word that repeats itself all through church history. Even the martyrs rejoiced.

And yet somehow, this word is focused on the Christmas season. Everything about Christmas seems to reflect joy. We see this particularly in the familiar customs of Christmas in the way we celebrate it today.

Take for example the Christmas carol. Joy certainly characterizes our Christmas songs. A well-known person of church history, Francis of Assisi, may have introduced the carol. The word "carol" means "to dance in a circle." Francis at Christmas time led people, especially children, in singing and dancing, and from this grew the Christmas carol. Francis—so the legend says—also introduced the idea of a crèche, the living picture of the nativity scene, using real animals and people, including a new-born baby.

Another joyful Christmas custom is the Christmas tree. In Martin Luther's time, there was no Christmas tree in the celebration of Christmas. The legend tells about Martin Luther—and you may or may not believe the story, but in this season it's a lot easier to believe all these legends—the legend says that Martin Luther was wandering thought he woods on Christmas Eve and marveled at the stars shining through the branches of the fir trees. And so he cut a fir tree for his family and set it up at home, and lighted it with candles to represent the stars. And so the custom of the Christmas tree began. Maybe. Oh... why not?

Another joyful Christmas custom introduced by a famous person in church history was Santa Claus. Yes, Virginia, there really was a Santa Claus. He was Nicholas, bishop of Myra, who lived in the early 5th century. He was particularly known for his generosity to children. One of the best stories about him tells of a father who had three beautiful daughters, but he couldn't arrange a suitable marriage for them because he was poor and couldn't afford a dowry. Then one night Bishop Nicholas climbed up on their roof and dropped three gold coins down the chimney to provide the dowry for the three girls. One of the coins—so the story goes—accidentally dropped into a shoe placed near the fireplace, and perhaps that was the origin of some of our quaint Christmas customs.

After his death, Bishop Nicholas was canonized as a saint, and eventually he became the patron saint of children in three countries: Greece, Holland and Belgium. As his fame spread to Scandinavia, Saint Nicholas picked up his reindeer and sleigh, and also his red suit (a hand-me-down from the Norse god Thor). His name, after going through several languages, became corrupted from Saint Nicholas to Santa Niclaas to Santa Claus. Dr. Clement Moore, in his famous poem "The Night Before Christmas," gave him his rosy cheeks, white beard, and a slightly overweight belly that "shook when he laughed like a bowl full of jelly."

There's plenty of joyful trivia in the origin of Christmas customs. Mistletoe, for example. The early Britons thought mistletoe had the power to heal disease, counteract poison, protect against witchcraft, and bestow fertility. If a young couple were married with a kiss under the mistletoe, they were supposed to have good luck and lots of kids. Because it is an evergreen, it became part of the decorations for Christmas, and kissing under the mistletoe became a joyful tradition—joyful, that is, depending on whether or not the kisser was liked by the kissee.

Holly and ivy are part of Christmas decorations, too. The ancient tradition said that holly is considered male and ivy female.

Whichever is brought into the house first tells who will rule the household during the coming year. Maybe that explains why Christmas decorations are done earlier and earlier every year.

The wassail bowl and the Christmas toast both have fascinating origins. The legend of the wassail bowl is a delightful story that is as not well known as some of the others. According to the story, a German chieftain decided to invade and conquer Britain. The German chieftain's daughter went to Britain before the invasion, and there she met the British prince. He offered her a cup of good British ale, and she held up her cup and said in German, *"Wassheil,"* which I'm told means "Here's to you!" The prince responded gallantly and offered to marry her, which turned out to be a pretty good idea, because the German chieftain called off his invasion and came to the wedding. And that, according to legend, is how the wassail bowl became a part of our joyful Christmas traditions.

The recipe, for those who are interested in that sort of thing, is a mixture of hot ale, sugar, nutmeg and ginger. For those of us who watch our weight, we will have to substitute fruit juice and diet ginger ale. (You get a little bit of everything when you come to this church!)

The word "toast" came into the language a little later because early wassail bowls sometimes had pieces of toast floating around on the top. They didn't care what they put in their wassail bowl!

All of these delightful Christmas customs and legends have one central theme: *Joy.* Christmas is a time to celebrate, to enjoy family and friends, to indulge in ancient traditions, to sing and laugh and dance. A truly joyous season.

But something happened to these joyous celebrations several hundred years ago in England. The celebrations went too far. They turned into wild parties and orgies as the lords and ladies overindulged in Christmas joy. That was the time when the expression "drunk as a lord" came into the English language. For the twelve days of Christmas, they celebrated with a little too much joy!

And then the Puritan movement swept across England, and they reacted against all this celebration of the season. For two reasons: one was the wildness of their twelve-day party, and the other was that Advent and Christmas was "popish." Anything the Roman Catholics did was bound to be sinful! And so these straight-laced Puritans decreed that anyone caught observing Christmas in any way would be severely punished. These Puritans weren't exactly the fun people of history.

A lot of the history of the Presbyterian Church reflects our Puritan heritage. Did you know that for many years Christmas was forbidden to Presbyterians? They never sang carols in church. They never used the word "Advent." Preachers might preach on the Incarnation at Christmas time, but that was the only way they observed the season. Good Presbyterians were not supposed to have Christmas trees, or teach their children about Santa Claus, or exchange gifts, or any of the other joyous Christmas customs.

I think it was the children who brought back joy to the Presbyterian Church at Christmas. Churches began having parties at the church building for children. Some of the more liberal churches went so far as to have a decorated Christmas tree in the Sunday School building, and they even invited Santa Claus to give out candy to the children. By the time I was a little boy, Christmas was acceptable in the Presbyterian Church. And only in my adult lifetime did we permit such things as the Advent candles and Christmas tree in the sanctuary, decorated with Chrismons. And I am certainly glad that the Presbyterian Church now celebrates the season with joy.

There are a lot more joyful traditions and customs that I could tell you about, but I think I should get to the main point of this sermon. And that is the reason for our joy at Christmas time.

This is a time when we celebrate the coming of Christ. And I do mean celebrate. It is a time of joy when we remember that God himself stepped down into our world and into our lives. And that is what makes this season so enjoyable.

It should be joy without guilt. Sometimes we divide Christmas into the secular and the religious. Have you heard people say, "Let's put Christ back into Christmas?" They try to make us feel guilty because we celebrate so much at Christmas time that we forget about the reason for our joy. But Christmas *is* a time of joy, and all that we do in the enjoyment of the season is a reflection of the joy we feel as we remember the reason for the season.

There are two words which should be defined at this point: *joy* and *happiness*. There is a slight difference, but that difference is important. "Happiness" comes from an old English word *hap,* which means circumstance, what is happening around you, outside factors. Sometimes we feel happy, sometimes unhappy, depending on the circumstances around us. But joy is different. It comes from within. We can feel joy at all times, because of an inner knowledge that Christmas means that God has stepped into our lives and has come to live among us. And that inner joy does not depend on the circumstances of life around us.

Christmas *is* a happy time, but it is also a joyful time, and that means a lot more. We are happy in the things that surround us: Santa Claus, gift giving, decorations, carols, etc. But the joy we have at Christmas time is far deeper than the happy circumstances.

As a matter of fact, there are a good many people for whom Christmas is not a very happy occasion. Perhaps death has taken the person with whom we most want to celebrate Christmas. Illness or poor health may take much of the happiness out of the celebration. Financial limitation may cut down on our ability to give gifts. For many people, Christmas means loneliness. All these things are outside factors, and let's not forget that for a lot of people, happiness is limited at Christmas time.

But joy is not! The deep abiding joy of the Christmas season is the realization of what Christmas really means. God has reached down into our lives. We are no longer alone, spiritual orphans in the universe. God is not just a vague being way up there; he is here, in our lives. And this gives us true joy, no matter what the circumstances.

The song that the angels sang to the shepherds is being sung to us again this season. Therefore let the angel's message speak to you . . . and rejoice!

*Behold! I bring **you** good tidings of great joy!*
*For unto **you** is born this day in the city of David a Savior, who is Christ the Lord!*

Therefore: *Glory to God in the highest,*
And on earth peace among men, with whom he is pleased.

Amen.

BAH! HUMBUG! TO NEW YEAR'S EVE, TOO

Scripture: *James 4: 13-15*, especially the verse that reads, *What is your life? For you are a mist, that appears for a little while and then vanishes.*

Psalm 90, especially this verse: *A thousand years in thy sight are like yesterday when it is past, like a watch in the night. Thou dost sweep men away . . . like a dream . . . like grass in the morning, which fades in the evening. For all our days pass away, our years come to an end like a sigh. Three score years? Four score? They are soon gone, and we fly away.*

The Preacher's Notes:

New Year's Eve is a time to think about those haunting words in the text. The brevity of our lives reminds us of our mortality. It's a time to think seriously about the meaning of life, and how to live it right.

This sermon was preached at a Universalist-Unitarian Church. Surprisingly, they did not tar and feather me!

BAH! HUMBUG! TO NEW YEAR'S EVE, TOO

I'm gonna go to bed early on New Year's Eve. So don't invite me to your New Year's Eve party.

I hate New Year's Eve. Do you know why? It's not those New Year's Eve parties; I never get invited to them anyway. It isn't the wall-to-wall football games on TV, which begin to look the same at this end of the season. Nor is it that it will take me a whole month to learn to write the proper date on my checks. It's something more profound than that.

What really bugs me about New Year's Eve is . . . *its frequency!*

It happens so often! Why, just the other day, we were celebrating last New Year's Eve. A whole year has passed. Sneaked by. Boy, this is going too fast!

My concern about the brevity of life is biblical. In an obscure little verse in the Epistle of James we read: *What is your life? For you are a mist, that appears for a little time and then vanishes.* And in Psalm 90 we read: *A thousand years in thy sight are like yesterday when it is past, like a watch in the night. Thou dost sweep men away . . . like a dream . . . like grass in the morning, which fades in the evening. For all our days pass away, our years come to an end like a sigh. Three score years? Four score? They are soon gone, and we fly away.*

I have always suspected, though I have no way of proving it, that the reason some people have a wild, bacchanalian party on New Year's Eve is to blot out the undeniable, inescapable reality that another year has gone by, that time is passing, and going fast. Perhaps in alcoholic fun this idea can be forgotten, and not faced, at least momentarily.

For what is your life? It is a mist, which appears for a little time, and then vanishes.

I used to think these morbid thoughts were peculiar to my life. However, a recent study shows that more and more people are concerned about the brevity of life, and their inability to adjust to life's brevity and do something significant. These thoughts are just as common among young people as older folk. We who are older seem to have come to terms with this brief flickering moment that we call life. But for everybody, these are haunting, nagging thoughts, which many people refuse to face, and sometimes we repress them. But they are still boiling around in the subconscious unexplored parts of our minds and come bubbling to the surface in various ways, and are often expressed in our attitudes and philosophy of life.

So as we head toward another New Year's Eve, let's not run away from this morbid thought. Let's face it boldly, uncompromisingly, bravely: Our life is soon gone, and we fly away. So what are we going to do about it?

One possibility: *Brood.*

Squiggle down into the black hole of depression. Breathe luxuriously in the sweet sadness of self-pity. Life is almost gone. And what have we done with it? Nothing.

We have all known depression. A few people have experienced what they call "clinical depression," which is far more serious and requires professional and medical attention and often hospitalization. But all of us have known hours and maybe even days when we have "the blues." Something like New Year's Eve, and thoughts about the brevity of life, can bring it on.

Remember Macbeth? He came to the end of his life, and looking back over it, he became depressed. All he saw was a life of ambition, scheming, murder, gaining a throne . . . and emptiness. Meaninglessness. And this is how he expressed it:

Tomorrow . . . and tomorrow . . . and tomorrow . . . creeps in this petty pace from day to day, to the last syllable of recorded time, and all our yesterdays have lighted fools the way to dusty death. Out, out, brief candle! Life's but a walking shadow, a poor player who struts and frets his hour upon the stage and then is heard no more. It is a tale told by an idiot, full of sound and fury, signifying... nothing.

Nowhere in history do we find this attitude toward the meaninglessness of life more prevalent than in the ancient Roman Empire. These Romans had conquered the world, and they were living it up and enjoying the fruits of world domination. They had no work to keep them busy; slaves did everything. They needed to be entertained, and so they attended great circuses; blood flowed freely on the arena sands, and emperors strove to outdo one another in putting on bigger and better spectacles, trying to satisfy a need for a thrill, for something new to experience, something to fill the emptiness of a life that was already too full. This was Rome, and the Romans. A meaningless existence.

Archaeologists discovered tombstones of ancient Rome with the letters written on them: NFFNSNC. They knew it meant something like RIP—"Rest In Peace"—but they couldn't find the key to their meaning. Then someone found it: it stood for the Latin words: *Non fui, fui, non sum, non curo.* Translated, that means: "I was not, I was, I am not, I do not care." That's quite an epitaph to describe a person's life: *I was not,* referring to the time before he was born; *I was,* referring to his life time; *I am not,* meaning his present state—dead—and then the summary of it all: *I do not care.* What tragic futility of life those Romans must have had!

And then something happened in the Roman Empire that turned all this around. Something amazing, something spectacular. In the first three centuries A.D., Christianity swept through the Empire. It offered them a chance to find meaning in life, to give themselves to a cause that was bigger than Rome, something worth dying for, something even bigger than death. It was a cause, a philosophy of life, a meaningful reason to live. It gave them something to do, something with values, something with hope, something they could pass down to future generations. It was a cause they were even willing to die for.

No longer were they depressed, filled with ennui, looking for thrills and something with meaning for their lives. These Romans began to smile again, to sing, and lift their heads. At first the government tried to stamp it out, but it proved impossible, as these people had found something that they were willing to die for. And so eventually the government accepted it. Perhaps that was not the best thing for this newborn religion, just beginning to flex its muscles and grow strong. For when the new faith became legitimized, and a papacy established, and an inflexible doctrinal standard set for them, it lost some of its vigor. But that didn't happen until the third or fourth century.

But those first two or three centuries A.D. must have been exciting. They taught us something that may be just the cure for the depression that sometimes accompanies New Year's Eve and those gloomy thoughts about the brevity and meaninglessness of life. The secret of a meaningful life is not just to live, but also to have something to live for.

Everybody needs a *raison d'etre*, a *summum bonum*, a world view, which you live by, which makes your life ultimately worth while. Even though brief, this life can be filled with meaning. But you have to have a reason for living. Have you discovered yours?

Let me tell you about mine. I struggled with this when I was young. Let me go back to age nineteen. During one of my summers when I was in college, I went to New England to spend the three summer months. I got a job working in a YMCA youth camp on Lake Winnepesaukee in Vermont.

To get this job, I showed the camp director a letter of recommendation written by the president of my college. The president didn't know me very well; he said some very complimentary things about me. He didn't know about the time I—well, never mind about that.

One of the things in that letter said I was a young man "of high purpose." That's nice. But I wondered at the time what this high purpose was that I was supposed to have.

And so I set for my goal that summer to find out what this high purpose for my life was. There, in the pine forest, beside the beautiful lake, and while on camping excursions to the White Mountains in New Hampshire, I struggled with my own *raison d'etre*, my philosophy of life. By the end of the summer, I had done this.

I determined that my life would revolve around three basic priorities: something worthwhile to do, someone to love, and something to worship. I have pretty much lived by those three priorities during my lifetime. The "something to do" consisted of a life of service to others, rather than serving myself. The "someone to love" was discovered a few years later, and *that* was one of the best decisions I have ever made in my life. The "something to worship" did not come easily, and caused me a lot of struggle, and energy, and agony, but eventually I came to a comfortable—and tailor-made-faith in God, rooted and grounded in the Christian faith I was brought up in. And that's pretty much how I have lived my life, and it has taken me though a lot of New Year's Eves.

That's mine. What's yours? Different from mine, I'm sure. I urge you, at whatever age, to find your own philosophy of life. You can have mine if you want; there is no extra charge for that. But it would be better to work out your own.

One final thought.

Every summer I went to Pennsylvania to visit my mother while she lived. I used to take an early morning walk out in the country. I would climb a hill and walk along the ridge overlooking farm country, with the newly risen sun shining over the green stalks of corn. At the end of my two-mile walk was the old Fenneltown Church, now deserted, the roof caved in, lonesome and forgotten. Across the street from the church was the Fenneltown Cemetery. It was well kept for an ancient graveyard.

I enjoyed walking through that cemetery in the stillness of early morning, looking at the tombstones. There was for example George Fennel, 1823-1888. Next to him was Martha Briggs Fennel, 1826-1900. Their grave markers were old, faded, and worn smooth by the passage of time.

The thought occurred to me, some day that will be all that is left of me: a name and date on a tombstone. These were people who lived and loved, worked hard, enjoyed life, worshipped in the church across the street, and died and were buried by their mourning family. For years they were remembered, and flowers were placed on their graves. But time passed, and their children and grandchildren died, and George and Martha were forgotten. *Is that how it will be for me?*

The approach of another New Year's Eve reminds us that we have such a short time to muddle through this life. So few years to live, to gather our rosebuds before the Master of the Game says to us, "Time to put away your toys and lie down for your eternal rest."

So few years. We only pass this way but once. So let's be sure to do it right!

BAH! HUMBUG! TO BIRTHDAYS, TOO

Scripture: *James 4: 13-15*, especially the verse that reads, *What is your life? For you are a mist, that appears for a little while and then vanishes.*

Psalm 90, especially this verse: *A thousand years in thy sight are like yesterday when it is past, like a watch in the night. Thou dost sweep men away . . . like a dream . . . like grase in the morning, which fades in the evening. For all our days pass away, our years come to an end like a sigh. Three score years? Four score? They are soon gone, and we fly away.*

The Preacher's Notes:

Yeah, I know. It's the same text and general theme as the sermon entitled, **Bah! Humbug! To New Year's Eve, Too!** But it's still a different sermon, although I hope these two won't be preached back-to-back at a church.

This sermon takes a light-hearted look at birthdays, and the inevitable fact that we're getting older. There are a few practical suggestions on how to avoid the "birthday blues."

BAH! HUMBUG! TO BIRTHDAYS, TOO

Just how long is a person's life? Modern medicine has pushed the longevity average now to the upper seventies. Now, that's an *average*. The Psalmist described that as the outer limits of a person's life: *The days of our years are three-score and ten* (seventy), *or possibly by reason of strength fourscore years* (eighty). And then he adds this ominous footnote: *But it is soon gone, and we fly away.*

Charles Lamb, in his essay on growing old, says that until a person arrives at middle age, he doesn't really feel the lapse of time. But from then on, he begrudges the steady relentless passage of the minutes, days, years.

What brought on these gloomy thoughts is the approach of my birthday. One of the major differences between young people and older folks is their attitude toward birthdays. The young person says, "Oh! Boy! Another birthday!" But the older person says, "Oooh boy. *Another* birthday."

It's not that I don't like to get mushy birthday cards, or useless presents, or a high-calorie cake. I do. That's a sign that somebody out there cares about me. What I really don't like about birthdays as I grow older is that they happen too often. Why, just the other day I celebrated my last one.

This is going too fast. Is that what being "over the hill" means? It's downhill from here on and gathering momentum. My life is the down side of a roller coaster, and I can't stop it.

So let's not run away from the morbid thought this morning. Let's face it, boldly, uncompromisingly, bravely: Our life is soon gone, and we fly away. So . . . when a birthday comes, what are we going to do about it?

Plan A: Ignore it. Pretend that the birthday never was.

One year, I tried to skip a birthday. I told everyone not to mention my birthday, under pain of death, torture, eternal damnation . . . or worse! I told myself that too. But it didn't work. I woke up that morning a whole year older than I was yesterday. I told myself that I was just one day older. But it wasn't true, and I knew it. I was a whole year older that day.

You can't solve problems by running away from them. So let's try some other approach.

Plan B: Accept it.

This year, look forward, not backward. Let your theme song be: "These are the days, my friend; these are the days!"

Normal Rockwell was asked once what his favorite painting was. His reply: "The next one."

That's the way to approach birthdays. The next time someone asks you what's the best year of your life, have the answer right there in your hip pocket: "The next one."

Instead of New Year's resolutions, why not make some birthday resolutions? Try something like these:

Birthday Resolution No. 1: Do something different this year.
Something new and exciting. Something you've always wanted to do but thought you were too old.

Take up painting. Go jogging. Take a trip to some new and exciting place. Collect butterflies. Find a new hobby, such as carpentry, cooking, bridge, or basket weaving. Become an expert on the sex life of horned toads.

You say you've done all these things? Well, think up something else then.

Birthday Resolution No. 2: Volunteer!

Many of us have arrived at the age when we put the making of money in its proper perspective. We no longer have to scratch and scramble to make a living. So what do we do now? We look around for something to do.

And there are so many opportunities! Many organizations are begging for volunteers who have time to give for the service of others. And there are individual opportunities also. So . . . volunteer!

This is the time to rediscover the joy of serving others. And it is a *very* reliable way to chase the birthday blues!

Birthday Resolution No. 3: Surround yourself with friends and loved ones.

Someone told me once that the curse of old age is loneliness. Being a grandfather to seven grandchildren—and one great-grandchild—I have observed that loneliness is a curse for teen-agers also. But nobody has to be alone, unless he chooses to.

The secret is to cherish the value of companionship. You have so many opportunities to surround yourself with cheerful loving companions. People are everywhere!

I have always liked what Robert Browning said:

Grow old along with me.
The best is yet to be!
The last of life, for which the first was made.

Now, I realize that many people in their old age lose their beloved spouse and companion. This is a devastating blow, and the loneliness of old age looms large for these people. But that's what the rest of us are for. We can never replace what you lost, but we can at least give you a little laughter, and companionship, and friendship. These are the ingredients for facing the last of life with peace and happiness, and surviving the loneliness of birthdays.

Birthday Resolution No. 4: Don't forget the best Companion of all!

He walks with you every day. He comforts you when you are sad, and rejoices with you when you are happy. He understands your needs. And he does not condemn.

He likes you!

This, I have discovered, is another difference between the faith of an older person and a young person. For us who are older, our faith is relaxed, enjoyable. I believe the best way to describe it is "comfortable." Like an old pair of slippers that have been molded to your feet, they fit just right for you. So relax and enjoy your faith now.

When you were young, faith was a compelling force. You felt guilty about not doing enough. You were challenged to do more. And you did.

But now, it's different. Relax. Find peace. And enjoy that loving Companion, who walks with you every step of the way, sharing the moments, savoring with you the beauty of life that you have discovered, and giving you a sense of serenity that "all's right with the world."

This is a time when many of us learn to live with the famous "Serenity Prayer" never too far from our thoughts. You know that Serenity Prayer, don't you? Let me say it for you, and you will agree that this is a good prayer to live with:

> *Lord, give me the serenity to accept what cannot be changed; the courage to change what can be changed; and the wisdom to know the difference.*

And when that last birthday comes, when death takes you by the hand and leads you into new vistas and new experiences, think of it as a joyful adventure. The One who was your companion in life is your strength and guide in death. He has prepared a place for you, and when he comes again, he will take you unto himself, that where he is, you will be also.

So . . . take *that*, birthdays! You don't scare me any more!

Here's what you do on birthdays: You laugh, and turn to embrace life, and offer the prayer of the Psalmist: *Teach us to number our days, that we may get a heart of wisdom!*

Or, as the Amish Dutch paraphrased it, *Ve grow too soon old, und too late schmardt!*

Amen!

THE PURSUIT OF HAPPINESS

Scripture: *Ecclesiastes 1:12-2:11,* a very gloomy passage of scripture talking about the vanity of life.

Matthew 16:24-26, which includes, *Whoever would save his life must lose it, and whoever loses his life for my sake will find it. For what does it profit a person if he gains the whole world and forfeits his life?*

The Preacher's Notes:

This is a Fourth of July sermon. It's also a history lesson. It centers on the phrase in the Declaration of Independence—written by Thomas Jefferson—that is so familiar to all of us: *The pursuit of happiness.*

You can't find happiness by pursuing it. It sneaks up on you. Try to define it for yourself. You'd be surprised what you'll find!

THE PURSUIT OF HAPPINESS

Webster's *Guide to American History* lists these facts:

> *June 11, 1776: Congress appoints a committee to draft a Declaration of Independence.*
> *June 28, 1776: The Declaration, written by Thomas Jefferson, is presented to Congress.*
> *July 4, 1776: After making some revisions in the Declaration, Congress approves it without dissent.*

Thus reads Webster's *Guide to American History*. These cold, Almanac-like facts can't begin to catch the excitement that must have prevailed in those history-making days, when the Continental Congress gathered to discuss something that they knew would be one of the major turning-points in world history. There are many little events in those exciting days that can conjure up in a person's imagination a thrilling scene. Such an event I would like to try to picture now, with a fiction writer's imagination.

I can see Thomas Jefferson, late at night, sitting at his desk, quill pen in hand, with a pot of ink on the desktop, writing slowly and carefully on a piece of paper. He writes very little; most of the time he is gazing into space lost in thought. On the paper before him he has written these words:

> *When, in the course of human events, it becomes necessary for one people to sever the bonds which have connected them with another, and to assume, among the powers of the earth, the separate and equal station to which the laws of nature and of nature's God entitle them, a decent respect to the opinions of mankind requires that they should declare the causes which impel them to the*

separation. We hold these truths to be self-evident: that all men are created equal; that they are endowed by their Creator with certain inalienable rights; that among these are life, liberty, and....

Here Jefferson pauses in his writing. He has been quoting the words of the English philosopher John Locke, who said that the fundamental rights of man are "life, liberty and property." Yes, muses Jefferson, *Life* is definitely an inalienable right, for in any kind of decent government the individual's life is sacred and must be protected by the government. And *liberty* is certainly a keystone, for a person ought to be free to say what he thinks, worship how he pleases—or not worship if he pleases, to enjoy protection from the rich and powerful, to have a fair day in court. *Life* and *Liberty*: two cornerstones on which to build a young, ambitious nation.

But *Property?* Yes, this is important, but it just didn't fit with those other two words, *Life* and *Liberty*. It is so bare, so cold, so... practical. Life, liberty, and... *property?* There ought to be a better word or phrase to express the American Dream.

Just then Jefferson is interrupted by a late-night visit from the Rev. John Witherspoon, a Presbyterian minister who is also a member of the Continental Congress. They sit in Jefferson's study and talk, and their discussion is animated and excited as they explore their favorite subject, the American Dream. In the course of their conversation Dr. Witherspoon uses the expression, "the pursuit of happiness." It doesn't register with Jefferson at first, but after Witherspoon leaves, it recurs to him. He tries it out on the page before him: *Life, liberty and the pursuit of happiness."* That's it! Not the bare, practical term "property," but something idealistic, something visionary, something intangible to express the American Dream: *The pursuit of happiness!* And so it became a part of the document that we prize so highly as a part of our American heritage, The Declaration of Independence, and also a part of the vocabulary of the American Dream.

The American Dream! It speaks to us of freedom, equal opportunity under the law, the ability to gather here this morning to worship in our own way, to live our lives openly and freely, without harassment or injustices by the rich and powerful. This is truly the American Dream, a part of which is the Pursuit of Happiness.

Or is it? Is that all there is to this phrase, the *Pursuit of Happiness?* I really think it is much more profound than that. How would you define that mysterious and elusive word: *happiness!*

Several years ago, an attempt was made to do just that. Eighteen prominent Americans, representing many different professions and vocations, spent several days together to draw up a statement that would interpret what Jefferson meant by "the pursuit of happiness." They came up with a truly startling declaration that, while everyone has the right to pursue happiness in America, a person seldom gets it by pursuing it! In fact, to go directly after it is one of the surest ways *not* to obtain it!

It reminds me of the time when I dropped a thumbtack on the floor and couldn't find it. I got down on my knees and hunted and hunted for it, to no avail. A few days later, when I was walking through the house in my bare feet, *I found it!*

That's the way it is with happiness. If you look for it, you'll never find it. It's when you're looking for something else, then happiness comes to you as a byproduct, an unexpected bonus. And most of the time, you're not even aware of the fact that you are . . . *happy!*

The writer of the Old Testament book of Ecclesiastes became aware of this. This writer—whoever he was—in his old age was reflecting on the pursuit of happiness during his long lifetime. He had certainly pursued it. He tried to find it in wealth, in wisdom, in pleasure, in hard work, in status, in a good reputation—he certainly pursued it! And his conclusion? It's all vanity—useless—like chasing after the wind!

A Twentieth Century version of the book of Ecclesiastes can be seen in a meeting that took place back in 1923. At the Edgewater Beach Hotel in Chicago, eight men were gathered to discuss the American business scene. They were eight of the most successful business men in America. Listen to the roll call of those present:

The president of the largest independent steel company.
The president of the largest utility company.
The greatest wheat speculator.
The president of the New York Stock Exchange.
A member of the President's cabinet.
The greatest bear on Wall Street.
The head of the world's greatest monopoly.
And the president of the Bank of International Settlements

These were some of the most successful men in America in the year 1923. This meeting was covered extensively by the press, who characterized these men as having fulfilled the American Dream. I'm sure the people of our country back then looked up to these men and said, "They're happy!"

Now let's see what happened to each of these men:

The president of the greatest utility company—Charles Schwab—died bankrupt and lived on borrowed money the last five years of his life.
The president of the greatest utility company—Samuel Insul—died a fugitive from justice and penniless in a foreign country.
The greatest wheat speculator—Arthur Cutten—died abroad, broke.
The president of the New York Stock Exchange—Richard Whitney—served a term in Sing Sing Penitentiary.
The member of the President's cabinet—Albert Fall—was pardoned from prison so that he could die at home.
The greatest bear on Wall Street—Jesse Livermore—committed suicide.
The head of the world's greatest monopoly—Ivar Kreuger—committed suicide.
The president of the Bank of International Settlements—Leon Frazer—committed suicide.

Each of these men, like the writer of Ecclesiastes, spent his life in the pursuit of happiness. They tried everything: the accumulation of money, fame, status, hard work, success, rising to the top. And each one found that life was vanity—useless—like chasing the wind.

Are you looking for happiness? Chances are, you won't find it. Not until you forget the pursuit of happiness and begin to pursue some other things that are more important.

Several years ago, the editor of a newspaper offered a prize for the best answer to the question: "Who are the happiest people on earth?" The following answers were judged to be the best:

> *A mother at the end of a busy day, bathing her baby.*
> *A craftsman whistling over a job well done.*
> *A little child building castles in the sand.*
> *A doctor who has just finished a difficult operation and saved a life.*

Each person was so absorbed in the task at hand that he or she forgot himself. They did not pursue happiness. It came as a by-product. They stumbled on it by accident. And they would never think of saying to themselves, "I'm happy." If you asked them, "Are you happy?" they would probably shrug their shoulders and reply, "I suppose so. I hadn't really thought about it. But yeah, I guess I am."

Does that remind you of something Jesus said? "Whoever would find his life must lose it."

Happiness comes—not when you are pursuing it—but when you lose yourself in something else, something more important to you than *you*. It comes as a by-product, an unexpected bonus, when you are in pursuit of something else that is bigger than yourself.

We have the privilege of spending our lives in the pursuit of happiness. In our country it has been guaranteed to us in the Declaration of Independence and our Constitution. If you were asked to define happiness for yourself, how would you answer? The answer to that question would be different for each one of us. Let me give you my own personal answer, but you will have to figure out your own. For me, happiness consists of a few pictures like these:

I walk into a room where my great-granddaughter is. She catches sight of me and her face lights up in a big smile, which says more than any words, "I like you." Now that's happiness.

A family dinner. Around me are children and their spouses, my grandchildren who are discovering their life's paths in maturity, a great-grandchild with her whole life ahead of her, and perhaps other family members and friends. At this dinner, there is a lot of laughter . . . and a lot of love. That, too, is happiness.

I watch a sunrise in the mountains. I see the sun coming up over the distant horizon, gradually seeping light into the broad vista below. Birds begin to sing, and I can taste the crisp clean air. And then I realize that my faith in God is satisfying and comfortable, for this God whom I have followed all my life, who knows the real me better than anyone else, has accepted me as one of his own, because of some arrangements he made for me a couple thousand years ago

This is my definition of happiness. What is yours? Each one of us must define it in his or her own way. Whether you realize it or not, you have spent your lifetime following Thomas Jefferson's dream for America in the pursuit of happiness. Now . . . define it.

Of course, in your definition, you must take into consideration the sorrows, the disappointments, the failures, the embarrassments . . . but all the tragedies of life will lead you to appreciate the positive experiences that have led you to happiness. If you have never tasted the negatives of life, how can you possibly appreciate the positives?

But now, as we approach the Fourth of July, look back on your own pursuit of happiness. That word, *happiness,* is elusive, enigmatic, indefinable. You've been pursuing it all your life. Now . . . maybe . . . you can define it. And then, having defined it, thank God for it.

LETTERS TO OUR PILGRIM FATHERS

Scripture: *Deuteronomy 26:1-4, 16:13-15,* showing some of the origins of Thanksgiving celebration in the ancient Hebrew tradition.

The Preacher's Notes:

This is a Thanksgiving sermon with a rather novel approach. I wrote some letters to our Pilgrim Fathers, and they replied! My letters asked them questions about what the first Thanksgiving was like, and their answers were both revealing . . . and surprising.

This sermon has always been well received wherever it was preached. At a Unitarian-Universalist church once, one of the speakers, dressed in a Pilgrim costume, read the letters of the Pilgrim Fathers. I wasn't there, but I heard rave reviews about that performance.

LETTERS TO OUR PILGRIM FATHERS

Recently, I carried on some correspondence with our Pilgrim forefathers, and it was quite interesting. Of course, you mustn't ask me how I did this; just be grateful that they answered my letters. So now I would like to share with you my correspondence with the Pilgrims.

Dear Honorable Pilgrim Fathers:

As Thanksgiving Day approaches, some of us in Florida would like to ask you a few questions about our national holiday. You are an authority on this subject, since you started it.

Or did you start it?

Every time a national holiday comes, some smart-alecky scholars tell us some weird facts. They tell us that Columbus wasn't the first to sail to American shores, and Santa Claus was originally a priest who helped children, and the word "Easter" comes from the old Anglo-Saxon referring to a pagan festival. All we need now is for some clown to tell us that you venerable Pilgrim fathers did not start Thanksgiving. So please, dear ancestors, confirm that it really was you who originated the wonderful tradition of Thanksgiving.

Sincerely,
A Modern American

P.S. Now we call it "Turkey Day." How many turkeys did you have on your table at your first Thanksgiving? And did you invent Cranberry Sauce?

Dear Mr. Modern American:

    Were we ever surprised to receive your letter! We have had a Town Meeting to decide how we should answer it, and a small committee of elders has been appointed. We knew that you remember us about once a year, but we hardly dared believe that you would ask *us* something about this national holiday. We are honored!

    First, let me say that we are quite amazed to see that a little celebration that we once enjoyed in July of 1621 and then didn't think much about has become a national event. We might have thought twice about inviting the Wampanoag Indians and asking our ladies to cook us a feast had we known what we were starting.

    Secondly, we were a little shocked to think that modern America actually believes that we Pilgrims started Thanksgiving. It's one of those legends that will not be destroyed by the facts. Actually Thanksgiving began as an ancient Jewish festival, and is described in the Book of Deuteronomy. Moses called for a feast of Thanksgiving for the Hebrews in celebration of the fall harvest. This feast is still carried on by the Jews in what they call their Feast of the Booths. If only the old practice of Bible reading had not been neglected in your time, you would probably know more about these things.

    Yes of course we borrowed the idea of a Thanksgiving feast from other sources. Not only were we aware of the Biblical feast of Thanksgiving, but we had recently come from England, where we observed the Michaelmas Celebration on Saint Michael's Day. We cooked geese and ate and drank our wine in Thanksgiving to God.

    If you want to know the truth, we had no intention of starting an annual Thanksgiving Day. It was many, many years later that official annual feasts were proclaimed in America. We just wanted to say thanks to God for being alive. And besides, this was about the first time in many months that we had enough food on the table to even call it a feast!

Your obedient and humble servants,
The Pilgrim Fathers

P.S. Our dinner on Thanksgiving Day was composed largely of wild duck, fruits and venison. But we seem to remember a few wild turkeys, too. They were pretty tough old birds, which didn't compare with venison in flavor. Perhaps if we had cranberry sauce to eat with it, we might have been able to eat them. But our Thanksgiving Day was definitely not a "turkey day."

Dear Pilgrim Fathers:

I was so delighted to receive your letter that I am answering it immediately with a few more questions. For one thing, we are very much interested and surprised by your comment on the menu for the first Thanksgiving. You even called it a "feast." Tough old turkeys, indeed, without any cranberry sauce! What kind of a Thanksgiving dinner was that?

What in the world did you have to be thankful for? We have read about some of the suffering you went through in those days: the cold winter, the lack of food, the many deaths. How could you possibly be thankful? I think I would have cursed God for the rough time.

Sincerely yours,
A Modern American

P.S. Your "not eating much turkey" at the first Thanksgiving shattered my picture of Thanksgiving Day in 1621. I envisioned a bunch of old men sitting around eating turkey. How could I have been so mistaken about the turkey?

Dear Modern American:

Last evening we had a special Town Meeting to decide

on how to reply to you. You certainly asked us an interesting question. Why *were* we so thankful? You're absolutely right; we didn't have much to be thankful for. In fact, as we look back on it now, our suffering was incredible.

You mentioned three things that caused our suffering: cold winter, very little food, and many deaths.

Yes, it was a cold winter; just about the worst that we can remember. But perhaps it was terrible because we were so poorly equipped for it. After all, we landed in the late fall, and we hardly had time to do any preparation. People who live in New England even today do far more preparation for winter than you Southerners can imagine. Do you realize what a job just getting firewood was? And especially when you consider that most of the time there were not more than one or two men who were healthy enough to swing an axe!

And food! Sometimes our daily diet consisted of a few grains of corn. You can't imagine how weakening it is, both physically and emotionally, to slowly starve to death. And worse, we had to watch our young ones, who should be growing, slowly waste away and die.

Yes, and death, too. You are always saddened when death comes to the family circle. But when you had to watch it like we did, it almost drove us insane. We started off with one hundred people at Plymouth, and before the winter was over, exactly half of us had died. We were so weakened with hunger and despair that one more death hardly mattered.

We talked for a long time last night in our meeting about why we were so thankful that fall. We have come to the conclusion that it was *because* of these hardships and sufferings that we could even begin to say thanks to God adequately. When we stripped away the things, we found that we had left the one thing that really counted: our faith in God. After that experience, never again will we measure our gratitude by how much we have. We are more grateful for the Giver than we are for his gifts!

Your humble and God-fearing ancestors,
The Pilgrim Fathers

P.S. Your comment about Thanksgiving Day in 1621 being "a bunch of old men sitting around eating turkey" made us so angry that we almost recommissioned Miles Standish to teach you a lesson! Old men, indeed! All of us were under forty, and most of us were this side of thirty. Most of the great events of history were accomplished by young people, not old fogeys!

Dear Young Pilgrims of 1621:

As we hear more about you, we are coming more and more to respect you. You must have really been great men, to endure what you did and accomplish so much!

We do have one question that we in our modern time would like very much to know. We have always heard that the main reason you came to American shores in the first place was for religious freedom? Is this true? And was it worth it?

Sincerely yours,
A Respectful Modern American

P.S. Is there any truth to those references in our history books to strong red wine on your tables, made from wild grapes? We have such a drug and alcohol problem in our time, and I don't think that's a good influence on young people.

Dear Mr. Modern American:

We appreciate the respectful tone of your letter, and we discussed at great length at our Town Meeting your question about religious freedom.

First, we want you to know that strictly speaking, it was *not* religious freedom that we wanted. We just wanted to be allowed to worship in our own way. We may be splitting hairs, but there is an important difference.

The difference is that we didn't really want religious freedom in our little colony in Plymouth. We wanted only to worship God the way *we* felt was right. When we lived in England, we tried to worship in our way, but the established church wouldn't let us. You really couldn't blame them; religious freedom as you know it in America today was unheard of then. We moved to Holland, because their religion was much closer to the way we liked it. But we didn't want our children growing up in Dutch ways, so we decided to take our little community to the new world where we could worship God in our own way. And you'd better believe that we kicked out of our colony anyone who wouldn't worship exactly the way we believed God ought to be worshipped!

Your concept of freedom of worship in modern America is one that we would never have tolerated in Plymouth. You don't enforce the Sabbath, you don't require church attendance, and you even protect atheists! Anyone subscribing to a Humanist belief would have been burned at the stake in our time.

But we also concluded in our Town Meeting that your concept of freedom is much better than ours. So guard it well, modern America! Thank God for the kind of country in which both the atheist and the ultra-fundamentalist are allowed to practice their beliefs in the same town without persecution. Because then—and *only* then—can you be sure that you can practice your religion in the way you want it, without being forced to conform to the religious practices of the majority.

Sincerely, your respectful and admiring ancestors,
The Pilgrim Fathers

P.S. Of course we had wine! Do you think that's evil? What hypocrites! You Americans consume more alcohol than we can imagine, but you still think that the fruit of the vine is somehow bad. We drank a little wine, simply because we enjoyed it! Our Bible tells us God gave us "wine to gladden the heart of man." Of course, our young people were taught to drink only in moderation, and we hope yours are equally educated.

Dear Pilgrim Fathers:

We have certainly enjoyed this correspondence with out honored ancestors, and we are grateful that you would share your views with us.

We have one final request. Please comment in whatever way you wish about the difference between Thanksgiving now and Thanksgiving then. How does our modern Thanksgiving celebration and attitudes compare with yours?

Sincerely yours,
A Modern American

P.S. I can't restrain myself; I must ask you this one question: did your women actually wear those silly-looking clothes that we see in pictures? They were so long that they must have tripped over them while walking!

P.P.S. On the same subject, please comment in general about the place of women in your time. Did you really consider them a husband's "help-mate?" In our time, women are equal, and we would have referred to Pilgrim Mothers as often as to Pilgrim Fathers. How do you feel about this?

Dear Mr. Modern American:

Your question about the difference between Thanksgivings then and now led to considerable debate in our Town Meeting.

Some felt there is no similarity between the two. You live in a complex industrial society, compared to our simple rural culture. Only the old-timers among you can remember what a harvest meant. You go to the super market and buy your groceries, and you get fresh or frozen foods year-round. You can't begin to imagine what the word *harvest* meant to us. It meant the difference between life and death as we faced the cruel winter. That's why we were so grateful to God; the harvest festival meant that life itself could be continued, and it was God who gave us life. We imagined it would be difficult for you to see the providence of the Almighty in the frozen foods counter at Winn Dixie.

However, there were some who did not agree with this point of view. They felt that basically our Thanksgivings were the same. Of course the outward expression has changed, as it must throughout the changing centuries. But basically you people are as grateful to God in your way as we are in ours. Is this true? Do you really say thanks to God—and mean it—in your modern celebration of thanksgiving. Or is it just "Turkey Day" to you?

Your humble and obedient servants,
The Pilgrim Fathers

P.S. Yes, our ladies wore long skirts, and a lot of other things, too. And for good reason: it was cold! How long do you think our women could stay warm in the kind of short skirt or shorts that your women wear? Also, the morality of our time was conditioned by the Puritan teaching, which to you seems harsh and strict. But these kinds of morals are traditions, which depend on the flavor of the times. There are many ways that the extremes of Puritanism were superior to *your* modern moral extremes, but not in the matter of tasteful clothing. When your young women wear a dress, at least they look like a young woman! In your time, you at least have *that* to be thankful for!

P.P.S. Yes, we honored our Pilgrim Mothers, but we interpreted the Bible differently when it came to our attitude toward women. Her place was in the home, caring for husband and children. She did not speak in public meetings, and had very little influence on men's affairs. Your women's equality movement took place only in your generation, but throughout history the role of women was to serve her husband and bear his children. I had planned to comment further on whether you have progressed or regressed since our time, but my wife said—

At this point, my correspondence with the Pilgrims came to an abrupt end. Perhaps these letters will give us some small insight into the life and times of our ancestors, enabling us to be a little more appreciative of our heritage. We are grateful to our Pilgrim Fathers—and Mothers—who corresponded with us so candidly. We salute you!

THE BEAUTIFUL—AND TRAGIC—STORY OF A MOTHER

Scriptures: *Luke 1:26-38, Luke 2:27,33-35, John 19:25-27.* All three Scriptures provide a glimpse into the life of Mary, the mother of Jesus. The first described events before Jesus was born, the second tells a fascinating incident that happened when Mary brought young Jesus to the Temple to be circumcised, and the third described Mary as she watched her son die on the cross.

The Preacher's Notes:

This is a Mother's Day sermon. Mary began her career of motherhood with high hopes and dreams, but it ended tragically.

The theme of the sermon is that we don't have complete control over the tapestry that our life weaves. We weave our dreams of happiness, but we must allow for some tragic threads that come unbidden into the tapestry.

THE BEAUTIFUL—AND TRAGIC—STORY OF A MOTHER

If you look closely at the tapestry of your life, you will see that it is woven of two-ply: one strand of your own choosing, and the other not of your own choosing at all.

When we were young, we were aware of only one strand. We never imagine that there is going to be another at all. Life is ours! We are to choose the thread, select the pattern, accomplish the weaving—*our way!* It is going to be all our own work. We will construct our life just the way we chose to make it.

But as the years pass, we discover that we are not as free as we imagined. We have to adapt our pattern, make room for colors we never anticipated, accept other threads, accommodate changes and events we never foresaw. We have to make something of two-ply: to weave together choice and circumstance, desire and destiny, our preferences and that strange thing our forefathers called fate. Some call it good luck and bad luck. But it's all woven and blended into the two-ply pattern of the tapestry of our lives.

For example....

There was once a young maiden of Nazareth in whose heart there were dreams and in whose mind were the shining expectancies of youth. But then, suddenly, the simple pattern of her life got complicated. She had to take into her life another strand.

She had to play a leading part in God's plan for his people. She was to be the mother of the Messiah!

Mary accepted this responsibility, and willingly. She said,

"Behold, I am, the handmaiden of the Lord; let it happen to me according to your Word."

Of all the things that could have happened to a young Jewish girl of the house and lineage of David, this was the greatest. I am told that throughout history and even today, Jewish mothers, when they become pregnant, offer the ancient ritual prayer that this child would be the Chosen One. Now Mary is told that the time has come. *She* has been designated *that* mother. What an honor! What great hopes she must have had for the child to be born! The idealism of youth, the sensitivity of pregnancy, and the emotion of a deep faith, combined to lift her sights to the highest level of expectancy for her child. The pattern *he* would weave in the loom of life would bring joy and peace to the tapestry of *her* life.

But she soon discovered that she was not the only weaver. Other threads thrust themselves into the tapestry.

It happened early. The hand of the government reached out and touched her, and she and Joseph had to take the long journey to Bethlehem to be enrolled in the census. And because of the crowded conditions in Bethlehem, this child—*this Messiah of great hopes*—was born out in the barn! That's not what Mary envisioned for her tapestry of life.

But stranger things were yet to come.

When the shepherds arrived at the stable that night describing the wondrous sight and the angelic message they had seen and heard, Mary's heart sang again. This was God's Son! Everything was going to be all right after all.

On the eighth day after his birth, Mary and Joseph took the child to Jerusalem for the ritual circumcision. There old Simeon spoke prophetic words to her, words that brought again to her mind the great future for her son. She almost missed the final prophecy from the old man; it was like a footnote, or parenthetical: *"A sword shall pierce your soul, too."*

What did that mean? But the brightness of youth and the joy of motherhood enabled her to forget that, as she returned to Bethlehem and was hostess for some strange visitors from the East—

astrologers—who had seen a star that meant a new king was born. They had come to honor him and give him expensive gifts.

But even then the other strand was weaving itself into the tapestry of her life. They had to rise one night and flee to Egypt to escape the wrath of a jealous king who sought the life of the child born to be a king.

Eventually they returned to Nazareth in Galilee, where Mary sought to restore some order to the pattern of her life. When her son was twelve, they went to Jerusalem for a religious holiday, and there she discovered her strange son in the Temple discussing theology with the rabbis. She spoke to him, saying something like, "Son, come on home to your father's house where you belong." He replied something like, "But Mother, I *am* in my Father's house where I belong!"

Nothing is known of the eighteen years that followed. Many attempts have been made to picture what might have happened then, but the one I like best was a picture painted by the artist Holman Hunt. He shows the youth Jesus standing in the doorway of the carpenter's shop in Nazareth, his arms wide to catch the dying rays of the afternoon sun. Behind him, Mary sees the shadow cast on the floor—the shadow of a cross—and her face reflects horror as she wonders what the future holds for him.

And then Jesus began his ministry at the age of thirty. How proud Mary must have been of him! Her son could do wonderful things! Like the time he turned the water to wine at the wedding feast at Cana. She didn't understand what he said to her: "Woman, what have you to do with me? My hour has not yet come." Do you suppose she thought, when his hour finally comes, it will be marvelous!

Then one day, her son came home, to Nazareth. He was invited to speak in the synagogue, to read from the sacred scroll. Proudly, the men of the family took their places in the synagogue, while Jesus, the honored rabbi, stood up to read. He chose a passage from the prophet Isaiah, which told of the coming of the Messiah. Then he sat down, and in the expectant hush that followed, he said, "Behold! This day is this Scripture fulfilled in your presence!"

What did this mean? Either it meant that he was the Messiah, or it was the most blatant form of blasphemy. The people of Nazareth had no doubts. They ran him out of town!

What a blow this must have been for Mary! Her own son, the popular rabbi, whom she knew to be the Messiah—disgraced in the eyes of her friends and neighbors in his own home town! There were those darker threads in the tapestry again.

Mary's other sons—she had four of them, James, Joseph, Judas and Simon—were appalled. The only explanation they could think of for such behavior was that he was demented. The proper thing to do with a demented member of the family in those days was to keep him locked up at home, so that he wouldn't bring more shame upon himself and the family—an attitude that we have grown out of in our time. That's probably what Jesus' brothers decided to do. They took Mary with them because they thought he might listen to her, and they went looking for Jesus. He wasn't hard to find—in a big crowd, preaching. They sent word to Jesus saying his mother and brothers wanted to speak to him. When he heard this, he said, "Who are my mother and brothers?" Then, indicating the people around him, Jesus said, "These are my mother and brothers." His brothers were probably more convinced than ever that he was demented.

But Mary, I suspect, was with him all the way. She had been pondering in her heart since birth all the strange things about her son. *She* knew who he was, even if nobody else did. She didn't understand him, but—mother-like—she stayed with him through everything.

And this brought her to the foot of the cross.

What a traumatic tragedy this must have been for her! It's agony enough for any mother to lose her child, but to stand there and watch him die in great pain and humiliation would be unbearable. I'm sure she must have remembered that day years ago, when old Simeon said to her, *"Behold, a sword shall pierce your soul, too!"* As Mary stood there at the foot of the cross, she learned how sharp that sword was.

I'm sure Mary did not understand the meaning of his crucifixion. I don't understand it very well myself. Better theologians than I have shaken their heads over its depth of meaning. John, the beloved disciple who stood beside her that day, didn't understand it either, not then. Maybe later, after the resurrection forced them to take a deeper look, maybe they could catch a glimmer of the profound significance of what he had witnessed. But at that time, to Mary, there was agony, and confusion, and dismay. Her son—God's Son—the Messiah—*on a cross! Dying!* What had gone wrong? What was happening?

The loom of Mary's life was weaving some very dark threads at that moment. These were events and circumstances over which she had no control. She had never expected anything like this! So much good could have been done, so much happiness could have been possible, so much success could have been woven into her son's tapestry of life! But instead—*this!* This unspeakable tragedy! Why couldn't things have turned out the way *she* wanted them to!

Mary, Mary . . . what can we say to her now, to bring consolation in this, the worst hour of her life? Shall we tell her to wait for three days, and see what happens then? Shall we tell her to wait a few years, and then look at this tragic event in its proper perspective? Shall we tell her to wait two thousand years, and see what has happened as a result of this life and this death? I'm afraid that wouldn't be very comforting to Mary in those moments.

In fact, probably the only comforting words that could be said to her were said by her son from the cross: "Woman, behold your son. Son, behold your mother." With those words, he assigned her care and comfort to the beloved disciple standing beside her. No words; only the comforting touch, the steady companionship, of a friend or loved one, could bring consolation to a grieving person in a tragic moment. John, the beloved disciple, don't *say* anything to her; just be there when she needs you.

The darkest threads of Mary's tapestry of life were being woven right then. But Mary, remember: *you* are not the Weaver. Nor is that young man beside you, who places a comforting arm around you. The Weaver is unseen, perhaps unnoticed in that traumatic moment. But he is there. He's always there. And he's weaving . . . weaving a pattern we may not be able to see . . . weaving with skill and understanding and love.

And the weaving goes on . . . .

HEAVEN AND HELL—AND CHRISTMAS

Scripture: *Matthew 2:13-23* Once again, the familiar nativity story, this time Matthew's version.

The Preacher's Notes:

This time, the familiar nativity story is presented with a twist. What is heaven? What is hell? Maybe the simple story of the baby of Bethlehem can give us a clue as to the meaning of heaven. And possibly King Herod, in his palace in Jerusalem, can show us what hell is like.

HEAVEN AND HELL—
AND CHRISTMAS

When I say the words "heaven" and "hell," what do you think of? What images come to your mind?

When I say "heaven," do you picture a celestial city, with streets of gold, gates of pearl, ivory palaces, jasper walls, clean, sweet smelling, glittering, and filled with joyous music?

When I say "hell," do you think of a dark, dreadful place where tortured souls are writhing in agony over sizzling flames, where there is a smell of sulphur in the air, and the demonic laughter of Satan in your ears?

These pictures of heaven and hell come from the folklore of the Middle Ages—Dante's *Foust* and Milton's *Paradise Lost*. They are materialistic images, based loosely on the symbolism of the Bible. Most thoughtful clear-thinking people of our time have rejected them as archaic, superstitious and meaningless.

Let me picture for you another way of thinking about heaven and hell.

One picture is a barn. There are animals in it: a cow, a donkey, perhaps a sheep. It is dirty. Musty. There's straw on the floor. The gate is rough-hewn wood. It stinks. This is heaven.

The other picture is a beautiful marble palace. It has ornate carvings, classical architecture, carpets on the marble floors, colorful tapestries on the walls. Pictures and sculptures and works of art from all over the world lend beauty and charm to each room. In the gardens and courtyards are pleasant fountains, green grass, cheerful flowers. There are slaves who bring in the best food to serve their masters. Everything clean and sweet smells. In the background skillful musicians play soft music. This is hell.

What I am saying is that the physical surroundings and furnishings have nothing to do with heaven and hell. What makes the difference is the kind of people who live there.

In that barn, a baby was born. The child's mother, a very young, pretty peasant woman, gently wrapped the baby in swaddling cloths and laid him in a manger.

How often we have seen paintings of the Madonna. She is usually dressed in blue, haloed in soft light, holding the small child in her arms. And the look on her face is pure love. I have seen that look on the face of many mothers. So have you. It is so beautiful, so loving, that even the most skillful artists cannot do it justice. It is the face of love.

Love surrounds that little family. Joseph is there, giving Mary his support and tender care. That night some shepherds come to see the newborn child, their faces filled with wonder as they see once again the miracle of new life. But they see something more than that. Perhaps they don't fully comprehend what is happening that night, but in their simple uncomplicated reasoning they know that somehow, in that baby, God has reached down and touched his people. And they offer their enthusiastic praise and spur-of-the-moment joy.

In that barn, there was no carpet on the dirty floor, no crystal chandelier, no upholstered furniture, no gold or pearls or any other sign of wealth. Yet . . . this was heaven.

Just six miles away, in the city of Jerusalem, a lonely old man lived in a beautiful palace. His name was Herod, and he was the king. They called him Herod the Great, and the historians say he deserved that title. His power was granted by the Roman emperor, and he had absolute power—life and death—a very unusual grant to a non-Roman in that empire, but granted to Herod because he was so capable. He had been king there for almost forty years, and he was the only ruler of Palestine in New Testament times who succeeded in keeping the peace and bringing order to that usually troubled land. King Herod was a great builder. He built the Temple. This was the third Temple in Jerusalem, and the last. One of its walls still stands, the famous "Wailing Wall."

Even the people called him "Herod the Great." He could be very generous. In times of difficulty he remitted the taxes to make things easier for the people—and it wasn't even an election year! During the famine, he actually melted down his own gold plate to buy corn for the starving people. He built roads, defended the borders, removed the threat of highwaymen, quelled uprisings and riots without massacres. He developed a workable system of courts, and his justice held the respect of the leading citizens. He was a great king, and is so recorded in history outside the Bible.

But . . . Herod was alone. In spite of the servants in the palace, in spite of the officials in the kingdom who obeyed his will, in spite of the vast powers he had—he was alone.

His problem was that he was suspicious of everyone, a classic case of paranoia. He had no one to share his longings, his dreams, his joys and sorrows. No one was close to him. He suspected everyone. He suspected his wife of infidelity, so he killed her. He thought his mother was plotting against him, so he killed her. He was afraid of his own children, whom he suspected of trying to overthrow him and usurp his throne, so he killed three of his sons. There was always someone who was being executed or assassinated because of his feelings of insecurity. He was always on guard, for he knew that when someone offered him friendship, or brought him a gift, that person wanted something, and might even be trying to bring him down.

When some astrologers from Eastern lands came to Jerusalem seeking a baby who was born to be a king, according to the signs they saw in the stars, Herod pretended outward friendliness, while inwardly plotting to get rid of this potential threat to his throne by killing all the male children in the area under two years of age.

Something of the savage, bitter, warped nature of this man can be seen in the provisions he made for his own death. His doctors told him, when he was seventy years old, that he had very little time left to live. This was just a few years after the birth of Jesus. He retired to Jericho, his favorite city, where he wanted to die. Then he issued orders that a group of the leading citizens of Jerusalem be arrested on trumped-up charges, imprisoned, and at the moment of his death, executed. He said grimly that he was well aware no one would morn for him when he died, and he was determined that some tears would be shed at the time of his death. Fortunately, his last order was never carried out.

This was King Herod—Herod the Great—who was very much alone.

Can you imagine the terrible loneliness, the suffering, the fear of death, the need for companionship when there was nobody he could turn to, the creeping cancer of suspicion, the horrible feeling of insecurity that must have gripped this old man in his beautiful palace, with its luxury, its plush surroundings, waited on by slaves, surrounded by the best of everything. This was hell.

Heaven and hell. These two concepts have nothing to do with the physical surroundings. They are not merely places to go to after we die. They are here-and-now concepts. We can be in heaven or hell right now.

The Middle Ages poets, Milton and Dante, did us a great disservice when they presented the concepts of heaven and hell in materialistic terms. Perhaps as a result of their writings, we have a mistaken notion that we can attain heaven here in this life—as well as in the next—by being successful and wealthy and surrounding ourselves with material possessions and luxury. We can avoid hell by escaping poverty, disease and suffering in all its forms. And so we strive for the material wealth that can bring us heaven and happiness. Often the price of our heaven comes high, if it means neglecting the family, cultivating friendships for what we can get out of them, and making sacrifices in our spiritual nurture to gain material success and wealth—just like King Herod. And perhaps the day will come when we discover that, like Herod, living in luxurious surroundings with plenty of money and power does not bring happiness at all. It brings instead loneliness. Hell.

Loneliness. What could be worse than being alone?

Loneliness does not depend on how many people are around you. King Herod was surrounded by people—important people—but he was still alone. You can be alone even when there are a lot of people around you. I have never felt more alone than those times when I have been jostled by a crowd of Christmas shoppers in a crowded department store. Loneliness is not the absence of people. Loneliness is the absence of love. And that's hell.

The antidote to loneliness is love. You are never lonely when you fill your mind with thoughts of others, or seek ways to do things for others rather than thinking about what other people can do for you. The person who centers his life on the theme, "What's in it for me?" is quite often a very lonely person. But the person who lives by the question, "What can I do for you?" is never lonely.

And this brings me to Christmas.

Many people in our time find Christmas to be a time of hell. There's a lot of unhappiness in this season. The suicide rate shoots up in December. Beneath the veneer of good cheer, laughter, busyness, and the "Christmas spirit," there are a lot of people who find Christmas to be a living hell.

Christmas is a time of emotional extremes. Either you plummet to the depths of hell, or you rise to the heights of heaven. It doesn't make any difference what the physical surroundings are: a rough stable, an ornate palace, a well-decorated home with wreaths and holly and mistletoe and a Christmas tree with brightly-colored presents beneath it. What makes the difference is whether there is love . . . or loneliness.

Christmas is the time to give the gift of love. The strange paradox of heaven and hell is that the only way to get love is to give it. The only way to avoid loneliness is to give companionship to someone else. Kahlil Gibran gave us something to think about as we give Christmas gifts. He said, *You give but little when you give of your possessions. It is when you give of yourself that you truly give.*

So . . . your Christmas this year can be either a heaven or a hell. It depends on you. It depends on how far you are willing to give love.

Christmas is a time of giving oneself. And come to think of it, isn't that the basic meaning of our doctrine of the Incarnation?

A SIGN UNTO YOU

Scripture: *Luke 2:12* Again, the familiar nativity story, focusing on the phrase, *and this shall be a sign unto you: you will find a baby* . . . .

The Preacher's Notes:

The point of this sermon is in the text (above). This event is the focal point of history. The Messiah has come. At last! How should this be presented to the human race? A sign! Something spectacular, epic, unforgettable. But no . . . the sign was a baby, born in a barn. Strange, how God chooses to do his work.

A SIGN UNTO YOU

There are many parts of the Christmas story in Mathew and Luke's Gospels that are fascinating. The more you read and think about them, the more interesting they are, and the more details you uncover that are colorful and engrossing.

There is the story of Elizabeth and Zechariah, and the birth of John the Baptist; the announcement to Mary by the angel Gabriel that she had been chosen by God to be the mother of the long-awaited child, and her response in the beautiful *Magnificat*; the relationship between Joseph and Mary; the trip to Bethlehem for the census-taking; the crowded inn, the birth in the stables; and later, the mysterious star, the strange magi from the East with their gifts, and the hurried flight to Egypt. These stories are captivating and delightful.

Today, let's look closely at one of the little, often-overlooked incidents that make up the whole pattern of the Nativity story. When the angel spoke to the shepherds out in the field, he told them to go to Bethlehem and see a new-born baby—the Promised One of Israel. The angel then anticipated their need for proof; some sign, which would assure them that this was indeed the long-awaited Messiah.

So the angel spoke these words: *"And this shall be a sign unto you: you will find a baby, wrapped in swaddling cloths and lying in a manger."*

I find this one of the most fascinating verses in the entire Nativity story.

Notice first the need for a sign.

How human these shepherds were—just like us. We too would like to have some kind of a sign. We want to be sure. How do we know that God really exists? That he is involved in our daily lives? Show us a sign that we may believe.

It reminds me of the familiar story Gideon. He was called by God to lead the army of Israel against the extremely large army of Midianite invaders. But he wasn't too sure about that. How was he to know that this was really God, and that God would be with him? He had to be absolutely positively for sure certain before he would undertake such a big responsibility. So he asked for a sign. Gideon even suggested what that sign would be.

"Lord," he said, "I'm going to put a fleece on the ground outside tonight. Tomorrow morning, if the fleece is dry and the ground around it is wet with dew, then I'll know for sure that you're with me."

He did, and sure enough, the next morning the ground was covered with dew but the fleece was dry.

"Now, Lord," he said, "don't get mad, but what say we try this again. Tomorrow morning, how about the fleece being wet, and the ground around it dry."

Well, it worked. Then he knew God was with him.

Doesn't that sound easy? If only it would work for us! And I wonder . . . how many people abandon their Christian faith because they have never had a sign from God to prove to them that he is really with them?

A line from one of Tennessee Williams' plays puts it this way: "I believe that the long silence of God, the absolute speech-lessness of him, is a long, long and awful thing that the world is lost because of. . . . "

Just where is God? Why doesn't he give us a sign?

Perhaps God *has* given us a sign, but we don't recognize it, because we are looking for something big, something spectacular, something . . . *miraculous!* Like Gideon's fleece. But maybe God's signs come to us in little, quiet ways, in common ordinary experiences of life, experiences in which you can see the hand of God only through the eyes of faith.

And maybe this is the way it was for the shepherds. The angel said to them, *"This is your sign: a baby, wrapped in swaddling cloths, lying in a manger."* What kind of a sign is that!

The sign was a *baby*. A baby is a big and spectacular experience to the parents, and a joyful happening to relatives and close friends, but hardly to strangers. To the shepherds, news that another baby born in a crowded world of suffering and poverty and taxes could hardly be a sign that God has come to earth. It happens every day. It is so common, so . . . ordinary. Isn't it fascinating that God chose to reveal himself in something as commonplace as a little baby?

Wrapped in swaddling cloths. That's diapers! Plain old ordinary diapers. Big deal! The Son of God is born, and a part of the sign for us is that he has to be wrapped in diapers!

And *lying in a manger*. A manger is the little wooden feeding-trough used to feed the animals. This is saying that the long-awaited Messiah has finally come, the Son of God is born, and they didn't even have a cradle to put him in, so they temporarily jury-rigged a crib by using the feeding trough of the cows. What kind of a sign is this for the coming of God to earth?

Isn't it amazing, the way God works! *My ways are not your ways, neither are my thoughts your thoughts, says the Lord.* This is the kind of thing God is always doing.

The Gideon story was an exception, not the rule. Instead of the Son of God entering the human race through the proud conquering Roman people, he was born instead to Jewish parents— Jews, a conquered people! *How odd of God to choose the Jews.* Instead of being born in a rich family of the noble class, he was born of peasants, in poverty. And why not in Rome, the capitol of the Empire, or at least in Jerusalem—why Bethlehem! And in a small inn—why not the Radisson or the Bethlehem Hilton, in the presidential suite? No . . . he was even born in a barn, down under the over-crowded motel.

Something tells me that if we Presbyterians had planned this great Incarnation event, we would have done it a little differently. We'd make something big and spectacular out of it. We'd have a huge parade—bigger than Macy's or the Rose Bowl. The major TV networks would cover the event, even pre-empting Monday night football. The young parents would be interviewed by Larry King, have some time with Oprah, and be the subject of a segment of Sixty Minutes. They would be invited to the White House for dinner. And the whole world would know, because this is truly a historical event: the Incarnation, the coming of God to earth, when *the Word was made flesh and dwelt among us.* Let's do it up right!

But . . . *my ways are not your ways, says the Lord.* It was all done so quietly, so softly, so un-spectacularly, that most of the world didn't even notice. Because that's the way God works.

Maybe this is why many of us slip through life wishing we could have some big sign from God, but never see him—because who would ever expect to find the Incarnate Son of God in a baby, wearing diapers, lying in a manger!

We keep looking for God to reveal himself in a dramatic event that is befitting his power and majesty, but he surprises us by speaking to us in the common ordinary events of our lives. We look for him to meet us face to face in a morning worship service at church, and then maybe we don't recognize him when we see him in the little things that happen every day. We keep listening for his voice through the preaching of Billy Graham, or some other famous preacher, when perhaps he speaks to us through our neighbor, or the person beside whom we work every day, or some member of the family or a close friend. The God who revealed himself through a baby, wearing diapers and lying in a manger, is the kind of God who can meet us any day, any time, any place—and usually where we least expect him.

Maybe this is why many things in our Christian faith are difficult for us to accept, because we expect the great God Almighty, creator of heaven and earth, to act only in spectacular ways. If he is that great, we say, and has that much power, why should he ever have to act in such common humble ways? But he does, and that's why it is so startling and unexpected . . . and unnoticed.

> *Prayerful souls may find him by our quiet lakes,*
> *Meet him on our hillsides when the morning breaks.*
> *In our fertile cornfields while the sheaves are bound,*
> *In our busy markets . . . Jesus may be found.*

Recently I watched for about the fourth or fifth time the movie *Oh God* starring George Burns. It's a delightful film, giving somebody's idea of what it would be like if God—played unassumingly by George Burns—would come to earth and once again tell his message of people through an assistant manager of a grocery store. I like that idea; it sounds like what God might do. But I didn't like how the movie ended. God—George Burns—was brought into court, placed on the witness stand, and asked to prove that he really was God. And he did—by a series of cheap little miracles. He made a deck of cards disappear, and then reappear, and then he himself disappeared, while his ethereal voice spoke out of nowhere. Cheap tricks. Maybe this is how some Hollywood script writer thinks God would give us a sign to prove that he really is, but that's not how I see the God of the Bible. The God I read about reveals himself in common ordinary ways. And in the greatest revelation of all, when he actually came down to be one of us, he came as a baby, wearing diapers, and lying in a manger.

And that's our sign, that he really is among us.

DO YOU BELIEVE IN THE VIRGIN BIRTH?

Scripture: *Luke 1:26-33* This portion of the nativity story tells the story of the Angel Gabriel coming to Mary, telling her that she will be the mother of the Messiah. But Mary was a virgin . . . .

The Preacher's Notes:

This sermon takes the form of a court trial, complete with a judge, a prosecuting attorney, defense counsel, witnesses, and of course the jury. The jury is you, the reader/listener. You will hear the evidence, and then you will make your decision. The question? That's the title of this sermon.

This sermon could be presented as a drama, with several people playing the roles of the judge, prosecuting attorneys, defense counsel, and witnesses.

DO YOU BELIEVE IN THE VIRGIN BIRTH?

Judge: Ladies and gentlemen of the jury:

You have been called to jury duty this morning to hear and render a verdict on the doctrine of the Virgin Birth. The question before you this morning is this: Do you believe in the virgin birth of Jesus?

This is a very appropriate question for the Advent season, for as we approach the day when we celebrate the birthday of Jesus, we need to ask ourselves: In what manner was he born? Was it a miraculous birth as some say, or was it a birth like any other? Many honest and sincere Christians are troubled by this question. Some would sooner believe in Santa Claus than in the virgin birth of Jesus. Therefore I am asking you, ladies and gentlemen of the jury, to sit in this courtroom this morning and hear the case of the Virgin Birth of Christ, and render in your own heart and mind a verdict on the question: Do *you* believe in the Virgin Birth of Jesus?

We have before us in this courtroom today the prosecuting attorney, the defense council, and a series of witnesses for both the prosecution and the defense. The prosecution will make an opening statement, and then the defense council shall be heard briefly, followed by the case presented by the prosecution, then the case by the defense. There will be a closing statement from both sides, and then the judge will charge the jury. If the prosecution and the defense are ready at this time, let us proceed with the case.

Prosecuting Attorney: Ladies and gentlemen of the jury:

It is the contention of the prosecution that the doctrine of the Virgin Birth of Jesus is a myth, a fabrication, a superstition, and no honest sincere Christian who cares to give it a second thought can accept it as truth. We will bring before you reliable witnesses who will prove to you that a virgin birth is medically and scientifically impossible, that it is a common myth among all religions of history, that a person can accept the doctrine of the Deity of Christ without accepting the story of the virgin birth, and that in this modern scientific age, an educated person living in our modern society cannot, if he is honest, accept this doctrine, yet he can reject it without at the same time endangering his faith.

The Defense Council: Ladies and gentlemen of the jury:

The Defense holds that his doctrine of the Virgin Birth of our Lord is true. It is clearly stated in the Bible, which is the source of all truth for the Christian's faith. It is held by intellectuals and common people alike. It is and has always been the belief of both professional clergymen and the laymen of the Church. It is a necessary doctrine if we are to believe in the doctrine of the deity of Christ. We ask you, ladies and gentlemen of the jury, to accept and believe in the doctrine of the Virgin Birth of Christ.

The Prosecuting Attorney: I call for my first witness Dr. R.C. Davis. Dr. Davis, will you please take the stand?

Question: State your name and occupation.
Answer: R.C. Davis, physician, specialist in obstetrics.
Question: Dr. Davis, do you believe in the virgin birth of Jesus?
Answer: No.
Question: Why not?
Answer: Because it is scientifically and medically impossible.
Qestion: Why do you say that?
Answer: Because the human body is so constructed that, in order for conception to take place in the womb of the female, the female ovum must be fertilized by the gene of the male, and this can happen only as a result of the conjugal act.
Question: Will you please explain what that means in layman's terms?

Answer: Yes. There has to be a father.
Question: Dr. Davis, you said you are an obstetrician. Just what is an obstetrician?
Answer: An obstetrician is a doctor who specializes in the care and treatment of women during pregnancy and childbirth.
Question: In your experience as an obstetrician, have you ever come across a case of a child being born who was sired by only one parent, or we might say, a virgin birth?
Answer: No.
Question: Have you ever heard of it before?
Answer: Yes. There are cases on record of a mother who gave birth to a child and then claimed that there was no human father. In most cases it was proven to be simply a convenient way to get out of what was proving to be an embarrassing situation for the young unmarried mother.
Question: You say in most cases. Have you ever heard of cases that have not been proven to be lies?
Answer: Yes, there are one or two in history. Some doctors accept them as reliable. I do not.

Prosecuting Attorney: That is all. You may cross-examine.

Defense Council: Dr. Davis, do you believe in miracles?

Answer: What do you mean by a miracle?
Question: An event that cannot be explained by medical science, and that you can explain by saying that it is an act of God.
Answer: Yes, I do. I suppose most doctors with any experience at all will admit to that.
Question: Then why do you say that the Virgin Birth of Christ is impossible?
Answer: I did not say that the Virgin Birth of Christ is impossible. I merely said that it is medically and scientifically impossible. If one is to believe in the Virgin Birth, he must do so in some other way, such as accept it by faith.

Defense Council: No further questions.

Prosecuting Attorney: I call as my next witness Dr. Thomas Campbell Smith. Dr. Smith, will you please take the stand?

Question: State your name and occupation.
Answer: John Campbell Smith, doctor of philosophy, professor of history at State University.
Question: Dr. Smith, as a historian, do you believe in the Virgin Birth of Jesus?
Answer: No.
Question: Why not?
Answer: In my studies of history, I have learned that many ancient religions construct myths based on a virgin birth to explain some outstanding hero or the founder of the religion. Buddha, Zoroaster, Lao-Tse, and Mahavira were all supernaturally born. So were Pythagoras, and Plato, and even Augustus Caesar. The mythology of Greeks and Romans are full of this sort of thing. For example, there is the story of how Alcempe, a human female, was beloved by Jupiter. The result of this union of a mortal and a god was Hercules. But Juno, Jupiter's goddess wife, was so jealous that she sent two great serpents to destroy Hercules as he lay in his cradle, but this remarkable child strangled them with his bare hands. There are a lot of stories like this to explain a remarkable person, and I class the Virgin Birth of Christ among them.

Prosecuting Attorney: No further questions. You may cross-examine.

Defense Council: Dr. Smith, as you compare the story of the Virgin Birth of Christ with those other virgin birth stories of history, do you see a difference?

Answer: Oh yes. The Virgin Birth stories of Christ are much better written. There is a mysteriousness and dignity about them that is missing in the other tongue-in-cheek stories. The story of Christ's birth is filled with people who questioned and doubted and had to be shown, which would be very natural. In the other stories all these miraculous events are accepted as a matter of course.

Question: If there is that much difference, then why do you class the Virgin Birth of Christ with all those other myths?

Answer: The story of Christ is better written, but it is still a virgin birth story. It belongs in the category with all other stories of this type. The only difference is that the writer was a little more serious, a little more eager to try to convince his readers that it really happened.

Defence Council: Thank you. No further questions.

Prosecuting Attorney: I call as my next witness Dr. John Mason Brown. Dr. Brown, will you please take the stand?

Question: State your name and occupation.
Answer: John Mason Brown, doctor of theology, professor of Systematic Theology at Presbyterian Seminary.
Question: Dr. Brown, do you believe in the Virgin Birth of Jesus?
Answer: No, I do not.
Question: Do you mean to say that a professor in a Presbyterian Theological Seminary does not believe in this doctrine? How do your fellow Presbyterians feel about this?
Answer: It caused quite a storm at the General Assembly a few years ago. The question of my staying as professor in a Presbyterian Seminary was debated long and loud on the floor of the Assembly.
Question: What was the outcome of that debate?
Answer: I was permitted to stay. You see, the real question there was not the Virgin Birth, but academic freedom.
Question: Dr. Brown, why don't you believe in the Virgin Birth of Jesus?
Answer: Perhaps I should modify my answer a little. I believe in

the Virgin Birth of Jesus. I just don't believe in the literal, historical, physical, biological Virgin Birth of Jesus.

Question: Then what kind of Virgin Birth *do* you believe in?

Answer: I believe in the symbolic Virgin Birth. You see, I believe that Jesus is the Son of God. The Virgin Birth is the best way I know to pictorially present this fact. When the writers of the Gospels came to the place where they wanted to present the doctrine of the deity of Christ, they said to themselves, "Let's see, now, what would be the best way to present this doctrine in a very clear way? I know—I'll tell the story of the Virgin Birth of Jesus. This will symbolize to all my readers that Jesus is really the Son of God." I believe that's how the Virgin Birth story came into Christian doctrine. And I believe it. It is the best way I know to symbolically tell the story of the Deity of Christ.

Prosecuting Attorney: No further questions. You may cross-examine.

Defense Council: Dr. Brown, you are saying, I believe, that the doctrine of the deity of Christ is symbolized by the mythical story of the Virgin Birth of Jesus. Would you also say that the doctrine of eternal life is symbolized by the mythical story of the resurrection of Jesus?

Answer: No, I believe in the historical resurrection of Jesus.

Question: Isn't this a contradiction? Why do you believe one but not the other?

Answer: Because the doctrine of eternal life depends on the actual, historical resurrection of Jesus in order to be true. The Bible says, *Because he lives, we too shall live.* But this is not so of the doctrine of the deity of Christ. I *can* believe that Jesus is the Son of God without believing in the Virgin Birth. However, I can *not* believe in immortality without believing in the resurrection of Jesus.

Defense Council: Thank you. No further questions.

Prosecuting Attorney: I call as my last witness the Rev. J. Ralston Scott. Mr. Scott, will you please take the stand?

Question: Please state your name and occupation.
Answer: J. Ralston Scott, pastor of the First Presbyterian Church of this city.
Question: Mr. Scott, do you believe in the Virgin Birth of Jesus?
Answer: Yes, I do.
Question: Do the members of your congregation believe it?
Answer: Some do, especially the older members. But the younger members, for the most part, do not.
Question: You say you do believe in it. Do you try to teach this to your members?
Answer: No, I do not. You see, there are many people who just cannot accept it. It is contrary to their training, their education, their experience in a scientific culture. If they had to accept this doctrine, it would do serious damage to their Christian faith. In fact, if I said to them, "You have to accept this doctrine in order to be a Christian," I'm afraid that many of them would leave the Church.
Question: Then you believe that a person can be a Christian—a *good* Christian—and still not believe in the Virgin Birth?
Answer: Yes, I do. In fact, I know of several young men in my congregation who are active in the church, deeply serious about their faith, fully committed to their Lord, but who just can't accept the Virgin Birth. That's all right with me, and I feel sure that it's all right with God. Our salvation does not depend on our getting every point of our theology correct.

Prosecuting Attorney: No further questions. You may cross-examine.

Defense Council: Mr. Scott, you say that you believe in the Virgin Birth of Christ. Don't you think that it is important to stand by the truth? Is this being true to your Christian faith?

Answer: I believe that it is. You see, I also believe in Predestination, the Second Coming of Christ, and a lot of other relative unimportant doctrines that many of my people cannot accept. What I ask them to accept are the really important doctrines of the Christian faith: the way of salvation through faith in Christ, the authority of Scriptures, the deity of Christ, and others. Let's distinguish between the major doctrines and the minor ones. I put the Virgin Birth among the minor doctrines, and I don't insist on my people accepting it. And besides, God is our Judge, not me.

Defense Council: Thank you. No further questions.

Prosecuting Attorney: The Prosecution rests its case.

The Judge: Is the Defense ready to proceed?

Defense Council: We are, your honor. I call as my first witness Dr. William Morgan Stanley. Dr. Stanley, will you please take the stand?

Question: Please state your name and occupation.
Answer: William Morgan Stanley, retired, professor of theology at Presbyterian Seminary.
Question: Dr. Stanley, do you believe in the Virgin Birth of Christ?
Answer: Yes, I do, and I believe that I stand with the testimony of the Presbyterian Church, both in its historical standards and also the belief of most of the people in the Church today.
Question: Why do you believe in the Virgin Birth?
Answer: I could quote from the Westminster Confession of Faith or any of the other doctrinal standards and creeds of our Church, which clearly state the official position of the Presbyterian Church. But I shall quote to you from an even higher authority: the Holy Bible. In Matthew's

Gospel we read: *Now the birth of Jesus Christ took place this way. When his mother Mary had been betrothed to Joseph, before they came together she was found to be with child of the Holy Spirit; and her husband Joseph, being a just man and unwilling to put her to shame, resolved to divorce her quietly. But as he considered this, behold, an angel of the Lord appeared to him in a dream, saying, "Joseph, son of David, do not fear to take Mary your wife, for that which is conceived in her is of the Holy Spirit, and she shall bear a son, and you shall call his name Jesus, for he will save his people from their sins." All this took place to fulfill what the Lord had spoken by the prophet: "Behold, a virgin shall conceive and bear a son, and his name shall be called Emmanuel" (which means "God with us.") When Joseph awoke from sleep, he did as the angel of the Lord commanded him; he took his wife, but knew her not until she had borne a son, and he called his name Jesus.*

Question: Is this the only place in the Bible that tells about the Virgin Birth?

Answer: No, the Gospel of Luke has a much longer and more detailed account of it.

Question: Granted that the Bible teaches the Virgin Birth, what does this have to do with your belief in it?

Answer: The Bible is inspired by God, and therefore without error. It is the source of all our doctrine.

Defence Counsel: No further questions. You may cross-examine.

Prosecuting Attorney: Dr. Stanley, as a scholar of the Bible, are you aware that when Matthew quoted Isaiah, *Behold, a virgin shall conceive and bear a son . . .* he was quoting incorrectly?

Answer: Yes, I know the criticism to which you refer. The Revised Standard Version more accurately translates Isaiah 7:14 this way: *Behold, a young woman shall conceive and bear a son.* The mistake was actually made when the Old

Testament was translated from Hebrew to Greek, in what we call the Septuagint Version. These translators mistakenly said "virgin" rather than "young woman," and this was the version that Matthew quoted from.

Question: If this was a mistake, then how can you say that Matthew was accurately talking about the Virgin Birth of Christ as an Old Testament prophecy?

Answer: I believe that the mistake was made in the providence of God. Even though Isaiah meant "young woman," yet under the inspiration of God, Matthew was led to use the term "virgin." It still does not deny that the Virgin Birth is clearly taught in Scripture.

Prosecuting Attorney: No further questions.

Defense Council: I call as my next witness the Rev. Robert T. Wilkerson. Will you please take the stand?

Question: State your name and occupation.
Answer: Robert T. Wilkerson, pastor of John Calvin Presbyterian Church.
Question: Mr. Wilkerson, how do you classify yourself as a theologian?
Answer: I am a Fundamentalist.
Question: What is a Fundamentalist?
Answer: A Fundamentalist is one who believes in *all* the true doctrines of the Bible: the verbal inspiration of Scripture, the blood atonement of Jesus Christ, the historical truth of the book of Genesis, and Jonah and every other part of the Bible, that every person must be born again or he will burn forever in a literal hell, and I definitely believe that Jesus was born of a virgin, and if you don't believe that, you are going to hell for eternity.
Question: Are you saying that a person who doesn't believe in the Virgin Birth is not saved?
Answer: That's exactly what I am saying. You see, if the Virgin

Birth is not true, then Jesus is not the Son of God, and if he isn't the Son of God, then he can't save you, so if you can't accept the Virgin Birth of Christ, you have no salvation at all, and you're going to hell.

Defense Council: No further questions. You may cross-examine.

Prosecuting Attorney: Isn't this viewpoint rather narrow?

Answer: Yes, it is. But Jesus in the Authorized King James Version said: *Straight is the gate and narrow is the way which leadeth unto life, and few there be that find it.*
Question: Mr. Wilkinson, how do you feel about drinking?
Answer: A sin.
Question: And dancing?
Answer: A sin.
Question: And going to movies, and wearing shorts, and wearing lipstick?
Answer: Sins, all of them.
Question: Tell me, Mr. Wilkinson, how do you feel about chewing gum?

Defense Council: I object, your honor, on the grounds that this is immaterial, irrelevant and incompetent, and any member of the jury who watches Perry Mason knows what I'm talking about. The Prosecuting Attorney is demeaning a person's sincere faith by this line of questioning.

Prosecuting Attorney: You're right. I have no right to ridicule a person's sincere beliefs. I apologize. But Your Honor, I'm trying to show that this witness has a theology that is completely unrelated to life, and while it may have been popular a hundred years ago—or more likely, in the Middle Ages—it is completely out of place in our day and age.

Defense Council: Your Honor, I object to the prosecution's attempt to classify all these silly questions with the serious doctrine of the Virgin Birth of Christ.

Judge: The objection is sustained. The jury will disregard any part of the cross-examination that attempts to equate these small moral questions with the theological question of the Virgin Birth.

Prosecuting Attorney: I have no further questions for this witness.

Defense Council: I call as my last witness Mr. John Doe. Mr. Doe, will you please take the stand?

Question: Please state your name and position.
Answer: John Doe, member and ordained elder in the Westminster Presbyterian Church in this city.
Question: Mr. Doe, do you believe in the Virgin Birth of Jesus?
Answer: Yes, I do.
Question: Do you believe, as the fundamentalist witness before you, that you have to believe in the Virgin Birth to be saved?
Answer: No, I do not. Salvation is by faith in Christ, not belief in the Virgin Birth.
Question: Why do you believe in the Virgin Birth?
Answer: I am neither a theologian nor a scholar. I'm just a Christian who is trying to serve God the best way I can in my church. I'm not interested in the deep theology of the Virgin Birth. I just believe Jesus is the Son of God, and this means that God is his father and Mary his mother. This is what the Bible says, and this is what I believe.

Defense Council: No further questions. You may cross-examine.

Prosecuting Attorney: Mr. Doe, isn't this rather naïve of you? Don't you think a good Christian should struggle with the hard problems of the Christian faith?

Answer: Perhaps so. I *have* struggled with it, and I admit that it's a little too deep for me. What I need is something practical, something meaningful, something that I can get my teeth into. I don't really care about such things as the symbolic Virgin Birth, or the myths of history, or the scientific problem involved here. What I want is a realistic way that I can believe in Christ as the Son of God, and when the Bible says that he was born of a virgin, with God as his father, that's good enough for me.

Prosecuting Attorney: No further questions.

Defense Counsel: This concludes the case for the defense.

Judge: In view of the lateness of the hour, let us wave the closing statements, and I will now give the charge to the Jury.

Ladies and gentlemen of the Jury, the question that you must face is, Do you believe in the Virgin Birth of Jesus? The Prosecution says that you do not need to accept it, because it is medically impossible, historically classed as a myth, that it can be accepted symbolically rather than literally, and that it will not damage your faith to do so. The Defense urges you to accept it, saying that it is clearly stated in the Bible, which is our source of theological truth, that it is meaningful to the average person who tries to believe in Jesus as the Son of God. This Jury will not be like most juries, who must render a single unanimous verdict. Each one of you will consider this case in your own heart and mind, and render your own verdict that is satisfying to you. Therefore I am asking each one of you at this Christmas season to consider the question: Do *you* believe in the Virgin Birth of Jesus?

WHEN THEY BEGIN THE BEGATS

Scripture: *Matthew 1:1-17* This is a Scripture reading I'll bet you have never heard in church. It is the "Begatitudes," that boring section of genealogy that reads "so-and-so begat so-and-so, who begat so-and-so." It tells the ancestors of Jesus.

The Preacher's Notes:

This is not what I would call a great sermon, but I include it because I suspect that never before has a sermon been preached on the Begatitudes. There are several fascinating facts hidden in them, and some precious lessons to be learned from these facts.

WHEN THEY BEGIN THE BEGATS

Recently I read something about deserts. They are bare, desolate wastes, dry and barren, and the traveler is sometimes surprised when he comes upon an oasis at how lovely it is. Perhaps after the contrast of the harsh wasteland, the oasis in comparison is lush and green and beautiful and comfortable.

And I have heard that reading the Bible is sometimes compared with traveling across the desert: it is dry and desolate, until you come upon a Biblical oasis that is interesting and inspiring. But the driest, most deserted wastelands of the Bible are usually such things as the "Begatitudes" that we read in our Scripture lesson. The Begatitudes are not to be confused with the "Beatitudes," that beautiful oasis at the beginning of the Sermon on the Mount, that begin with *Blessed are those who* . . . . We're talking about the "Begatitudes," which are a desert. And when they begin the begats, there are no oases.

I heard once that a Bible study group decided to study the book of Matthew. It was their policy (or method in Bible study) to read a chapter each time they met and then work together on that chapter. As soon as they opened the first chapter of Matthew, they knew they had made a mistake. The Begatitudes! So-and-so begat so-and-so, who begat so-and-so, and on down the line. What could be more like a desert than that? But as they began their study, they were pleasantly surprised to find several oases along the dry desert way. Before they were through they agreed that it was as interesting a Bible study as they had ever had.

What in the world can you find of interest in the Begatitudes?

Where are the oases in this barren desert? Let's explore this boring wasteland, and see if we can discover an oasis or two along the way.

The first thing let's look at in our search for oases in this genealogical desert is the genealogies in Luke's Gospel. Wow! Another desert! But don't worry; I'm not going to read to you Luke's list. But it is interesting to compare the genealogies in Luke and Matthew, which are the only two books of the Bible that mention the list of Jesus' ancestors.

But they *are* two different lists. Between David and Joseph, the only names found on both lists are two men who lived at the time of the return from the Exile. Maybe Matthew and Luke copied their list from two different places, perhaps one from the synagogue records and the other from family records. Another suggestion is that Luke's list is the genealogy of Mary, while Matthew's is the family tree of Joseph, one to show the blood line, the other the legal inheritance.

Still another suggestion is that the list is too long to include everybody in the family tree, so the writer merely chose certain ancestors to list, and left the others out. Matthew and Luke chose different representative ancestors. I don't know . . . what do you think?

However, more important in this comparison of the two lists is the fact that Matthew begins his list with Abraham, the father of the Hebrew race, while Luke traces his line clear back to Adam, the father of the human race. Evidently Matthew was primarily concerned with telling the Jews that the Messiah was a product of their own race, with the proper credentials, while Luke was intent on telling the world that the Messiah was not just a private god of the Hebrews, but belongs to everybody.

The next interesting insight in a study of the Begatitudes is the thought that there are several women mentioned in the genealogy of Jesus. Women in the genealogies? First Century Women's Lib! This was most unusual for that time. Back then, women were regarded as second class citizens, almost as slaves. Those were the days when men commanded, and women obeyed.

I wanted to comment on whether we have progressed or regressed since them, but I'm not allowed.

Not only is it amazing that four women appeared in the genealogy of Jesus, but what is even more amazing is the kind of women these were. Tamar, Rahab, Ruth and Bathsheba. There was a scandal connected with each one of them. Tamar was a deliberate seducer and adulteress. Rahab was a professional prostitute. Ruth was a Gentile, which to the Jews was a scandal in itself. And Bathsheba was the wife of the man whom King David murdered so that he could legitimately marry her and be the father of their child.

If Matthew had ransacked the pages of the Old Testament for shady characters, he would have a hard time finding four more incredible ancestors for Jesus. It is as though Matthew were trying to tell us that God's message through all this genealogy is this: "Behold, my son. He is one of you. The ancestors that produced him were both good and bad. Women and Gentiles and scandalized sinners were among my Son's ancestors. I am their Heavenly Father; I love them all."

I don't know about you, but this makes me breathe a little easier. I haven't lived a perfect life either, and if you will be honest with yourself, neither have you. It's a good thing to know that the God who did not hesitate to claim the likes of Tamar, Rahab, Ruth and Bathsheba as the ancestors of his Son, would not hesitate to claim a person like me.

There will come a time some day when you and I will have to stand before the great judgment throne of eternity and own up to the lives we have led. Has your life been perfect, without blemish? Mine hasn't. Can you read the verse in the Sermon on the Mount that says, *You must be perfect, as your Heavenly Father is perfect,* and not cringe a little as you realize what's in store for you? You see that ledger that has been kept in heavenly places about your life, and on the left hand side are all the debits: the time you did this or that, or failed to do something you should have, and so on and on, the list is endless. And then you look over in the other column, the column of assets, and you find only one entry . . . one entry . . .

but more than enough: the atoning sacrifice of Jesus Christ. And you breathe a sigh of relief that he has come to your aid. Without him, you would never have made it.

And so, when I read that the immaculate Son of God numbered among his ancestors some pretty shady characters, without censure, with loving acceptance, then I feel a little better about my chances. And I'm sure glad that a loving God has made the arrangements this way. If I had to depend on my own goodness, I'd be lost. But I, like Tamar, Rahab, Ruth and Bathsheba and everybody else who walks through he pages of Scripture, don't have to depend on ourselves. Now, *that's* an encouraging thought from the Begatitudes!

We have found two oases so far in the barren desert of the genealogical tables: a comparison of the two lists in Matthew's and Luke's Gospels, and the fact that some shady women were lurking in those lists. But let's not forget the main point of the Begatitudes: that Jesus was a direct descendent of King David. The long-awaited Messiah, the Annointed One, had come! Before these Gospel writers could write about the birth of the one who claimed to be the Messiah, he had to establish that he had the right family connections. No pretender to the throne could ever be accepted as king unless he established first of all that there was royal blood in his veins.

Matthew, being a man with an orderly mind, groups the genealogy in three groups of fourteen each. Seven was the perfect number for the Jews, so twice-seven would be twice as perfect. Right? Okay, and these three groups fall very neatly into three categories, which are meaningful in Hebrew history. The first was from Abraham to David, from the birth of the Hebrew nation to its height under its greatest king. The second group is from David to the Exile. This traces the downfall of the nation, from its highest peak to its lowest valley, when they were conquered and carried away into exile. The third category begins at this low point and builds up, until fulfillment is reached in Jesus.

Whether Matthew grouped them this way deliberately, or found them this way in the Synagogue records out of which he copied them, his point comes through very well. History is very well planned by an all-powerful God. And everything that happened in the long and meaningful history of Israel led to this one great event: the coming of Christ.

This is the point of the Genealogy: that Jesus is the One. He is the One who was expected, the One whom prophecy said was coming, the One who would be the center of sacred history. This is the One, said Matthew, and *he has come!*

Once a little child with a magnifying glass went out into the sunshine and focused his glass on a pile of dried grass. The sun's rays pointed down to a pinpoint of light on that grass, and in a few seconds it began to turn brown, then a wisp of smoke appeared, and then a spark of fire, which the child blew on until it flared up into flame. And to that child's mind, a miracle had occurred. He had taken the sunlight, which is everywhere, and focused it into one small place, and produced fire!

This is what happened when Jesus was born: God was focused on the human race. This great God, who is the God of the vast universe, whose hand guides the course of history . . . this great God has been focused on one small planet, into one small event on that planet, the birth of a child in an obscure village in an unimportant little country. The great silent God has broken his silence, and he says:

> *I am the Child.*
> *All the world waits for my coming.*
> *All the earth watches with interest to see what I will be.*
> *Civilization hangs in the balance,*
> *For what I am, the world of tomorrow will be.*
> *I am the Child.*
> *I have come into your world.*
> *Now . . . what are you going to do with me?*

To that child of Bethlehem, the descendent of kings, be ascribed honor and glory, by his Church and by all peoples everywhere . . . forever and ever! Amen.

LOOKING FORWARD TO EASTER

Scripture: *Mark 10:32-34* This brief Scripture reading presents a picture of Jesus and his disciples going to Jerusalem. Jesus seems anxious to get there, even when he predicts that there he will suffer and die.

The Preacher's Notes:

This is a sermon for the first Sunday in Lent, or on Ash Wednesday. It is about preparation for Easter.

Many people believe that Lent is a time of fasting, of austere discipline, and giving up things you enjoy doing. This sermon presents a more positive approach to Lent. Instead of giving up things, why not add a few things to your life, so that Easter will be more meaningful to you.

LOOKING FORWARD TO EASTER

I can recall very vividly one February morning many years ago when I was in high school, I walked up to a friend of mine at school and said to him, "You have a little smudge on your forehead. You'd better go wash it off."

The look on his face reflected disgust. "It's the first day of Lent, stupid!" he barked.

Well, how was I to know? Born and bred a Presbyterian, we just didn't observe Lent in those days in the Presbyterian Church. But I'll tell you this: I never made that same mistake again!

This past Wednesday was Ash Wednesday, the first day of Lent. This was the day our Roman Catholic friends attended Mass early in the morning, and the priest daubed their forehead with a little smudge of soot, symbolizing the ancient custom of strewing upon their heads dust and ashes as a sign of repentance and humbling oneself before God. It marks the beginning of the Lenten season, which is a time of prayer and fasting, of discipline and self-denial, as one prepares for the Easter season.

When I was a boy growing up in the church, we didn't observe Lent, or even talk about it. That was something those Catholics did. But times have changed. Now our Worshipbook recognizes Lent, designates the liturgical color purple for the season, and prescribes prayers and worship programs for Ash Wednesday and Lent.

Once a few years ago, I attended an Ash Wednesday service in a Presbyterian Church. The Confession of Sin was the central part of the service. We were each given a small piece of paper as we entered the church and were told to write on it one word, one sin, which might stand between us and a healthy relationship with God. Then we folded the piece of paper and dropped it into a large can in the center aisle. That was our Confession of Sin. The papers were set on fire, and at the conclusion of the service as we walked out, one of the ministers touched his finger in the ashes and daubed a little bit of it on my forehead. This was the Assurance of Pardon. Who says Presbyterians don't observe Ash Wednesday anymore! On that day, you couldn't tell us from the Catholics!

Today is the first Sunday in Lent. This is Shrove Sunday on the Liturgical Calendar, the time for confession and assurance of pardon. It marks a beginning of the season of Lent leading up to Easter.

The word "Lent" comes from an old Anglo-Saxon word meaning "springtime" and is the root of our English word "length." It is the time when the days begin to lengthen, and there is a freshness of renewal in the air. Smell the freshness of the breeze, let the sunshine envelop you, and watch the grass green up. The flowers brighten up the roadsides and the trees begin look a little more like trees. You feel better during these lengthening days, and there is rejoicing in the color and freshness and beauty that surrounds us. Nature is telling us that the old winter is dead, and Spring is here, fresh, new-born, vigorous.

It says something to us about our Lenten season. Easter is a time of resurrection, too, and the Lenten season calls us to preparation for it. Many have said that Easter is the most important date on the Christian's calendar, even more important than Christmas. And Lent says: *prepare!*

When I attend the symphony, I like to arrive early enough to read thoroughly the program notes for the performance. I absorb these notes carefully: which instruments would be used, the composer's interpretation, the climaxes, and by the time the conductor lifts his baton, I am ready. Isn't this true of just about anything you do? Preparation enhances the experience.

The purpose of Lent is to prepare for Easter. What kind of Easter experience do you want to have? Are you willing to prepare yourself for it?

But let's not cheapen the Lenten season, as is so often done. I think it is cheapened when you say to yourself, "I will give up something for Lent," especially if it is something that you ought to give up anyway, Lent or no Lent. I shall never forget a college friend of mine who said to me, "I'm going to give up swearing for Lent." Sure enough, he did; but after Easter, he was cussing just as much as ever! Let's not cheapen Lent. Someone once said, "I'm giving up Lent for Lent." What he meant was that if there is something in his life that he ought to give up anyway, he would give it up for good, not just for Lent. Lent doesn't mean much when it is only a seasonal break in the usual pattern of life.

In New Orleans last week, they had a blast. Mardi Gras, a time of revelry when everyone casts aside his inhibitions and has a big time, when the Lord of Misrule rules, when anything goes. The reason for Mardi Gras, which literally means "Fat Tuesday," is to have a last fling before Ash Wednesday, when Lent begins, for Lent is a time of austerity, of fasting, of self-discipline, when you do without things you enjoy. Somehow this view of Lent cheapens the season. Lent is not a time of self-denial, but rather of spiritual preparation.

When we observe Lent, let's do it in a positive way. Instead of giving up something, let's add something worthwhile to our lives. Let's try to decide on something that we could do that would lead up to Easter: some way to prepare of this season to make it more meaningful to us.

For example, try something new in your approach to the Sunday morning worship. Think up something. Maybe it will be a way you say some of the prayers, or sing the hymns, or open your mind and heart to the Scripture reading, or perhaps just your general attitude and frame of mind. Perhaps in some way, you can make the routine of Sunday morning worship service a special event each week for you.

Or maybe you might want to read something special this month, some book, some magazine articles, anything that would enrich the season and make your preparation for Easter more meaningful. Maybe this is a good time to read the Bible, especially those events of the last week of Jesus' life that cover so much of the Gospel narratives. Try reading these familiar stories in one of those exciting new versions. Now, *that* could be a great spiritual experience!

And sometime during this season of preparation, think about the life of Jesus, especially that last week of his life that we call Holy Week or Passion Week. Passion Week is an appropriate term for it; it implies the passion or suffering of our Lord. Constantly ask yourself, *What does this mean to me?*

It is most appropriate at this time to bring to our minds a scene in the life and ministry of Jesus. I am referring to that time during his ministry when, in Luke's words, he *set his face steadfastly toward Jerusalem*. Mark's description is equally fascinating: *And they were on the road, going to Jerusalem, and Jesus walked ahead of him; and they were amazed.*

The disciples must have wondered abut this strange man whom they had followed for the last two or three years. He had his face set resolutely toward Jerusalem, and he seemed in a hurry to get there. But Jerusalem was a place of danger; the enemies of Jesus would like nothing better than to get their hands on him. It was even stranger to them when Jesus explained what he saw ahead of him there. What strange compulsion drove him? What madness led him into the very city where suffering and death lay waiting?

But nothing could dissuade him. *He was going to Jerusalem!* So are we; not in a geographical sense, but in the figurative or spiritual sense. Let us, with Jesus, *set our faces steadfastly toward Jerusalem* in anticipation of the great worship experiences that await us there.

As we prepare ourselves for the Easter season, let us keep our eyes on him who walks ahead. Look closely at him, for he is the central person in all these events. Let's follow him into the city on Palm Sunday, casting palm branches before him and shouting "Hosanna to the Son of David! Blessed is he who comes in the name of the Lord!" As we follow him into the week, let us reverently go with him to the Last Supper and watch him there as he administers the first Sacrament of Communion. Let's follow him then to the quiet Garden of Gethsemane, and listen for his prayer,

"Father, if it be possible, let this cup pass from me; nevertheless, not my will but thine be done." How will you feel when Judas betrays his Master with a kiss, and the soldiers lead him away? What are your emotions as you stand there in front of Pilate's porch and listen while the crowd shouts, "Crucify him! Crucify him!" Let's go with him out to that hillside just outside the city gate, where he is nailed to the cross. Listen to his seven last words, and then watch thoughtfully as he dies, and let us ponder what this event means for us. And then . . . let us go reverently to the tomb on Sunday morning, and discover with great joy that he is not dead, but risen! Then let us worship the risen living Lord, and affirm once again that he is not dead. He lives!

Let's approach this season with thoughtfulness and devotion. This is the meaning of Lent.

JESUS IS UNIQUE

Scripture: *Luke 24:1-12, I John 1:1-4* The story of the Resurrection as told by Luke. The opening words of John's first epistle present to us the unique character of Jesus.

The Preacher's Notes:

This sermon was preached at a sunrise service with several denominations in attendance.

Jesus is unique in four ways: his birth, his life, his death and his resurrection.

JESUS IS UNIQUE

There are many ways to drink coffee, and all but one of them are wrong. Some people drink it black. Wrong! Some drink it with cream only. Wrong again! Some . . . *ugh!* . . . with sugar only. And then there are those who drink it correctly: with cream *and* sugar. Anyone who drinks it any other way has no business drinking it at all.

However, I suspect that you did not get up this early on Easter morning to come here and learn about the proper way to drink coffee. I'm not sure why you did come this morning—maybe I'd be happier if I never found out—but I suspect that some of you came this morning not to hear about how to drink coffee, but rather because of some motivation springing from your Christian faith. Now, it would be just as absurd for me to tell you that there is only one legitimate way to be a Christian—*my* way!—as it is for me to tell you the only legitimate way to drink coffee.

Each one of us is different. I suspect that there are represented here many different ways of being a Christian, and many different nuances of doctrine. I am quite willing to let you approach God in your own way, with only one exception: I object strongly to the person who says, "Your religion must be the same as mine, or you are not a Christian at all. Your beliefs must be like mine, your methods of worship must be the same as mine, and your approach to God must be the same as mine, or else you have no faith at all." Somehow, I believe that God is big enough to recognize our differences, and to accept us, each in our own way.

Then, let me tell you about my beliefs. I can no more insist that your beliefs must be exactly the same as mine than I can insist that you have to drink coffee the same way I do. Nevertheless, let me tell you what I believe, and invite you to consider it. It means a lot to me, and I would like to share it with you.

I believe in Jesus Christ.

Without him, my religion topples and falls, and I have nothing. Christ is the center of my faith. Anything that I have to say about my religion must be centered in him.

I believe that Jesus is unique. Never has there been a man like him, and I believe, never will there be another like him. He is unique.

He was unique in his birth.

That child who was born in a manger in Bethlehem in the first Century—I believe that somehow the fullness of God dwelt in him. I don't know how; in fact, there is a mystery here that is beyond my ability to comprehend. But we believe that somehow—in that Bethlehem manger—Incarnation took place. God was in Christ.

It is not enough to say that there is a little bit of God in each one of us. Incarnation means a lot more than that. I have never ceased to be amazed at what Incarnation does mean. Think of it—God, the mysterious, vague, far-away being, so far beyond any concept that a finite person can grasp, let alone put into words—this God has come, and dwelt among us! Without Incarnation, God is nothing but a big question mark, a blur, as we wonder—what *is* that vague, mysterious being in the universe, if there really is one. But with Incarnation, the mysterious has been revealed, the unintelligible has become known, the blur has been focused. And this I believe, for without Incarnation, I would have no idea who God is.

Not only was he unique in his birth, but also he was unique in his death. He lived as no other man before or since has lived.

Of course, there are many ways in which his life was very much like ours. He shared in a humanity that all of us know. Physically and emotionally and spiritually, Jesus lived the same life we all live. He hurt. He played. He fussed and fought with his brothers and sisters. He had to learn. He could be afraid as well as self-confident. He could feel lonely and deserted not only by other people but by God. He was one of us—a human being.

And yet, he was different. The Bible says that he was like us in every way except one: he was without sin. Now what in the world does that mean?

I'm not sure, but wiser theologians than I have said that this means simply that Jesus lived his life for others rather than for himself. Sin is self-centeredness. It is, as William Barclay said, "thinking that you know better than God." One of the biggest mistakes we Christians make is to think of sin as all those bad things we do that are on a list of things we shouldn't do. That's not sin; sin is much deeper than that. Maybe we could say that all those bad things we do are symptoms of a disease, but the disease that infects all of us is simply self-centeredness. We have a tendency to glorify the pronoun "I." This is what Jesus never did. He lived completely and unselfishly for others. In this way he was different from all the rest of us.

Not only was Jesus unique in his birth and his life, but he was also unique in his death.

He died well. Of course, the cross was a very ignoble way to die, but the cross is no longer a symbol of shame. Jesus changed that. He died so well that a callous Roman soldier, standing before the cross, shook his head and muttered, "Surely this was a godly man!"

Yes, Jesus died well. But this in itself is not unique. Many others in history died well. Even some criminals about to be executed have gone to their deaths with poise and calm. This is not what makes Jesus' death unique, but it should be noted in passing that he did die well.

What makes Jesus unique in his death was something intangible, something theological, that is pretty hard to put in words other than the theological jargon in common use. The theology textbook says that his death made atonement with God, bought us redemption, propitiated God and reconciled man and God. Now, that is a theological mouthful. What does it mean?

In some strange and mysterious way, that one solitary death in a moment of history had vast and unique theological implications. I'm not sure that I understand too clearly exactly what happened, but because of that specific death, my relationship with God was established. In that sense, his death was unique.

Jesus was unique in his birth, his life, and his death. And he was also unique in his resurrection. This is the message of Easter: that Jesus arose from the grave.

This means two things to me. First, it means that Jesus conquered death on our behalf. As Jesus himself put it, *"Because I live, you too shall live."*

This means that I can stand beside the graveside of a loved one and not despair, for death is no longer the mysterious end of all. It is a beginning, an open door, a new life, an opportunity for future reunion. This is the first thing that Jesus' resurrection means to me, that death is dead, for Jesus has conquered it!

And secondly, it means that Jesus is alive. We do not worship a dead man. We worship a living God.

In the former Soviet Union, the Communists of the country we now call Russia celebrated as a national holiday the first day of May. May Day was observed throughout the Communist countries, but especially in Moscow. A large throng gathered in Red Square to parade around the mausoleum of Lenin, the founder of their party, the leader of their faith. But Lenin was dead. His body lay cold and useless in a tomb.

Not so with our leader! His tomb is empty! On this great festival of the Christian faith, we rally around an empty tomb, for our leader is alive! And this makes a big difference to me, to realize that the one whom we follow is not dead, but alive. In this he is unique.

Jesus was unique in his birth, his life, his death and his resurrection. These are the great claims of the Christian faith, and I have accepted them. Have you? I can no more insist that you believe these things than I can insist that you drink coffee the way I do. But these beliefs mean a lot to me, and I invite you to consider them.

On a scroll of marble over a Byzantine figure of Christ in St.

Mark's Church in Venice, there are inscribed some words that may well speak to us on this Easter Sunday:

> *Who he was*
> *And for what purpose*
> *And at what price*
> *He redeemed thee*
> *And why he did this for thee*
> *And gave thee all things—*
> *CONSIDER!*

DO YOU BELIEVE IN THE RESURRECTION?

Scripture: *I Corinthians 15:12-20* In Paul's first letter to the Church at Corinth, he very logically explains his reasons for believing that Jesus rose from the dead.

The Preacher's Notes:

This is an Easter sermon, basically confronting the question in the title. The logic is not as important as our need to believe that death has been conquered once and for all.

DO YOU BELIEVE IN THE RESURRECTION?

One of the most fascinating stories to capture the imagination of people throughout history is the story of Marco Polo. The novel, *Messer Marco Polo* by Donn Byrne, is supposed to be an authentic account of Marco Polo's adventures in the court of Kubla Khan, the mighty emperor of China. The story tells how Marco Polo seeks the hand of the daughter of Kubla Khan, whose name was as beautiful as the girl herself: Golden Bells. He decided that before he would ask for her hand, he would tell the emperor and his court the story of Jesus Christ. And now quoting from the book:

> High on his throne, so high that his feet were above the heads of the tallest captains, sat the emperor; and beside him on a little throne sat Golden Bells, whose simple charm and beauty were all that the stories of her had foretold. From her throne she smiled at Marco Polo, and as the Khan smiled also, he began his story, starting with the teachings of the Master, beginning with the Sermon on the Mount.
>
> One by one he went through the Beatitudes, and everyone listened respectfully; little Golden Bells leaning forward with her chin on her hand, and Kubla Khan leaning backward, his eyes half closed. The young explorer spared no detail, and when he came to the words, "But I say unto you that ye resist not evil, but whosoever shall smite thee on the right cheek, turn to him the other also," there was a restless movement among the fighting men in the hall.
>
> Then he turned from Jesus' teaching to the Master's life and death. He told of Bethlehem and the star and the shepherds, and

the poets nodded their heads. He told of the healing deed and the casting out of devils, and the magicians raised their eyebrows and wondered. He told of the little band in the Upper Room, of the Last Supper, and the betrayal of Judas, and the captains of arms shifted in their seats. He told of the judgment, of the scourging, the scarlet robe, and the crown of thorns, and the great Khan flicked his dagger in and out of its sheath, and Golden Bells looked through a mist of tears.

And then he told of the crucifixion between two thieves, and out from the lips of Kubla Khan there ripped a great oath, and silver tears dropped from the eyes of Golden Bells. Then, in the hush that followed, he added, "And on the third day he rose from the dead."

And with a great shout, Kubla Khan stood up and cried, "He came back from the dead and showed himself to the Roman Pilate in all his majesty and power, he . . . ."

"No," said Marco Polo.

"Then he showed himself to the thousands who had seen him die on the gallows tree; he showed himself to them; he . . . ."

"No," said Marco Polo.

A frown hovered upon the brow of the Emperor. "Then to whom did he show himself?"

"Just a few of his friends and followers—a fallen woman named Mary, and to some fisher-folk, and a man named Peter."

Kubla Khan sank back and said no more, and silence reigned over that great assembly. And Marco Polo was aware of two things—the great politeness of the Chinese people, and Golden Bells' pitying eyes.

That's the end of the story. Marco Polo did not win the hand of Golden Bells, nor did Kubla Khan and the Chinese people accept Christ. And the reason is obvious. The story of the resurrection is unbelievable.

Do you believe it? I do. You'd better believe I believe it. And I'll tell you why. There are three reasons why I *must* believe the most unbelievable fact of the Christian faith.

The first is that if Jesus did not rise, if the resurrection is not true, then I would be afraid to die. Are you afraid to die? Death stands at the end of the journey of life, and not one of us can escape it.

A famous doctor said that there are three reasons why people fear death. The first is fear of suffering and pain at the end. The second is concern about the loved ones you leave behind. And the third is fear of the unknown.

He went on to say that as to the suffering and pain at the end, medical science has pretty well taken care of that, and a person's sufferings may be eased considerably at the end. As to the people you leave behind, some careful planning and good insurance will relieve your mind considerably there. But when it comes to that part about the unknown, the doctor had nothing to say.

But our Lord Jesus Christ does! Listen to what he said: *I am the resurrection and the life. He that believes in me, though he die, yet shall he live; and he that lives and believes in me shall never die!"*

A famous explorer, now retired, was addressing a group of people, and he described how he had traveled all over the world and had had many adventures. And then he concluded his talk by saying, "My greatest adventure is still ahead of me." The people looked wonderingly at him. He was about 80 years old, and had lived a full life. What greater adventure was still ahead of him? And then he said: "The first few minutes after death!"

Are you afraid of death? If the resurrection of Jesus is meaningless to you, you may well be. You may be like the king of France who refused to allow the word death to be spoken in his presence. No one could tell hem when someone died, and he would never think of it himself. Is this your experience? Do you avoid even thinking about death, because you are afraid of it? Not if you believe in Christ! He conquered death. It is no longer a threat to us. *Because he lives, we too shall live!*

The second reason why I must believe in the resurrection is that otherwise I would find no comfort when I stand beside the grave of someone whom I love. For each one of us, there is a grave somewhere that means a lot to us: a mother or father, a wife or husband, a brother or sister, son or daughter, a close friend or loved one. How do you feel about this? If you do not believe in the risen living Christ, then that grave to you means the end, no hope, nothing to look forward to, no anticipation of reunion, just despair, fear, dread of the unknown. But believe in Christ! He has conquered death! In this faith, there is peace, hope, joy, anticipation. How can you describe the feeling of security in the thought that because of Christ, that loved one has gone to a heavenly home!

The third reason why I must believe in the resurrection of Jesus is that I must believe in a *living* God. Any kind of a faith you might have would be meaningless if the God in whom you trust is dead.

A Moslem taunted a Christian by saying, "You Christians do not even have a tomb to which you can point, where your Jesus is buried. We have a tomb of Mohammed in Mecca."

The Christian replied, "That is just the point. Your prophet is dead and lies buried; our Christ is risen and alive, and with us always."

This single fact is what makes the Christian faith what it is. We believe that Jesus is still alive and well, and living in Melbourne, Florida *(or whatever city you live in)*. We gather here today at his Table to eat a piece of bread and drink a cup of wine, symbols of his death. But this is called a *Communion* service, when we commune with our living Lord.

This means different things to each one of us. It means that when we turn to him in prayer, he is here to listen and answer in his own way. It means that when we are weak, he is near to give us strength. It means that when we are lonely, he stands by us as our companion. It means that when we grieve, he is there, to tell us what death is all about, and give us comfort.

He is risen! He is alive! He is *here!*

THE EMMAUS STRANGER

Scriptures: *Luke 24:13-35* This scene is set outside Jerusalem on the day after the resurrection of Jesus. Two men are going home to Emmaus, and then they were joined by a stranger who talked with them about what had just taken place.

The Preacher's Notes:

This sermon is designed for the Sunday after Easter. It tries to reconstruct what that stranger told the two men as they walked toward Emmaus. Well . . . maybe it is fiction, but it tries to make sense out of the whole theological history of the Christian faith.

THE EMMAUS STRANGER

If you had a time machine that could take you back in history to be present at any time and place in the past that you choose, what would you set it for? What great event in history would you like to witness with your own eyes? Would it be the people of Israel, newly escaped from bondage in Egypt, crossing the Reed Sea with its wall of water on each side? Would it be the strange handwriting on the wall in Belschazzar's palace in Babylon? Would it be one of our Lord's miracles, or perhaps his Sermon on the Mount?

I think, for me, it would be that day just outside Jerusalem on the road to Emmaus, when two people walked and talked with a stranger.

I imagine it would have been a day something like this one: Springtime in Palestine, perhaps just after a gentle shower, when everything is fresh and moist and sweet smelling, and the flowers are bravely smiling at the world. It was such a day as this that the writer of the Song of Songs wrote: *For lo, the winter is over and past, the rain is over and gone, the flowers appear on the earth, and the time of the singing of birds has come, and the voice of the turtle-dove is heard in our land.*

But these two men were insensitive to the glorious day and the pleasant springtime. They were in shock, stunned by the tragic violent death of their Master a day or two ago. The song of the birds fell on deaf ears as they plodded along the familiar road toward home. It was all over now, that glorious dream that had sprung up overnight, it seemed, but was now shattered, and they might as well go home.

And then they were joined on the road by this stranger. He inquired about their gloom on this pleasant day, and they began to tell him. Encouraged by his interest and friendliness, they told their sad story. As they talked, the words tumbled out, they interrupted each other, they could hardly keep their story straight. They told him about Jesus of Nazareth, a prophet mighty in deed and word before God and all the people, and of their shattered hopes that it would be he that would redeem Israel. But the priests and rulers delivered him up to be condemned to death, and the Roman soldiers crucified him. And then there is this strange rumor floating around this morning, that his body is missing from the tomb....

Then the stranger spoke. *"O foolish men, and slow of heart to believe all that the prophets have spoken! Was it not necessary that the Messiah should suffer these things and enter into his glory?"* And he began to talk to them, so that their hearts were strangely warmed within them, interpreting to them in all the Scriptures the things concerning the Messiah.

Right there! That's where I would set the dial for my time machine. Wouldn't it have been exciting to hear from the lips of this stranger the wonderful story of what had happened! Well... maybe we can reconstruct that story this morning. Maybe... just maybe... what the stranger said went something like this:

O foolish men, and slow of heart to believe all that the prophets have spoken! Was it not necessary that the Messiah should suffer these things and enter into his glory?

Do you recall the beautiful story that comes to us from the dark mists of our heritage? In the beginning, there was the Spirit of God, brooding upon the face of the waters. All the creatures of the sea and the birds of the air, and all the animals and other living things that inhabit the earth, were waiting for God to finish his creation. Then God brought it to pass: he created a human being, and set him in the beautiful Garden. God gave to the man a woman, and told them to live happily and prosper in the land the Lord God had given to them. And he cautioned them to always remember who their Creator really was.

There dwelt the man and the woman, happily, innocently, knowing that they were God's children. And then something happened in the Garden.

The man and the woman became aware of themselves. They had a power, and that power gave them the ability to choose. They could choose to obey God, and live happily in the Garden forever. Or they could turn aside from their Creator, disobey him, and live for themselves. The two human creatures could go their own way, or they could go God's way. This was their choice.

They chose to go their own way, turning their backs on their Creator. The story is beautifully told: they were tempted by the serpent to eat of the fruit of the tree that God had expressly forbidden to them. They ate. And thus it began. Their relationship with their Creator was shattered, and they were banished from the Garden.

And God saw what his creatures had done, and the path they had chosen to follow, and he felt a deep sorrow. So he set in motion a plan to redeem his people.

It began with the story of a man named Abraham. He was the father of the Chosen People. God called him to follow, and Abraham obeyed. He didn't go the way of Adam and Eve; he walked with God. And God made a Covenant with Abraham, a binding agreement between Abraham and all of his descendents, that they would be God's special people.

You remember the familiar story: how Abraham's great-grandson, Joseph, led them into Egypt, where eventually they became slaves. Then God raised up Moses, who led the people to freedom. They were promised a new land, and through the long hard journey through the wilderness they were molded into a people who lived by the Covenant between God and Abraham. They established the Passover, the worship rituals, the Laws, and they became a nation, the people of God.

Were they ready for the final redemption of the human race? No, not yet. There was more to come.

They established themselves in their promised land by tribes at first, and the lessons they learned were harsh. They would soon forget about God and the Covenant that bound them to God, and they would be brought back to it by some tragedy, some invading army, some period of suffering. They were learning, but it was slow, and hard.

Then they asked for a king, and as a kingdom, Israel began to grow in material wealth and power. And once again they began to follow the old familiar way, the way of Adam, which led them away from their covenant faith with God. Troubles came upon them. The kingdom was divided by warfare, and still they turned from God to go their own self-centered ways. Prophets came and went, preaching repentance, turn back to God, remember the Covenant, but they wouldn't listen. Something big would have to happen to them, something drastic, before they became the kind of Covenant people to produce the salvation of humankind.

First came the Assyrians from the north, devastating the land as they went, killing, burning, destroying, taking captives. The Northern Kingdom was overrun, and the people either killed or taken into Exile, from which they never returned. The Southern Kingdom frantically turned back to God, and received respite for a while. But a hundred years later, they had forgotten again, and were following the old familiar way of self as much as ever. So the Babylonians invaded, and this time the Kingdom fell. Jerusalem was destroyed, the beloved Temple leveled to the ground, and the people carried off into Exile.

They weren't in Exile long—about two generations—but in that time they began to rethink the meaning of a Covenant people. They were suffering. These proud children of Israel, who believed that God had chosen them for his own, given them a Promised Land, and prospered them, were now a conquered people, away from home . . . deserted by their God? Or just being led by their Covenant God to prepare for something big to come? One of their prophets, Isaiah, spoke to them comforting words, about a time that is coming to return home, about renewing their ancient Covenant, but this time as a New Covenant, written on the heart, a Covenant of life and deeds, not just of lips. They must learn that being a Covenant people entails not just privilege but responsibility. They must forsake the way of Adam, of serving themselves, and return to serving God, for a Messiah would come who would fulfill all their hopes and dreams and bring salvation to all of God's people.

And so they returned to their homeland, rebuilt the Temple, and rededicated themselves to being the Chosen People of God. They had been chosen for a purpose. Through them God's salvation would come to all. And they must be ready.

It was a long time before it happened, but when it did, everything began to fall into place. Let me quote to you from the ancient Scriptures to show you how this pattern was working out:

> But you, Bethlehem of Judea, though you are least among the cities of Judah, out of you shall come a governor who shall rule my people.
>
> Behold, a virgin shall conceive and bear a son, and you shall call his name Immanuel.
>
> Out of Egypt have I called my son, and he shall be called a Nazarene.

It was beginning to happen. The Covenant was being fulfilled. And now these tragic events of the past week have come upon you. But they are not as tragic as they seem. They are all part of the pattern. Our Scriptures speak of it, and now that these things have happened, you can understand what the ancient prophecies were talking about. Do you recall the prediction that the Messiah would enter Jerusalem, meek and lowly, seated upon an ass? That he would be betrayed by a friend for thirty pieces of silver? That he would be beaten, crowned with suffering, stretch out his hands in death, die with malefactors, given vinegar and gall, his enemies would cast lots for his garments, his side would be pierced, but not a bone of his body would be broken, that he would be buried by a rich man? That the Messiah must suffer and die, and on the third day he would rise? Now think about the events of this past week. Do they fall into place for you? It was all a part of the pattern, and predicted in our ancient literature. The pattern is working out. The ancient Covenant is being fulfilled, and a New Covenant is being established.

Remember the way of Adam, the way the human race chose to go? That was now met head on with the way of the Messiah. The way of disobedience met the way of obedience. The way of self met the way of God. The sin of Adam, the way of the human race, has found atonement and redemption in the events you have just witnessed. This is the way it was planned, and this is the way it has worked out.

O foolish men and slow of heart to believe all that the prophets have spoken! Was it not necessary that the Messiah should suffer these things and enter into his glory?

The walk to Emmaus had come to an end. The two men's hearts burned within them, and their eyes were opened. Somehow, the day was different. Everything was new, like the springtime. They hurried back to Jerusalem to tell the disciples. Everything was different now, since talking to that Emmaus stranger. It was like springtime in their souls.

A VISIT TO FIRST CENTURY JERUSALEM

Scriptures: *Mark 14:16-26* This is the story of the Last Supper, located in the Upper Room of a wealthy lady's home in Jerusalem. The lady is the mother of John Mark, the author of this Gospel. Her name is Mary, but to distinguish her from the other Mary's of the New Testament, she is known as Mary, John Mark's mother.

The Preacher's Notes:

The title of this sermon tells it all. Fictionally, we visit Jerusalem in the First Century, and enjoy the sights and sounds and smells of this ancient city. We visit the Upper Room of the house of Mary, John Mark's mother, and watch in awe the celebration of the Passover by Jesus and his disciples, and we are witnesses to the first Communion service.

This is a Communion sermon, and could well be used on the Sunday during Lent when Communion is celebrated.

A VISIT TO FIRST CENTURY JERUSALEM

Come with me this morning, back across the years to the first Century A.D. Let's fly backward in time on a writer's imagination, and see if we can catch a glimpse of how things were in New Testament times, and especially glimpse that one whom we have read about over and over again in the pages of Scripture.

Jerusalem!

The city looks old, even in these ancient times. It *is* old at the time we visit it; more than a thousand years old. How many cities in America are over a thousand years old? None. Not even St. Augustine is that old.

It looks old. Dirty. Smelly. The city fathers ought to do something about sewage and garbage disposal. The walls of the small houses are mud-and-brick, eggshell white, square-shaped with flat roofs, and a wall surrounds the courtyard in front. The streets are hard-packed dirt, and follow no organized pattern.

We're standing outside a two-story house in a residential suburb. A large wall surrounds it, but as we look through the iron gate, we can see that the courtyard is well tended, the clay floor swept clean. The oven in the courtyard is still warm; a meal was recently cooked there.

We pick up a small mallet and bang the gong. A muted metallic tone resounds in the courtyard. First Century doorbell!

Here comes a middle-aged lady from the house, her body covered by a single flowing garment, and a long white headdress that completely covers her hair. Only her face is showing. Her robe is not quite white, even though it's clean; more like a faded gray. But we didn't come here to study the fashions of First Century Jerusalem women; we came to see Jesus.

"How may I serve you, sir?" she asks.

"We would like to see Jesus."

She frowns. "He's in the upper room, sir. He and his disciples are busy. They're celebrating the feast of the Passover."

She opens the gate for us, and we come in. Don't ask me why she does this; after all, it's my writer's imagination and I can go anywhere I want. She points us to the stairs leading to the second floor, and we go up.

On the second floor, we cross the open balcony and go into the room. It's an average sized room by our standards, but large by theirs. Simply furnished: a table and benches, no pictures or tapestries on the walls. Even the table is bare; we can see the worn grained wood.

Seated on the benches are a group of men. Several things assault our senses at once. The men are short. I stand six feet tall, and if they would stand up, I would be looking down on every one of them, even that burly fisherman with the black beard—we can guess who *he* is. Their clothes are all a dirty white, patched, a little ragged. Their hair and beards glisten with the oil they rubbed into them.

We have no trouble picking out the one we came looking for. That's him, seated at the table. Everybody is staring at him. Gasping. Because he has just made an outrageous statement: "*One of you will betray me!*"

Now, let's take a good look at him; that's why we came to First Century Jerusalem. He doesn't look at all like they portrayed him in movies and paintings. His hair and beard are oiled, and neatly brushed, trimmed long. His face is weather-beaten, and his nose is a little large. His lips are thick. He looks like . . . *a Jew!* There is no resemblance to Warner Sallman's "Head of Christ," or that actor who played his part in the movie.

Now, what's he doing? Ah, yes: he's taking the bread in his hands. It's a long loaf, the crust somewhat brittle as he breaks it in half. Then he hands it to the men on either side of him, saying, "*Eat this. It's my broken body.*"

We're a little surprised at his manner of speaking. We have read his words and heard them from the pulpit so often that we have become accustomed to the King James English that he spoke, or at least the academic English of a cultured gentleman. Usually we hear those words of Jesus translated: "*Take. Eat. This is my body, broken for you.*" But Jesus spoke in the vernacular. His language was Aramaic, although it was first written in the Gospels in Greek, then translated into English for us. In our imagination, we'll translate. But let's not be too surprised to hear him contract words, slur sentences. It's done in every language in casual conversation.

Silently the pieces of bread pass around the table, and each one tears off a chunk and begins to chew. Then Jesus picks up the cup before him. A black, squat vessel about six inches high. A piece of pottery. This is the Holy Grail? He pours wine from the pitcher on the table. Everyone watches him.

"*Drink this,*" he says. "*It's my blood.*"

He looks around at them. Anyone can tell they haven't the foggiest notion what he's talking about. So he elaborates. "*This is a New Covenant, sealed in my blood. I'm telling you, I won't eat or drink with you again until I can drink fresh wine in the New Kingdom.*"

That was no help. Look at the disciples. They just stare at him. They're surely wondering, what is this all about? They join in as Jesus begins an ancient hymn—we recognize the words, they're from Psalm 118: *O give thanks to God, for he is good; his steadfast love endures forever!*"

It's a mournful, dirge-like tune. Some of the disciples sing off-key. Too bad we aren't hearing this sung by the trained Levite choir. Jesus rises now; the Passover feast is over . . . and so is the first Communion Service.

As Jesus leads them out of the room—they walk past us without seeing us—we look closely at him as he goes by. The disciples are confused, of course, but what about Jesus? How much does *he* understand of what is to happen in the next few hours?

Does he know that he will be betrayed by Judas and denied by

Peter within the next hour? Surely he does; he has already spoken of that. Does he realize he will face an agonizing, torturous death in the morning? He has talked about that, too. Does he really know that he will come back to life three days later and break out of his tomb? He has predicted all these things. And is he aware that the little ritual of breaking the bread and sharing the cup will be reenacted millions of times in the years to come? He must—why else would he have done it?

He walks down the stairway, leading the disciples out the gate. He walks slowly, almost reluctantly. Yes, he knows. He surely knows.

Let's follow him. Just who is this man, in whom we have invested so much of our lives—twenty centuries later?

All my life I have struggled with the doctrine of the Christian Church that says Jesus was fully man and fully God. What does that mean? I confess I don't understand it. To be both human and divine at the same time is a concept that is beyond me. If he is fully human, as our doctrine states, then he was limited to the characteristics and qualities of a human being. Physically. Mentally. Emotionally. A man—fully a man.

He was fully a man physically. Tomorrow morning, he will suffer, and it *will* hurt. Like it would for any of us.

He was fully a man mentally. That means that, like us, his mental powers would be limited. *Limited.* No one who is fully man can see into the future. But he did. Now, that's amazing. He must have had some mysterious second sight, some ability to foresee events. Pre-cognition, I believe it's called. But that doesn't mean he was omniscient, having the mind of God. He had the mind of a man, or our doctrine of Christology is false.

He was fully a man emotionally. If he really knew what was facing him the next morning, he would have been scared to death! Well, look at him. We're climbing the Mount of Olives now. Look at his face, his pinched eyes, his firmly set lips, the little muscle tics at the back of his jaws. See his clenched hands? *He's scared!*

But he's not a coward; that's something different. Every human being has fears; a coward lets his fear conquer him. A brave man may be scared, but in control of himself. Maybe Jesus was afraid, but . . . well . . . look at him as he enters the Garden of Gethsemane. He's going through with it.

Let's stand here in the quiet garden, in the dark shadows of nighttime, and think a moment about Church history. Go back to the Fourth Century A.D. The Church struggled with difficult doctrines, including the nature of Christ. Who was he . . . really? Their conclusion, as reflected in the Apostles and Nicene Creeds, was that he was fully man and fully God at the same time. This has stood as the doctrine of the Christian Church ever since, and it is clearly affirmed in the Confessions of the Presbyterian Church that we subscribe to today.

Those early theologians branded as heresy a group known as the Docetists. Docetism comes from a Greek word meaning "to appear," and their doctrine was that Jesus only appeared to be a man. Don't let that human body fool you, they said. That was only a shell, an outward appearance. Inside, it was really God.

Not so, said the Church, and it still does. Jesus was fully human. *Fully.* Not half-and half, not sometimes man and sometimes God, not just man in some ways and God in others. No, he was *fully* human. That's the Church's unchanging belief.

But—at the same time—he was also God. Somehow, in a mysterious way, the fullness of God dwelt in him. I accept that; it's the heart and soul of Christian doctrine. Yes, I accept it . . . but I must confess, I don't understand it. I just stand in awe before it.

And now . . . as we watch him kneeling in prayer in the shadows of the quiet Garden, we shake our head in wonder. Just who is he? Just how much does he know in this moment? Is he aware that all the hosts of heaven are holding their breath right now, watching him? Can he possibly have any idea of the cosmic revolution he will cause in the next few hours? Does he know how much he is changing the course of human history in those crucial days? Does he have a human being's awareness of what is about to happen? Does he know that hundreds of years in the future, a group of his followers will gather in a small church, and think about who he is, what he did, and what it all means to us?

I wonder. There are mysteries in those pieces of broken bread and in that small cup of wine that we will never understand. We can look, we can taste, we can feel. But always, there is an elusive mystery, an ineffable enigma, which leaves us shaking our heads and wondering.

As you touch that bread, as you taste that wine, be in awe. You are dealing with ancient mysteries that no one can fully understand. You approach a God who has come to earth to suffer and die and rise again.

Whatever you do, don't take Communion as though it is just another routine part of your everyday life. Eat and drink—and be aware!

THE SHEPHERD

Scriptures: *Matthew 18:12-14, John 10:1-18* These Scriptures describe Jesus as the Good Shepherd. In the Matthew reading, the Shepherd has ninety-nine sheep safe in the fold, but one is missing, and he must find it. In the John reading, the Good Shepherd describes himself, using the language of a herder of sheep.

The Preacher's Notes:

Not only is the story of the Ninety and Nine told dramatically in this sermon, but it is also updated to modern times, slightly changing the metaphor but not the meaning. Jesus is our Good Shepherd, whether the metaphor describes the profession of shepherding or our modern concept of family life.

THE SHEPHERD

The shepherd of First Century Palestine is a very interesting person. Can you picture him standing there in the night? The mood scuds in and out among the clouds, alternating periods of grim darkness with silvery light. See him there in the moment of bright moonlight, leaning on his staff, his rod not far away in case he needs it... sleepless... alert... motionless... watchful. His weather-beaten face and grizzled hair blend in with the comfortable tatters of his robe. He leans on his staff, and the sheep are on his mind. He watches them, brooding over them.

Each sheep is an individual. There is the one who is a little too inquisitive; he'll have to watch that one when they go through the Valley of the Shadow of Death tomorrow. That one was limping a little today; that foot should be bathed in olive oil before they start out in the morning. The mother of those lamb twins will need some help. And there's the weakest one of all; he'll have to be watched, to make sure he doesn't fall behind and get lost.

The hours pass, and the shepherd keeps watch. This is an honored profession. He's not rich, but he isn't exactly poor either. He's not one of the nobles of the land, but he is respected and looked up to as a competent professional. His steadfastness, his endurance of hardship, his concern for his flock, have won him universal respect. No wonder when the poets sought for a metaphor to describe a good king, they called him shepherd. No wonder the theologians began to apply this metaphor to God.

Now picture another scene. It is the next day, very late in the afternoon. Here is the communal sheepfold, where several flocks have come together for group safety at night. All the flocks are in now... except one. And here comes that one, in the setting sun, the last flock of the day. The shepherds in the sheepfold shield their eyes from the setting sun as they scan the incoming flock, looking for the shepherd. Where is he? There's the hired man, leading the flock, but where's the shepherd?

"Where is he?" one of them calls.

The hired man lifts his head. "He has gone back," he says. "One of the sheep is missing."

All those veteran shepherds know what that means. They've been through it before themselves. It is something that only the shepherd could do; only the shepherd *would* do it. It doesn't take much imagination for these experienced shepherds to picture what is going on out there, somewhere in the dark wilderness. The shepherd is looking for his sheep.

The grim wilderness is no place to be after dark. There are cliffs and boulders and crevasses and deep holes, shifting sand with no bottom, sharp thorns, blind canyons, rockslides, sharp rocks. There are lions, wolves, wild dogs, poisonous snakes. And there is the unknown, the darkness, the loneliness, the fear. They are all out there in the dark.

But a sheep is missing, and every shepherd knows what that means. They are poor businessmen, these shepherds. Out of a hundred sheep, ninety-nine are safely in the fold. Is it worth it, to search for one lost sheep? From a profit-and-loss viewpoint, no. But none of the shepherds here at the sheepfold look at it from a profit-and-loss viewpoint. One sheep, one precious sheep, is missing. And that was reason enough for the shepherd to be out there in the darkness.

All through the night, they wait. There is tenseness among them, in the lonely hours of the night. The sheepfold is quiet, except for the occasional bleating of a sheep. The shepherds alternately doze and watch, and anxiety hovers over the group. Where is the shepherd? When will he come?

Dawn begins to streak the eastern sky behind them. The shepherds gather at the sheepfold gate, straining their eyes into the western darkness, waiting, hoping, praying.

And then . . . *here he comes!* He moves out of the darkness with a confident stride, weary but strong in the morning light. And on his shoulder is the lost sheep.

Instantly the spell of anxiety and tension evaporates, and a loud shout goes up. Smiles replace frowns; laughter replaces silence. There is great rejoicing and celebrating in the sheepfold. *The shepherd has found the sheep that was lost!* Praise God!

When Jesus told this story, which we now know as the Parable of the Lost Sheep, he told it simply and without frills. The people who listened to the story understood him and filled in the missing descriptions in their imagination. They knew about shepherds and the honest profession of shepherding. In their minds, they could picture all this.

But it's different today. In our time and our culture, shepherding is not an everyday occurrence in our way of life. We enjoy hearing the story in its quaint, picturesque setting, but it is not a picture we are familiar with.

Nevertheless, across the centuries, the Word of God speaks to us through this story. We may not know much about the art of shepherding, but we know the Shepherd about whom this parable speaks. We understand the message Jesus was speaking through this parable. We know who the Shepherd is, and who the sheep are. The Word of God speaks to us, loud and clear.

Maybe in our time we should change the picture and adapt it more toward the culture we *are* familiar with. We can picture, for example, a young couple starting out in marriage. Fresh from their parents' watchful care, where they were surrounded and protected, they are thrust into a world where they have to take care of themselves. New responsibilities call for maturity and judgment. There are relationships that are much more than casual. There are pressures, temptations, anxieties, fears—that young couple needs a Shepherd. And the Shepherd is there, with his rod and staff, his steadfastness, his love. He's always there.

Now look again at this young couple. Picture them a few years later. There are small children in their home. They have weathered the early storms of marriage, of adjusting to one another, of taking their place in adult society. The Shepherd has helped them. And now they have children. What an awesome responsibility! One day it dawns upon them. They love their children, they are fun to be with; but then one day, it occurs to them what they are doing. *They have children!* They have in their hands these little lives, to lead them and mold them and prepare them for a life of responsibility ahead. They need help. They need courage and strength and high principles. They need a Shepherd. And so they turn to him, and he doesn't fail them. His rod and his staff comfort them. He's there; he's always there.

The years go by, and the children grow. The picture changes; they're teenagers now. These are the difficult years, when there is a natural tendency to rebellion, to try their wings, to experiment with life. These young people need a Shepherd. Through the years of their childhood, their parents have introduced them to the Shepherd. They have led them to the sheepfold of the Church, where their faith has been carefully nurtured. All this has not been lost on these young people. They may not show it or express it, but they have seen it. They have seen what the Shepherd has meant to their parents, and they know he is there for them. Sooner or later, they come to him. Sometimes it is later, after many experiences in the wilderness. But the Shepherd never leaves them.

One by one they all come back to the sheepfold—all but one. One young person, the black sheep if you will, has gone astray. He has decided to face life alone, without the Shepherd, and he turns his back on the Christian ways that his church and his parents have so carefully taught him. His parents pray. His brothers and sisters have returned to the fold, setting an example that he will not follow. He is going his own way, wasting his life, out there in the wilderness, a lost sheep.

And so the Shepherd goes out to look for him. Something happens to that young man, something strange, something unexplainable. Call it conversion, call it a return to sanity, or coming to himself—call it anything you like, but something happens. Maybe it's just plain maturity catching up with him. The boy becomes a man. He has changed; he's not the boy he used to be. He shoulders his responsibility now, and he returns to the sheepfold. He settles down to mature living. The Shepherd has brought back his own.

Time goes by, and the picture changes. A crisis comes to this family. I won't say what it is; it could be anything. You fill it in. Something happens to upset the normal way of life. There is anxiety, fear, pressure, emotional distress. But that family knows the Shepherd, and they find once again that the Shepherd is with them. He leads them in green pastures and beside still waters. And when they weather the storm—whatever it is—and a new day dawns, bright and clear, they give thanks to the Shepherd who has led them all the way.

One final picture. The family gathers around an open grave, where one of the parents is being buried. They stand there quietly and with dignity, but inside each one, there is turmoil. They half-listen to the words of the minister, but their minds are stunned by grief. They need the Shepherd.

And the Shepherd is there. He's always there. He walks with them through the Valley of the Shadow of Death. He prepares a table for them. He understands, and he cares.

The picture we see at that graveside is only half the pcture. Think of the picture we don't see. I have no earthy idea how to describe it, so I fall back on the Biblical picture of a heavenly Sheepfold, and the celebration that takes place there when the Shepherd brings home his sheep. The picture *we* see is one of quiet sorrow; the picture we *don't* see is one of rejoicing. The Shepherd has brought back one of his own.

In all of life and death, the Shepherd is there. Picture him, then, standing there leaning on his staff, brooding over his sheep. No sheep is too small or too weak for his watchful care. Sometimes we don't see him there, but he's there. He's always there.

The Lord is our Shepherd; we shall not want. Surely goodness and mercy shall follow us all the days of our life, and then comes the bonus: we shall dwell in the house of the Lord . . . *forever!*

WHO THE DEVIL IS THE DEVIL?

Scriptures: *Luke 10:17-20 Isaiah 14:12-15* Both these Scriptures refer to the ancient story of Lucifer, the fallen angel, describing his fall from heaven. Or does it? It depends on what versions of the Bible you read it from, and what commentaries you study.

The Preacher's Notes:

Yes, this is definitely a fictional sermon. The preacher assumes the identity of the devil and tells his own story.

This is a scholarly though irreverent look at Ol' Scratch. It may upset some of your cherished beliefs about Satan, and you might not like the final conclusion of this sermon, which points out who the devil really is. Maybe you won't like the preacher's theology, but I hope you enjoy the writing style.

WHO THE DEVIL IS THE DEVIL?

Just who the devil *is* the devil? Today's message is about this mysterious but well-known figures of Scripture, literature and superstition: **The Devil.**

Now, I could stand here and preach *about* him, and with some authority, too, because I've known him for quite a while. But I thought it would be more interesting for you if I were to invite him to come and speak for himself. So now I have the privilege to present to you this morning the Devil himself: Satan.

(At this point, the minister turns completely around.)

Thank you, Jim. It's a privilege for me to stand here in person and present my case to you. I'm glad of this opportunity to tell you who I really am, because I am probably the most misunderstood person in the world.

You're probably wondering right now: *Is he for real?* People often ask this question; they've been asking it for ages. Am I a real being, or merely a symbol, the "personification of evil," like some other symbolic persons such as Lady Luck or John Barleycorn? Well, I'm not gonna tell you. It doesn't really make much difference, does it? Whether I am a symbol or a real person, it all comes out the same. I have the same effect on your life one way or the other. My powers of temptation are just as strong either way. Believe what you wish; it really doesn't matter. You'll have to deal with me either way.

But I would like to tell you what I'm really like. Nobody understands me. All through history I have had a bad press. Maybe

I should have a public relations department. People through the ages have maligned me, columned me, libeled me, denigrated me, vilified me, belittled me, deprecated me, and not only that, but they've said some mean things about me. It's awful! And 99% of them are not true.

It all started several hundred years before Christ. Over in Persia, the people there developed a religion that had some very strange ideas. They divided everything into good and bad, and in the good kingdom there was a God, with his seven archangels and millions of angels. In the bad kingdom there was a bad god, with seven archdemons and millions of demons. These good guys and bad guys fought more than in a John Wayne western, and their battleground was the planet earth. The poor people of earth were caught in the middle, and either were led into the right way by the angels, or the wrong way by the demons.

This was a religion in ancient Persia. Meanwhile, back in Palestine about the 7th or 8th Century B.C., the Jews were defeated by the Babylonians and carried off into exile into this same country. They were there for a couple of generations, and while there they were influenced greatly by this strange religion. When they were finally released from captivity and came home to Palestine, they brought back with them all those weird ideas on angelology and demonology. You can find it in many of their Apocryphal books of that time. In these books there were all kinds of weird stories about me. They called me many names: Beelzebub, Beliel, Asmodeus, Abaddon, Apollyon—which are almost as bad as some of my contemporary nicknames: Old Nick, Old Scratch, and Robert Burn's favorite name for me: Auld Clootie, for my cloven hoofs. There is one name that I find particularly amusing: *Lucifer!*

Let me tell you about Lucifer. This is a story that is not found in your Bible, although many people believe it is, and they swear it is true.

The story goes like this: Once upon a time, before the creation of the human race, there lived in heaven with God and all his angels a very beautiful and talented angel named Lucifer. Lucifer began to get some exalted ideas about himself, and one day he decided to rebel against God and set himself up as the big boss in heaven. His plot was unsuccessful, and he was kicked out of heaven. He fell like a fallen star to earth. There he dug himself a big hole . . . deep, deep into the ground, all the way down to the fiery regions, and there he set up his own kingdom that he called "Hell."

As I said, that story is not in the Bible. Yet many people think it is. There are three passages of Scripture that they point to that they believe refer to this old myth. I want to show them to you.

The first is from the 14th Chapter of Isaiah. The King James Version reads: *How art thou fallen from heaven, O Lucifer, son of the morning! How thou art cast down to the ground, which didst weaken the nations! For thou hast said in thine heart, "I will ascend into heaven, I will exalt my throne abouve the stars of God. I will sit also upon the mount of the congregation, in the sides of the earth. I will ascend above the heights of the clouds. I will be like the Most High." Yet thou shalt be brought down to Hell, to the sides of the Pit.*

The name "Lucifer" is a mistranslation of the Hebrew word, a mistake first made by the translator Jerome in the Latin Vulgate Version and continued in the King James Version, which is based on the Vulgate. It is translated correctly by every other version of the Bible as "Day Star, son of Dawn." It refers to the Babylonian god of the Dawn Star, which they could look at in the early morning and say, "See, our god is still with us." In this passage, properly translated and read in its context, it is putting down Babylon and telling them, "Your god, the Dawn Star, who would like to be the equal of our Hebrew God, will be cast down to earth." This passage thus gives hope and encouragement to the Jews whose greatest enemies at the time were the Babylonians. But as you can see, these verses have nothing to do with me.

The second passage of Scripture that is often quoted out of context is the 10th Chapter of Luke's Gospel, just after the seventy had returned from their evangelistic mission with great success. Jesus was so elated over their success that he said in poetic language, *"I saw Satan fall like lightning from heaven. Behold, I have given you authority to tread upon serpents and scorpions, and over all the power of the enemy, and nothing shall hurt you."* These symbolic statements by Jesus are not to be taken literally, whether about seeing Satan fall from heaven, or about treading upon serpents and scorpions, which you may do at your own risk. This is what happens when you interpret the Bible too literally and out of context.

The third passage of Scripture that is often quoted to support this ancient myth about Lucifer is Revelation 12:9, which reads, *And the great dragon was thrown down, that ancient serpent, who is called the Devil or Satan, the deceiver of the whole world. He was thrown down to the earth, and his angels were thrown down with him.*

Now, nobody knows how to interpret the Book of Revelation, except, it seems, the people who give the wildest interpretations. In the most popular interpretation, this book describes the *final* battle between me and the forces of good under the archangel Michael, and it predicts my defeat. But it has nothing to do with the old Lucifer story.

As a matter of fact, the book of Revelation has a lot to say about me. I am described as a huge dragon with seven heads and ten horns. But really, I don't look like that. These are symbols, and are not to be taken literally. *Seven heads and ten horns?* That sounds more like Rome than me, with its seven hills and ten emperors who were the enemy of the early Christians.

As you can see, the old Lucifer myth damaged my reputation. But I think the most damage to my reputation came during the Middle Ages, when certain writers began to describe me in *awful* terms. There was Milton in his book *Paradise Lost,* and Dante in *The Divine Comedy,* and Goethe in *Foust* (who called me *Mephistopheles!*)

What a horrible picture they painted of me! According to them, I am completely red all over, I have a pointed tail, cloven hoofs, a short goatee and mustache, horns, and I carry a pitchfork. My home is a place of fire and brimstone, where people are constantly being tortured. I wouldn't mind all this so much (it *is* a little amusing), except for the fact that it is often taken seriously and literally. This Middle Ages picture of me has influenced the thinking of Christian people through the centuries and is even believed by some today.

This is a brief review of how I have been maligned throughout history, and I'm still misunderstood today. In our time, the most popular belief about me is a philosophy or world-view called *Dualism*. It has some resemblance to that ancient religion in Persia.

In Dualism, people believe that there are two great powers in the universe: a Good God and an evil power, or Devil. These two powerful beings are constantly fighting with each other, and the battleground is the human heart. Both want the allegiance of people. Now, the good God has a slight advantage, which he gained through Christ. But the Evil One is still working away, tempting everybody, even the staunchest pillars of the Church, and doing all he can to throw a monkey wrench into the celestial works. Does this sound like I'm trampling on some of the things you have always believed?

If you believe this, then you should listen to what one of your own theologians, John Calvin, had to say about God. He said that your God is *sovereign*. There is only one God in the universe, and he is in complete control of all things. This sovereign God allows evil things to happen—he doesn't cause them, but he allows them to happen because it somehow fits into his long-range plans. But there is only one sovereign being in the universe: God. This viewpoint makes sense, and sort of annihilates the philosophy of Dualism, doesn't it?

Well, then . . . who am I? The time has come for me to tell you who I really am. Therefore . . . who the devil *is* the Devil?

My real name is *Satan*. That word comes from an ancient Hebrew word meaning "The Adversary." That's who I am: Satan, *the Adversary.*

Now, this meant more to the Old Testament Jew than to you. An Adversary in Jewish legal terms was someone appointed by the court to bring out the other side, to make sure the other side was presented fairly. That's me, the Adversary. I'm the one who tries to show you how nice the other way is. It doesn't matter whether I am a symbol or a real person. I can do my job either way.

That was what I was doing in the Garden of Eden when I was symbolically described as a snake. I wasn't there to make Eve eat that forbidden fruit. All I wanted to do was point it out to her, and tell her the other side of the story. And that's all I did. When it came to disobeying God, Eve did that herself. So did Adam. Don't blame me for the Original Sin; blame your first ancestors.

And when the Spirit of God led Jesus into the wilderness, it was for the purpose of testing. I was there, to point out to him that if he were hungry, he had the power to turn stones into bread. If he wanted to, he could use his power to serve himself. Or, he could jump off the pinnacle of the Temple and land unhurt before all the people, who would believe him then after seeing such a spectacular miracle. Or, he could take the easy way to bring in his Kingdom, by worshipping me; that's certainly a lot easier than the long, hard road that led to a cross. Notice I didn't force him to do any of these things; I merely pointed them out to him. The decision to refuse them was entirely his.

It's the same thing I do when I come to you. And I do come to you, you know; every day, almost every hour. Whether I'm real or symbolic, I *do* come to you. I place before you an alternative. I show you how nice it would be to do the other thing, which you're not supposed to do. But if you succumb to that temptation, don't blame me. You have no one to blame but yourself. I think that's why nobody likes me, because you would like to blame me for the things that *you* do wrong.

Nobody likes to take the blame for himself. Have you ever noticed a child who does something wrong, who is very anxious to shift the blame to someone else. "Don't blame me," he says. "It wasn't my fault. So-and-so made me do it." The mature person says, "It was *my* fault; I'm sorry."

In like manner the immature Christian says, "Don't blame me, God. It wasn't my fault. *The devil made me do it.* After all, I'm only human!" The mature Christian says, "It was my own fault. I have no one to blame but myself. I deserve whatever judgment God gives me."

That's what the mature Christian says, and I don't have much influence over that kind of person. He won't blame me for *anything!*

I said a few moments ago that you have to deal with me often in your life. That's almost true. What is truer is that you will have to deal with yourself. All I do is point out the alternative. What you do is up to you.

Well, that's what I wanted to tell you about myself, and I thank you for the opportunity to do so. And I think you should know: I intend to visit each one of you this week—many times. Look for me every day, every hour. I'll be there. Whether you go my way or not is up to you. But I will surely give you a decent choice.

(At this point, the minister makes a 360 degree turn in the opposite direction than he had turned in the early part of this sermon.)

Hi. It's me again. I'd like to express my appreciation to Old Scratch for being with us today and telling us about himself. You recognize this, I hope, as a tongue-in-cheek presentation—my tongue in his cheek! Now that we have met the Devil face to face, maybe we can recognize him when he calls on us.

As that great theologian Pogo once said, *"We have met the enemy, and he is us!"*

THE VIEW FROM THE TOWER

Scriptures: *Habakkuk 1:1-6, 2:1-4, 2:20.* Who? The prophet's name is unpronounceable! These representative verses from this obscure Old Testament book give you the flavor of this prophet, and definitely set the scene for a fictional look at this guy.

The Preacher's Notes:

Picture Habakkuk standing on the watchtower, with the enemy down there. The scene takes place during the siege of Jerusalem, and Habakkuk is a soldier standing guard in the middle of the night.

What the prophet has to say is what God spoke to him during the lonely hours of his watch. It was a message for his people in Jerusalem, but it is also a message for us today. A very real and up-to-date message.

THE VIEW FROM THE TOWER

The fourth watch is the lonely three hours before dawn. The soldier who stands guard during that watch finds it awesome in its slow, frightening loneliness. The darkness is darker, the stillness more ominous, the burdens heavier, the hours longer, and the loneliness almost unendurable.

I have a tendency to look at Old Testament characters through the eyes of a fiction writer. I can see Habakkuk standing the fourth watch. He was probably a soldier as well as a prophet; every able-bodied man was in those days because of the national emergency. All the men were called up to guard the walls of Jerusalem.

Habakkuk was assigned the watchtower on the wall, and I can see him there, pacing restlessly from one corner to the other, pausing now and then to look out into the darkness and listen. They were out there in the darkness. He could see the campfires of the enemy.

They had come at last, the Chaldean army, these Babylonians. Their reputation for cruelty and ruthlessness had preceded them. Wherever they went, they killed, and plundered and destroyed. Now they were here. They laid siege to the city of Jerusalem, the last bastion of the Kingdom of Judah, and their intent was total destruction.

And Habakkuk was bewildered. At that time of the night, everything looks dark, hopeless. The enemy was upon them, the city could not hold out much longer, and the people would be killed or carried off into captivity. Maybe with daylight and sunshine, he could look at things a little more optimistically, but now, in the fourth watch, everything looked hopeless.

What's going on, God? What's happening? Where are you? Aren't you supposed to be in control?

And then, slowly, in those lonely hours, Habakkuk became aware of an answer. The message seeped into him, and it was startling. Mark it well, Habakkuk, and write it down: *Thus says God, "Look among the nations, and see; wonder, and be astounded. For I am doing a work in your time that you would not believe if told!"*

Habakkuk may have realized in that dark hour that he was too close to the situation to see it clearly. But *we* can see it. We who look back over twenty-seven centuries to Habakkuk's time can see what God was doing in those days. And it was awesome. We can see a pattern in it, the hand of God that guided the nation of Judah to defeat, to Exile, and a hundred years later, to return from Exile, to rebuild, to grow even stronger than before, preparing themselves, until finally the day would come when a baby would be born in Bethlehem, and the long-range plans of God would come together and make sense. We can see it, twenty-seven centuries later. But Habakkuk in the fourth watch couldn't. All he knew was that somehow God was at work. *"Behold,"* the voiceless words came to him, *"I am doing a work in your time that you would not believe if told!"*

God says the same thing to us in our time. We too stand on our watchtower looking out into the darkness, and we, like Habakkuk, can see clearly the campfires of the enemy. These are times when we can multiply in our imagination all sorts of things: the ominous menace of terrorists, the constant threat of nuclear warfare or biological warfare, the unrest of third-world countries. We have seen what a fanatical terrorist can do, and it could easily happen again. And we might have to watch again that horror of an attack on America that could destroy us.

We need to hear, as clearly as Habakkuk heard on his watchtower, the voice of God saying to us in our time: *"Look upon the nations and see; wonder and be astounded. For I am doing a work in your time that you would not believe if told!"*

And so Habakkuk waited through the lonely hours of the fourth watch, seeing only the campfires of the enemy so close, so dangerously close, hearing only faintly the whisper of God's voice. God was at work in his time; yes, he knew that. But when he looked out over the wall, they were still there, in the night, the glowing embers of their campfires a constant and ominous reminder of the seriousness of the situation. Habakkuk's restless mind leaped into the future. *What future? Was there any future for him and his people?*

As the darkness softened in the eastern sky, he began to be aware of a further word of assurance from God. It was a vision that he would eventually write down, in bold letters, plain enough for all to see. Habakkuk's phrasing of God's answer was this: *Still the vision awaits it time. It hastens to the end—it will not lie. If it seems slow, wait for it. It will surely come.*

Wait! That was his answer: *Wait!*

Someone once said that there are three answers to prayer: yes, no and wait. Of these three, wait is surely the hardest. But the vision awaits its time, and if it seems slow, wait for it. That was Habakkuk's answer, that God will answer him when *God* is ready, not when Habakkuk wants it.

Wait for it, Habakkuk. You can't see it in your life time. What you *will* see is the destruction of the city of love by the Babylonians, the burning of your beloved Temple, the enslavement of your people, and the long lonely years of exile in a foreign country. Wait for it, Habakkuk. Your answer will come, but not in your lifetime. It will come when God is ready, and not before.

I know of nothing harder than the answer to prayer that says "Wait." It would be a lot easier to accept a plain "No," because at least then you would know. But when the answer is "Wait," then you are left up in the air, and it calls for more patience than we human beings normally have. But it is often the answer God gives to us, as he gave it to Habakkuk.

I heard a story once about an artist who invited a friend to look at his latest painting. As the friend looked at the picture, he saw an elderly lady sitting in her chair reading a book. Her face reflected a radiance and joy as she read, and that look on her face impressed the visitor. Then the artist asked his friend to describe his feelings as he looked at the picture.

"Obviously," said the friend, "this is a picture of an elderly person finding great comfort and pleasure in reading her Bible."

"No," replied the artist. "That was not my intent. This is a picture of someone who has died. She is in heaven, and the book she is reading is the book of her prayers that she offered during her lifetime, prayers that have been answered, and she never know how they were answered. The look of joy and pleasure on her face is one of surprise."

How hard it is to wait. Habakkuk was told that the vision awaits its time, and he must wait. And so must we.

But there is another word for Habakkuk in the stillness of early dawn, a word that ties everything together. This is what made it all make sense: *Thus says the Lord: "Behold, he whose soul is not upright in him shall fail, but the righteous shall live by his faith!"*

There was Habakkuk's final answer, rising in his mind like the sunrise. It was not an explanation of what God planned to do. It was not setting forth the rationale of God's actions. Habakkuk would never know that. Instead it was a word of trust. *Trust me,* says God. *I know what I am doing, even if you don't! Maybe some day you will know, Habakkuk . . . or maybe not. But trust me. Live your life by faith. Put your future in my hands. I know what I am doing. I am God, and I am in control of your planet. Trust me,* says God.

Can't you see it, Habakkuk? It is so obvious to us, who live in the 20th Century. After 27 centuries, we can look back on your times and see exactly what was happening. The sovereign God was in charge. It was all a part of his plan. The city of Jerusalem would fall . . . as planned. The people would go into captivity . . . as planned. The Babylonians would then be conquered a hundred years later . . . as planned. Their conquerors, the Persians, would send the captives home . . . as planned. Everything was planned. The Remnant would return home, rebuild Jerusalem, rebuild the Temple, and be strengthened by this experience. Eventually would come the fulfillment of the Messianic Promise, which states that through these chosen people, carefully prepared, would come the One through whom all the people of the earth would be blessed. That baby will be born in Bethlehem, and the Messianic Promise will come true. It's all there, in God's plan. He's in charge. Can't you see it, Habakkuk? It's so clear to us, twenty-seven centuries later.

I wonder what some future Christian historian will say about our time. Perhaps he will say, "Why couldn't you see what God was doing in your time, you foolish people in the early part of the 21st Century? It's all so clear to me. Why can't *you* see it? You must be standing in the fourth watch," says the future historian, "because everything is as clear as daylight to me."

We can apply this to our personal lives too. Can you understand what is happening to you . . . *now?* Where is God in your personal situation? Is he in charge? Is this all a part of his plan? You'd better believe it! The sovereign God is in full command of your personal situation. Maybe some day you'll see it . . . maybe not. But in the meantime, remember what God said to Habakkuk: *The righteous shall live by his faith.* "Trust me," says God. "I know what I am doing, even if you don't."

Habakkuk's watch was over. The sun's red rim thrust itself above the Judean hills and bombarded the darkened sky with rays of light. The campfires of the enemy grew dim in the morning light, and Habakkuk turned around and looked toward the city. It was all there before him, in the freshness of the dawn's sunlight. And there, on a hill in the center of the city, he saw it. *The Temple!* Solomon's Temple. The Temple that had meant so much to these people who followed the God of their fathers.

And suddenly Habakkuk knew it was true. The God whose hand held the past also held the future. The righteous person *can* live by his faith. Even though the vision awaits its time, and seems slow, he could wait. His trust was in God, who was doing a work in his time that he would not believe, if told.

As he saw the Temple in the middle of the city, gleaming in the brilliant sunshine, there came to his lips a word of praise for the God whom he trusted:

> *"Behold,"* he said, *"though the fig trees are destroyed, and there is neither blossom nor fruit, and though the olive crops fail, and the fields are barren; even if the flocks die in the fields and the cattle barns are empty . . . nevertheless:* **The Lord is in his holy Temple; let all the earth keep silence before him!"**

LEAH, THE GIRL WITH LOVELY EYES

Scriptures: *Genesis 29:1-35* This is the story of Leah, Jacob's first wife. The story focuses on one verse (17), which compares the two sisters, Leah and Rachel.

The Preacher's Notes:

The character of Leah so captured my imagination that I wrote my first novel about her. Well, first, I wrote this sermon, then the novel. I hope you can see in this fictional approach to Leah why I fell in love with her. I hope you will, too.

LEAH, THE GIRL WITH LOVELY EYES

Every once in a while, I come across a verse of Scripture that holds such a fascination for me that I can't let it go without preaching at least one sermon on it. Such a verse is Genesis 23:17, which not only inspired this sermon, but also my first novel. In the Living Bible this reads: *Leah had lovely eyes, but Rachel was shapely, and in every way a beauty.*

I want to direct your attention to Leah. She reached out to me many years ago, and I have never been able to let go of her. Leah, the girl with the lovely eyes.

I appreciate this historian, the author of Genesis, whoever he was. He was very kind. What would you have said if you were writing this love story? Here are two girls, sisters. Now look at them. What would you have said if you were writing this story?

First, look at the younger one. She outshines her older sister in every way. She is beautiful! She has that golden glow of youth that the cosmetics can never hide. She is bubbling with life, bursting with springtime energy. Her name is Rachel, and no wonder Jacob fell in love with her.

Now, look at Leah. What would you say about her, if you were writing the story? Be nice. Look her over. What do you see that you can about her that is positive? Her hair? Her figure? Her nose? What do you say about a girl whose name in Hebrew means "Wild Cow?"

Ah, but look closely. Look at her eyes. Look again. They're captivating. They're deep, filled with character, thoughtful, understanding. They're *lovely*. Concentrate on her eyes. Don't say anything bad about her. I know, you have to say a lot about Rachel, but you can't leave out of the story something about Leah's eyes: *Leah had lovely eyes, but Rachel was shapely, and in every way a beauty.*

Isn't it fascinating that translators had trouble with that one Hebrew word, that adjective that describes Leah's eyes? The New English Bible said "dull-eyed," and the Jerusalem Bible said they "had no sparkle." The Revised Standard Version said they were "weak." The King James Version and the Anchor Bible both called them "tender eyes," which could mean either they were soft or sore. Both the Good News Bible and the Living Bible simply translated the word "lovely."

So . . . this is Leah, the girl with the lovely eyes.

I know her. Don't you? I see her every day. She crosses my path time and time again. She is the person who is not very good looking, or who has something about her that is not very appealing. Maybe she has a weight problem, or her features are not cast in the classical mold, or her teeth are crooked. Maybe her hair is wispy or stringy or poorly kept. Maybe she has some arrogance of personality, a permanent built-in sneer at life, a hostility that says, "I dare you to like me." Or maybe she talks too much. Or too little. Compared to Rachel, she's not much. Have you met Leah? I have. Every day.

What can you say about her? There's plenty to say. You can talk about her hair, or her features, or her verbosity, or her personality, or her big feet. But there's a better idea. Let's talk about her eyes.

Oh, it may not be her eyes specifically. But if you look at her—really look at her—you'll find something about her that will be fascinating, and very appealing. Somewhere in Leah, you'll find it, if you look long enough and carefully enough. It's there. It's always there. Just keep looking, and when you find it, talk about that. Her lovely eyes.

There's an old proverb that goes, *There's so much good in the worst of us, and so much bad in the best of us, that it hardly behooves any of us to talk about the rest of us.* That's why we need to look at Leah's eyes. With everybody we meet.

Now that we have discovered the most fascinating and appealing thing about Leah, let's go on and look for some more nice things to say about her. We're talking primarily about the daughter of Laban in the Bible story that is before us this morning, but we are in an incidental way also talking bout the Leah's we meet every day. So let's look more closely at Leah.

How sad she is! So melancholy. Maybe her eyes are lovely because she cries so much. What right does she have to be so sad? She has a wealthy father, a wealthy husband, and a lot of children. Why so sad? Let's think about that.

It's one thing to be Rachel, with all that beauty and sparkle and fresh natural youthfulness, but when you're Leah, looking like you do, it does put a different color on life. All the boys who come to your house are coming not to see you, but to see your younger sister. When the two of you go out somewhere together, everybody clusters around Rachel, and you're always out on the edge. Maybe it's no wonder she has that melancholy look about her.

And then Jacob walks into her life. The man of her dreams! Everything about him is just perfect. If she could only marry him, she would be perfectly happy. But is he interested in Leah? With Rachel there?

With a little scheming by her father, however, she marries him. Now she can be happy! Of course she has to share her husband with her sister, but what hurts so much is that he gives Rachel all his love and has none left over for Leah. And then she thinks, *If I can be the mother of his children, then he'll love me.* And that's what happens; the children of the family are born to her, not to Rachel.

So much is reflected in the names she gave her children. Reuben, the first-born. The name Reuben, in Hebrew, means "God noticed," because, she said, *"God noticed my trouble and gave me a son, and now my husband will love me."*

Then came Simeon, the second son. It means, "God heard." She said, *"God heard that I was unloved, and so he has given me another son."*

Levi, the third son. It means "affection." She said, *"Surely now my husband will feel affection for me, since I have given him three sons!"*

Then Judah, the fourth son. Now here is a strange name. It

means simply "Praise God." She said, *"Now, I will praise God."* What did she mean by that? Could this mean that, having failed to find fulfillment in her marriage, or any response in love from her husband, she now turns to God for consolation?

The story doesn't tell us that, but there are some indications that Leah had a very deep and meaningful faith in God. Remember that she was raised in a home where the God of the Hebrews was not worshipped. Laban was an idol worshipper who had his own household gods.

Rachel apparently never forsook the religion of her childhood. In fact, when the time came for Jacob to take his family and wealth and move back to his Palestine homeland, Rachel stole the household gods from her father's house and took them with her.

But Leah, from the time of her marriage, turned to Jacob's God. Her children were named with God in mind. She prayed to God, according to the Biblical record, for many things, including the love of her husband and strong healthy children. There is something quite admirable about this woman, who—given her looks and inferior position in the marriage—would rise above all this and become a very solid wife, a steady mother, a fulfilled woman. She rose above her jealousy of her sister, she accepted her husband's preference for his other wife, and she became a very fine person. She built a life for herself out of what little building material she had, but she built well, and it was a good life. It was Leah, not Rachel, who was buried beside Jacob in the family tomb at Machpelah in the land of Canaan, the acknowledged matriarch of the Hebrew clan. And, as we can see now, it was Leah, not Rachel, who was the mother of the son of Jacob who established the line of descendents that led to the Messiah.

God bless you, Leah. We know you well. We see you often; in the people we meet every day. Each one has a story to tell, a life that is full—full of good things and bad, full of attractive things and unattractive things. Each Leah we meet has pockets in her life that are sad, and unsatisfied, and lonely. She is struggling with herself. And she has to put up with the little burdens and embarrassments and emptiness and loneliness and responsibilities and dull routine—so many things that we can only guess at.

But let's look at her eyes. Such lovely eyes. *Everybody* has lovely eyes. Let's look at them.

MARY'S HARD QUESTION

Scriptures: *John 19:25-27 Luke 2:19 Genesis 50:15-21* The John Scripture describes the crucifixion, as witnessed by Mary, Jesus' mother. The verse from Luke mentions that Mary kept all these things, pondering them, in her heart. And the Genesis passage describes Joseph confronting his brothers in Egypt, with emphasis on the 20th verse, when he told his brothers that they meant their actions for evil, but God meant it for good.

The Preacher's Notes:

I couldn't decide where to classify this sermon. I considered placing it under "Seasonal Sermons," because it could fit into Mother's Day or Christmas or Holy Week. It could fit just as easily under "Theological Sermons," because it grapples with the very difficult question, Why does God allow bad things to happen to good people? But because of the writing style, I am placing it under "Fictional Sermons." I try to see things from Mary's viewpoint, as she pondered all the events of her life in her heart.

Mary's life was both happy and tragic. This sermon focuses on the tragic. She asked herself a question: Why? It's a hard question. And it is often our question, as well as Mary's.

Is there an answer to it? Well . . . maybe. Maybe not. At the end, the sermon quotes from a minister I admire very much, who comes as close to an answer as I have ever heard.

MARY'S HARD QUESTION

My mother, who died several years ago at the age of ninety-six, used to scold us when her sons sometimes tried to shield her from hearing about any problems in the family. Sometimes we didn't tell her about illnesses or difficulties because we didn't want to upset her. That was a mistake, as we soon learned. She may have been old and frail in body, but her mind and spirit were tough, and it hurt her to be shut out of her old familiar role of counseling her children when we needed her wisdom and experience. She wanted to be very much a part of anything that happened in her sons' lives, and she was this way until her death.

I think that's how Mary the mother of Jesus must have felt that day she stood at the foot of the cross and watched her son die.

What was she doing there? She had been brought there by the disciple John, who in the Gospel record is referred to as "the disciple whom Jesus loved." Didn't he know better than to bring this sensitive lady to watch the crucifixion of her son? She should have been told to stay at home, to be shielded from reality, to be comforted with smooth talk about how "everything's going to be all right."

I wouldn't be surprised if John tried to do just that. He probably argued with her as hard as he could that a crucifixion was no place for an old lady, especially when the victim was her own son. And I can just hear her firm reply, "Well, if you don't take me, I'll go by myself!" And she would have, too. She wasn't the frail weakling John thought she was. She was a mother, and nothing would keep her from her son's side in that critical hour.

I wonder what Mary's thoughts were as she stood there watching her son die in agony? Could she feel in *her* hands and feet the pain of the nails? Did the strength flow from *her* body as the blood drained from her son's? Did she empathetically experience alternate periods of pain and weakness that washed over her body like a wave? How much did she suffer during those hours?

What did she think about as those slow, painful minutes ticked by? I wonder if she remembered that magical moment when, as a teenager, she had an intense angel-vision in which she was promised to be the mother of Israel's Messiah? *"Hail, Mary, favored one; the Lord is with you!"* said the angel. And Mary ecstatically responded, *"Behold, the handmaiden of the Lord. Let it be to me according to your word."* She was so happy then. She had no idea of the pain and suffering that lay ahead of her. *"Favored one,"* the angel had called her. *"The Lord is with you,"* he added. Was he really?

I wonder if Mary remembered also, while she stood there at the foot of the cross, that hurried trip to Bethlehem with Joseph, and the frantic search for a place to stay in that crowded town. The baby was born in the stables, and I'm sure Mary must have thought about that a lot during her lifetime. The birthplace of the Son of God—*in a barn?* But it turned out all right, with shepherd visitors and strange oriental magi at the child's bedside. God knew what he was doing. Even that hurried flight to Egypt to escape the wrath of a jealous King Herod had been part of God's plan. Looking back, she could see that everything worked out all right. Retrospect always seems to do that; you can see how it fits into the total picture, even if you couldn't see it at the time.

But this? Here on this lonely, windy hillside outside Jerusalem? Is this all a part of it?

I wonder too if Mary remembered the time when they brought the baby to the Temple in Jerusalem for the purification rites when the child was eight days old. The old man, Simeon, had taken the child in his arms and strange words came from his lips. *"This child will cause the rise and fall of many in Israel,"* he rambled on. And then he turned to Mary and his eyes bored into hers as he said, *"And a sword shall pierce your soul, too!"* How right he was. And that sword was sharp and cruel.

As she stood there before the cross, I wonder if Mary remembered another time, when Jesus was twelve, when she and Joseph were returning home after Passover in Jerusalem, and they realized their son was not with them. He wasn't with any of the others, either. Where was he? Frantically they hurried back to Jerusalem to search for him. When they finally found him, in the Temple, he was surrounded by the theologians and rabbis, astounding them with his wisdom. *"Mother,"* he said, *"Don't you know that I must be about my Father's business?"* What was that all about? His Father's business? And was *this* awful scene before her now his "Father's business?"

And I wonder too if she thought back to that happy wedding in Cana of Galilee when he changed the water into wine. What was it he had said then? *"Woman, what have you to do with me? My hour has not yet come."* His hour? Well, was *this* his hour? The pain and suffering and death? Did it all come down to this?

Perhaps Mary recalled also the time he came to Nazareth as a young itinerant rabbi. The home-town folk honored him by asking him to read from the sacred scroll in the synagogue on Sabbath. All eyes were on him as he unrolled the scroll and read from Isaiah: *"The Spirit of the Lord is upon me, because he has anointed me to preach good news to the poor, and recovering of sight to the blind, and release to the captives, and to set at liberty those who are oppressed, and to proclaim the acceptable year of the Lord."* And then he sat down. In the stillness that followed, they heard him say, *"Today, this prophecy is fulfilled in your presence."*

But now, as she watched the blood drops fall from his hands and feet, did she ask herself: "Is the Spirit of the Lord on him now? Is this really the acceptable year of the Lord? How could that be?"

If those were Mary's thoughts as she stood there in torment and watched her son die, then they are thoughts common to all of us when tragic events happen in our lives. No one can slip quietly through life without being touched—and sometimes touched traumatically—by the hand of tragedy. We must all see our share of suffering and pain. And the questions Mary was raising in her mind are questions all of us raise when that happens.

So now you know what Mary's hard question was that day. The Bible doesn't say she was thinking about these things, but she was a mother, and she was bound to have those thoughts. We can easily imagine Mary's question, because we too have asked it.

Mary's question takes different forms, but it is all the same question. We ask, "Why is this happening to me?" Or we say, "Why, if God is good and loving and all powerful, does he let this happen?" Or, "What is the divine purpose behind this tragedy?" *Why, Lord? Why? Why? Why?*

Mary's question is one that people have been asking through the history of the human race. It takes many forms, different words, but it is basically the same question. Each one of us has asked it before, perhaps many times.

Nowhere is Mary's question posed better, or answered more clearly, than in the Ben Lacy Rose column in the magazine *Presbyterian Survey*. Dr. Rose was an editor and pastor for the *Survey*, and for many years until his death he wrote an incisive column that I read regularly. I clipped this one in the March, 1980, issue. Someone had written to him and asked this question:

> *If, as you said in your December column, "God carries us through life like a baby in its mother's arms," then why would this wise and loving God foreordain that a minister and his wife, still in their youth, be crushed to death in a car crash less than a year into their first pastorate? Is that an example of the "deep affection" of a God who "always gives what is best for his children?" Why don't you get down from behind some of those superficial answers and address reality?*

That was the question in Dr. Rose's column many years ago. Did you recognize the question? Isn't it the same question Mary must have been asking as she stood at the foot of the cross? And isn't this the same question we constantly hear from bewildered people in the face of suffering? Isn't it a question you have asked a few times in your life? Now let's listen to Dr. Rose's answer:

> *Let me begin with your last question. I have seen and dealt with my share of reality. When I was in college, my mother was*

injured in an auto accident that was the result of the bad driving of another woman. Mother's back was broken and she lay in a hospital, conscious of the gravity of her condition, until she died three weeks later.

My father died because of a doctor's mistake. My wife and I had twins, but both of them died a few hours after birth. Another son was born to us, but he lived only two weeks.

During World War II, while serving as chaplain of mechanized cavalry squadrons in Normandy, I carried to the Graves Registration Center the broken bodies of a score of my good friends. One of them was so mangled by a mortar shell that I had to pick him up with a shovel and bury him in a shelter half.

In forty years and four pastorates, I have suffered and cried with countless numbers as they experienced pain, tragedy, sorrow and death. And it was out of these very experiences that my faith in the wisdom and power and love of God was formed.

I have said often, "How do I know that God is good? I don't. I gamble. I bet my life upon one side of life's great war. This life stinks in places, but I back the scent of life against its stink! I bet my life on Christ—Christ crucified!

(I'm still quoting from Dr. Rose's column.)

Have you ever really looked at the cross of Christ? **There** *was evil at its worst. The religious leaders of the most devout nation, by suborning false witnesses and perverting Roman justice, caused the perfect man to suffer the most horrible death! Yet, God allowed it—because he knew he could work through it, around it, over it and under it for the good of those who love him. And out of the crucifixion of Christ, the most monstrous deed in the world, God brought the most marvelous thing in the world: the salvation of humankind. If God can do that for the worst event, then surely he can take the tragedies of our lives and bring good out of them, if we trust him and give him time.*

You ask, "Why did God foreordain the young minister's death?" Remember that "foreordain" does not mean "cause to happen." It means only that before it happened God said, "So let it be." That is, God allowed it. As to why he allowed it, I do not know. But I believe he will bring good out of it for those who love him.

(I'm still quoting from Dr. Rose's answer to the hard question of the reader.)

Now let me ask you a question: What is *your* faith? How do *you* reconcile all the evil in the world with a wise, loving and all-powerful God? One answer is to deny God is good. I rejected that because I found it helped no one. Another answer is to say God is good but has limited himself by giving free will to persons, and therefore cannot prevent evil from happening. That answer satisfied some persons, and since it helps them, I would not shatter it if I could. But it does not satisfy me, because I then end up with a rather powerless God who, in the jungle-world in which we live, can only wring his hands helplessly, like an old lady on the curb watching a street brawl. All she can do is plead, "Boys, don't fight. Please, be good." I prefer the faith of Joseph in the Old Testament. His brothers sold him into slavery in Egypt— a dastardly thing! But Joseph said to them, when they trembled before him remembering what they had done, "Do not be angry with yourselves that you sold me into this place, for God sent me before you to preserve you as his posterity . . . . As for you, you meant to do evil to me, but God meant it for good." Aw, Joseph, don't be so naïve. Face reality! Your brothers sold you into Egypt only because they hated you and meant to do you harm. Yes, Joseph would answer, they intended it for evil, but God intended it for good, and he saved his people by it.

Maybe Joseph's answer was "superficial." Maybe it failed to "address reality." But I'll stick with it until I find something better. So please, if you have a more helpful answer, write and tell me.

This is the end of Dr. Rose's column of March, 1980, and it gives as good an answer as any I have ever heard to Mary's question in the face of tragedy. Mary never did get a satisfactory answer, and to tell the truth, neither do we. But in the last few gasping words from the cross, Jesus made provision for her to be cared for and loved the rest of her life. The love that came down from the cross that day is beyond our ability to comprehend.

That cross amazes me. For us, it embodies the worst tragedy the world has ever known. We, like Mary, stand there at its foot, wondering, asking the hard questions. And the answer seems to be hidden somewhere in that cross itself.

There is a depth and profundity of meaning in the cross that astonishes and humbles us. We look at it again and again, not understanding what happened, wondering how this fits in to the pattern of our lives. There is no answer. And yet the cross itself is an answer. Not a perfect answer. But enough of an answer to enable us to live with the question.

EVERYTHING YOU ALWAYS WANTED TO KNOW ABOUT SIN

(but were afraid to ask)

Scriptures: *Genesis 2:15-176, 3:1-6* This Scripture tells the ancient story of Adam and Eve and their temptation in the Garden of Eden. Note particularly the symbolism of the two trees in the garden.

The Preacher's Notes:

What is sin? Is it, as most people believe, all those bad things you do? No, says this sermon. It's much more profound than that.

This sermon grapples with a very difficult question. But it does so in a light-hearted way. Why not? Try struggling with a very difficult theological definition of sin, but have some fun doing it.

EVERYTHING YOU ALWAYS WANTED TO KNOW ABOUT SIN

(but were afraid to ask)

This is a sermon about sin. And believe me, this is one time when I practice what I preach.

When I was a college student, about a hundred years ago, I learned what sin was. Now, don't misunderstand what I meant by that statement. I learned what sin was *theologically*. What I learned by experience was . . . well, never mind about that.

Everyone at this small church college I attended was required to take Bible 101. Our professor was an ancient throwback to the Stone Age who must have studied under John Calvin himself. In that course, he told us what sin is.

"Sin," he pontificated, "is any want of conformity unto, or transgression of, the Law of God." He was quoting from the Shorter Catechism, one of the doctrinal standards of the Presbyterian Church.

A simplified version of that catechism is: "Sin is all the bad things you do, and all the good things you don't do." We smart-mouth college students immediately paraphrased that to read: "Sin is all those bad things *other* people do."

Then our ancient professor told us that we were all sinners, though I don't know how he knew about *that!* But then he quoted the Bible to prove it. He threw at us all the Scriptures that are commonly quoted to prove it, such as, *All have sinned and come short of the glory of God*, or *If we say we have no sin, we deceive ourselves, and the truth is not in us.*

I greeted this statement with a typical college student's attitude. Who me, as sinner? Well . . . maybe I have done a few things I should not have done. And maybe I failed to do some good things I should have done. But who hasn't? Now you're talking about being sinners—I mean, *real* sinners—you can't mean me. I have never murdered anybody. I've never robbed a bank. I've never committed adultery, or molested children, or done drugs. I don't drink, I don't smoke, and I don't cuss (unless it's absolutely necessary). Who, me? A sinner? No way.

I used to believe that when I was young and foolish, and I'm not young any more. Now, I believe what he said about us all being sinners. Maybe, in the next few minutes, I can show you that he was right. But the only way I can do that is to re-define the definition of *sin*.

What I learned about sin during that course of study called Bible 101 came not from Professor Ancient John Calvin, but from one of the students in that class. And it has influenced my definition of sin ever since. I do believe we are sinners, but it depends on the definition of sin.

One of the students in that class challenged the professor. That was a daring thing to do—especially by the student who challenged him. He was the president of one of the fraternities. There were three fraternities on campus in those days: the good one that I belonged to, the egg-head one with all the guys who made straight A's, and the wild fraternity. And they *were* wild. Every weekend they held a non-stop drinking party at their frat house, and the orgies and debaucheries there were legendary (although, I suspect, exaggerated).

The president of the wild fraternity now challenged Professor John Calvin on his definition of sin. Why not? Who would know more about sin than he did?

The Westminster Shorter Catechism says, *Sin is any want of conformity unto, or transgression of, the Law of God.* In other words, the bad things you do, and the good things you don't do.

The fraternity president said no. That definition depends on what a person *does*. Sin, he said, depends on what a person *is*.

"Sin," he said, "is self-centeredness."

By that definition, he went on to tell us, we are all sinners. We are born sinful, always demanding something for ourselves. The baby, crying in his mother's arms, wants something for himself. We grow up that way, always looking out for Number One. Everything we do, without exception, is motivated by a desire to serve or please ourselves. And, he added, we will always be that way. It's our nature, and we can never change.

Professor Ancient John Calvin challenged him. "What about the mother taking care of that baby? Isn't that pure self-less love?"

"No," replied the fraternity president. "Even she is motivated by self-centeredness. The baby makes her feel good. The response the baby gives to her, with smiles, giggles, coo's, etc., is her reward. She's taking care of the child for herself."

Professor Ancient John Calvin then asked, "What about the person who gives his life for someone else? Like the soldier who throws himself on a hand grenade and is blown to pieces, but he saves his fellow soldiers by doing so."

"Even he," said the frat president, "is self-motivated. He has an in-born desire to want people to like him, and so he unthinkingly sacrifices himself to gain a kind of immortality—he will always be remembered fondly by his buddies."

Then Professor Ancient John Calvin played his trump card. "What about the Christian, whose life is touched by God? His life is turned around. From then on, he does his best to please God and turn aside from sin."

The fraternity president had an answer for that. "The Christian is more self-motivated than Christians will admit. He wants God on his side. He wants to go to heaven when he dies. Sure, he accepts Christ. Think of how much he gets out of it."

The discussion went on and on. The professor had the last word—when the time came for grades to be given for the class. But the fraternity president sure got me to thinking. And I have believed ever since that the common definition of sin from the

Westminster Shorter Catechism is flawed. Sin is not what you *do*, but what you *are*. And the word "self-centered" accurately describes it.

On some of the examples in that debate, I agree with the professor. A mother (or father, for that matter) taking care of her baby *is* an example of self-less love, even though there is a lot of self-gratification in it. But that self-gratification can't possibly explain the sleepless nights, the countless sacrifices, the hardships involved, which the child is totally unaware of until he or she becomes a parent. Of course, we hear in the news about mothers who mistreat or even kill their children, but they are exceptions, startling enough to be newsworthy. What we don't hear in the news is the image we all have in our minds of the mother and child, with pure self-less love flowing between them.

And I agree with the professor on another example in that debate: the life-sacrifice a person makes for someone else, such as the soldier throwing himself on a hand grenade. If self-centeredness were really the motivating factor, would he go that far? Or would there be more in it for him to run away and let his buddies take the brunt of that grenade?

And what about the Christian who is a Christian for what he can get out of it? Well . . . there's a tough one. I'd like to come back to that later.

I do believe that sin is really something you are, not the things you do. We *are* basically self-centered, and much of our life is spent gratifying ourselves.

Over the years, as I have thought about this, I have gone back to the third chapter of Genesis, to try to understand what it really means. I don't care whether you accept this literally as a historical event, or a beautiful story from ancient Hebrew mythology. Don't waste your time arguing such irrelevant matters. Rather, take a good look at what this story really means.

The theological meaning of this poignant story tells us something about ourselves, and about what sin is. The narrative describes the introduction of sin into the human race. And the sin was not what Adam and Eve did. Eating fruit of a tree was no sin.

What was sinful was that the tree just happened to be the Tree of the Knowledge of Good and Evil. And God told them not to touch it, lest they also take of the Tree of Life and live forever.

What was their sin? It was turning away from God. It was saying to God, "I don't belong to you. I belong to me. And I'm going to do what I please, not what you want me to do."

And that's what sin is. Self-centeredness.

Now, when you define it that way, I will have to admit that I am a sinner. In fact, that's what I did when I first joined the Church: I admitted it. So did you. The exact wording of the question I answered in our Profession of Faith was this: *Do you confess that you are a sinner in the sight of God, justly deserving his displeasure, and without hope save in his sovereign mercy?* I said yes, I admit that, and so did you. Maybe the wording has changed in recent years, but the meaning hasn't. To become a part of God's family, each one of us must first admit that we are sinners. That we are self-centered. I'm not sure I can do that if the definition of sin revolved around the bad or good things I do or don't do. But if I have to admit that I am basically self-centered, I can honestly say that I am. And so can you.

Now let's return to the unanswered question that I left hanging a moment ago. Professor Ancient John Calvin asked the fraternity president, "What about the Christian whose life is touched by God? His life is turned around. He no longer tries to do what pleases him, but rather what pleases God."

That's an interesting question. The basic meaning of conversion is to turn around. Your life is going in one direction, and then God touches you in some way, and your life is turned around and goes in the other direction. Of course, not all of us had a sudden dramatic conversion experience. God touches each person's life differently, and there is no stereotype religious experience. Sometimes it is sudden and instantaneous; but quite often it is a life-long process. But does this turn you around, so that you are not self-centered any more, but rather God-centered?

Well . . . you know, and I know, that self-centeredness does not go away. Ever. When God touches your life—in whatever way he chooses—you do not all-of-a-sudden become a perfect saint who never sins. It's part of our nature, to be self-centered. We *are* sinners in the sight of God, and we always will be.

Then what *does* happen when God touches your life?

I'm not sure I understand it very well, but something does happen to you. Maybe not instantly; maybe it's over a long period of time At least you are aware of the fact that you are a sinner in the sight of God. You can recognize your own self-centeredness, and you want to do something about it. You realize what God has done for you. And so now, you want to please God.

And this—in some strange and mysterious way—*does* make a difference in the way you live. Of course you still say to yourself, "What's in it for me?" But then you stop and think. You have experienced the self-less love of God for you. You remember what he has done for you in Jesus. And so you ask yourself, "What does God want me to do?"

Somehow, this affects the way you deal with other people. In a situation dealing with others, your only thought once may have been, "How can I get what I want?" Now, you think, "What does God want me to do? How can I help this person?"

When you say a prayer, maybe you used to pray nothing more than "God, give me this or that. God, do this for me. God, get me out of this mess." Self-centered prayers. But your prayers have matured. Oh, you still ask God for things for yourself, but now your prayers are becoming more like, "Thank you, God." And... "God, what do you want me to do?"

And then comes the time when you stand before that mysterious curtain that separates life from death. You look at that curtain, and you find yourself being very self-centered. You want to experience whatever it is that God has promised you after you have passed through that veil. You want to see your loved ones again. You want to experience the joys that future life holds. You are very self-centered about this. It's what you want. And then you look at me and ask, *Is that a sin?*

All right. So I don't have all the answers. So I too have a self-centered motivation for wanting God to take care of me when I die. So . . . I guess I'll just have to admit that I am a sinner in the sight of God, justly deserving his displeasure, and without hope save in his sovereign mercy.

I'll admit that, if you will. Together, let's stand before God and confess our sin. And together, let's put our trust in him, that he will accept us as we are, do what he can to make us a little better, and when we don't . . . well, God, just love us enough to keep us always in your hand, even if we don't deserve it.

And by the way, God, thank you for that.

MY FAVORITE DOCTRINE

Scriptures: *Romans 8:28-39* The Apostle Paul puts on his heaviest theological cap and makes some profound statements on the doctrine of Predestination in this mysterious passage of Scripture.

The Preacher's Notes:

I'll tell you in advance what my favorite doctrine is. It's the Grace of God. Really? Yes, definitely. I've tried in this sermon to dress it up a little bit, so that it really isn't as stuffy as it sounds. And at the end, I have used my favorite illustration.

MY FAVORITE DOCTRINE

My favorite doctrine is . . . *the Grace of God.*

A long, long time ago, when I was a young man, I went to the theological seminary where I learned the doctrine of The Grace of God. I learned it in a course entitled "Systematic Theology," from a textbook of the same name written by Dr. Augustus Horatio Strong. Dr. Strong's definitions of certain doctrines were just as stuffy and obscure as the title of his book. In fact, our ancient theology professor would begin his classes with a brief prayer, and in most of these prayers he would say, "Lord make us *strong*," and we knew exactly what he meant.

That's when I learned the doctrine of the Grace of God. I passed that course, incidentally; that is, I memorized all those stuffy definitions and gave the correct answers on the tests. And I believed those doctrines. But I didn't fully appreciate the meaning of the doctrine of the Grace of God until it sunk in. I had to rearrange the words for it to have some meaning for me. Just the words . . . not the meaning. But when it dawned on me what a great doctrine this is, it gave me a sense of freedom and well being that made a big difference in my life. I hope I can express to you this morning my understanding of this doctrine, so that you too can experience the freedom and satisfaction of believing this extraordinary doctrine.

As we studied Strong's *Systematic Theology,* and also John Calvin's book entitled *The Institutes of the Christian Religion,* we learned the essence of Calvinism, which is the backbone of Presbyterian theology. That book, Calvin's *Institutes,* became known to the students as "The Gospel According to Saint John the Calvinist." Sometimes we liked the doctrines presented in it, and sometimes we didn't. We debated them long and loud among ourselves, although on our test papers we of course wrote down the proper answers.

But as I came to appreciate the doctrines of Saint John the Calvinist, I changed some of the words. Not the meanings. I kept those. But I put them in my own words, so that it would mean more to me. And they do. This is my favorite doctrine. I'd like to share some of my definitions with you now, in my own words. In fact, you might call this "The Gospel According to Saint James the Shott."

Let's begin with the definition of the word *foreknowledge*.

This doctrine tells us that in the beginning of time, before the sovereign God began his mighty work in the creation of this particular planet, he planned ahead. He knew everything that was going to happen, and he knew each and every person he would create in the future. This is God we're talking about, not a human. God is not limited in his mental capacities like we are, so he can have this foreknowledge of everything and everyone.

And so, in the beginning of time, God planned. He planned my life. He knew in advance my name and everything about me.

The problem comes in the second definition of Calvinistic theology: *Foreordination.* I suppose you could call it *Predestination.*

This doctrine says that God not only foreknew about me and my life, he also foreordained that I would be one of his special children. He would love *me.* He would provide for *me.* He had my life all planned out before he even put into motion this grand scheme of creation. He would provide for my eternal salvation, and he had some very elaborate plans for that, including a very unselfish sacrifice by his Son.

I like this definition of Foreordination. It tells me that I don't have to worry about my salvation. It has been taken care of—in advance. I don't have to earn it. It's free. God *gives* it to me. That's the doctrine of the Grace of God.

Let me tell you, that's a relief. My salvation doesn't depend on me; it depends on God. Am I ever glad of *that!* You see, if it were up to me, I'd be scared to death. I know what kind of a person I am. So does God. I'd never make it, on my own. But it's not up to me. It depends on God, and God is dependable—much more so than I am. If the Bible presents an accurate picture of God, then I know God loves me. How do I know that? Well, just look at what God did for us in Christ. So . . . I can count on God to make all the arrangements for my salvation, which I could never do all by myself. What a relief!

But then, when you read the Gospel According to Saint John the Calvinist, there pops up a complicating factor. This is something that is known in the stuffy theology book as . . . are you ready for this? . . . *Double Predestination.*

This doctrine says that not only did God choose from the beginning those whom he would save; he also chose those whom he would damn. I'm not sure I like that. I part company with Saint John the Calvinist at this point. I don't think that's the way a loving God would do things.

Let me give you the picture the doctrine of Double Predestination conjures up in my mind.

In the beginning of time, before the creation of this planet, there was a great big lottery. God put all the names in a big turning basket, like you see in the lottery—all the names of people who would ever be born. He would draw out a name from the basket and place it in the pile of those whom he would save. He would draw out another name and place it in the pile of those whom he would damn. And it was the luck of the draw whether your name would be drawn for the salvation pile rather than the damnation pile.

This is what a lot of people think the doctrine of Predestination means. This is why many of the Reformation theologians turned away from Calvinism. The doctrine of *Free Will* became popular. Our salvation, they said, is not up to God; it's up to us. We have a choice. We can choose to be saved. If we do, we are; if we don't, we aren't. And that, some think, is a safer way than leaving it up to the divine lottery.

But not me. I would much rather place my salvation in the hands of a loving and dependable God, rather than leaving it up to me.

I can go along with Saint John the Calvinist on his doctrine of foreordaining those whom he would save. I like that. But I don't like that other part, the next logical step, which says he therefore chooses those whom he would damn. I'll just put my salvation in his hands—and go no further.

This doctrine of the Grace of God gives me freedom. I can do as I please, because I don't have to worry about my salvation. It doesn't depend on what I do; it depends rather on the Grace of God.

Now, just a minute. Does that mean that I can sin and get away with it? The way the Apostle Paul asks the question in one of his Epistles is: *What then shall we say? Shall we sin, that grace may abound?*

Well . . . yes. We can sin, and get away with it. Because it doesn't work that way. The amazing thing is that those who have realized the full impact of the doctrine of the Grace of God on their lives are the people who are doing everything they can to please God and do right. That's just the way it works. The difference is that when we slip up, and make mistakes, we can relax. It won't hurt us in the last Judgment. Our salvation doesn't depend on our mistakes. It depends on the Grace of God. And that's a relief, because I know *I've* made a few mistakes in my lifetime. How about you?

And do you know, our salvation doesn't even depend on whether or not we are on the right side of all theological issues. Maybe I have it all wrong about my rejection of the Calvinist doctrine of Double Predestination, or some of my reactions to other conservative doctrinal beliefs. I don't think I am, but even if I am, my salvation doesn't depend on getting it right; it depends on God's Grace.

Or maybe our Presbyterian approach to the doctrine of Baptism is wrong, that we shouldn't baptize infants; we should wait until they are old enough to decide for themselves, and then should be immersed. I don't think so, but what if we Presbyterians have that doctrine all wrong? Will it nullify our salvation because we weren't dunked? *No!* Our salvation depends on God's Grace, not on our getting everything right in our theological thinking.

Does this mean that even a liberal Christian can be saved, or are only conservative Christians in the heavenly fold? Of course it does. God's Grace is sufficient even for us poor liberals.

Now... let me try another example. This may come as a surprise to some people, but our salvation doesn't even depend on our being on the right side of the abortion issue. I'm not sure which side God is on, but I have known people who *are* sure. But my salvation doesn't depend on my getting even that right; it depends on God's Grace.

And that's why I can relax and enjoy life. Because I know that I am one of God's own, and he has made provision for me. He made these provisions for me a long time ago. And now that I realize that, I can smile at life... and death.

Let me tell you my little fantasy about death, which comes directly from the pages of The Gospel According to Saint James the Shott.

The day has come when I must present myself before those Pearly Gates. I stand there before the Gate, and just outside is a desk at which sits Saint Peter. He has a scroll and a quill pen, and he looks up at me as I approach.

"What do you want?" he asks.

"I want in," I reply. "I have heard your accommodations are much better than that other place."

"Well... let's see." He frowns, as he looks me over. "What credentials do you have that qualify you to get in here?"

Hey, I'm ready for him. I pull out of my pocket my letter of transfer from the First Presbyterian Church, signed by the clerk of the Session, and hand it to him.

"Sorry," he says. "Not good enough."

Oh, really? Not good enough... from a *Presbyterian* Church?

All right, I've got something else. I pull out of my other pocket a letter of recommendation, written on church letterhead stationery, and signed by the minister of the church. It says what a good boy I've been, and that I have never caused any trouble in the church, and I attend church fairly regularly, give generously to support the budget, and don't park on the newly sodded grass.

"Nope," he says, shaking his head. "Not even this."

"I'm getting desperate now. I glance down over the balcony railing to that other place, and they're having carrot sticks and celery for dinner tonight. No dip. And there's no chocolate anywhere down there!

I pull out of another pocket a list of all the good deeds I have done in my lifetime. It's a long list, and I have very carefully kept it over the years. I have on that list everything possible, including the time I helped an old grandmother across the street, even if she didn't need any help, and even if she didn't want to go across the street in the first place. I have hundreds of these incidents, and they're all there on my list.

Saint Peter shakes his head. "Not even this," he says.

I've run out of pockets. There's nothing left. I glance down over the balcony to that other place, and they're showing Seinfeld reruns down there now.

And so I decide to be honest with him.

"I guess I just don't deserve to be here. Sorry. I have nothing left to earn my way in. So . . . I guess I'll just have to put myself in God's hands. If I'm going to get in, it will have to be by God's Grace, because I just don't have anything else to give you."

And then Saint Peter smiles and says, "Why didn't you say so in the first place? How do you think any of us got in here? Your admittance has been pre-arranged. That's why God sent his Son to planet Earth two thousand years ago. He took care of everything. Now, if you had just accepted that a long time ago, you could have relaxed and enjoyed your life a lot more, without being afraid of death. So . . . come on in!"

And those Pearly Gates swing wide open, and I walk in on the golden streets, and there are mansions and ivory palaces and angels on wings, and a Frozen Yogurt stand on every corner. And chocolate everywhere!

Aw, listen. I don't know what heaven looks like. You make up your own fantasy.

And now you know why the doctrine of the Grace of God is

my favorite doctrine, and you have just heard it presented in the Gospel of Saint James the Shott. Maybe I have been talking about myself in this sermon. But don't kid yourself. I was talking about you, too.

BEHOLD, THE FACE OF GOD

Scriptures: *Palm 42, Matthew 28:16-20* The Psalm is used to introduce the subject. The Psalmist feels a need to behold the face of God. The Matthew Scripture contains the final verses in the book. They describe Jesus' commission to his disciples, sending them into all the world to evangelize and baptize " . . . in the name of the Father, and the Son, and the Holy Spirit."

The Preacher's Notes:

The best way I know to behold the face of God is very simple: the Doctrine of the Trinity. But how can that be? The Trinity is one of the most difficult doctrines to understand. Three? Yet one? How can this doctrine make clear the face of God? But it does, and that is the point of this sermon.

BEHOLD, THE FACE OF GOD!

There is something very real and very appealing about the 42nd Pslam. The Psalmists seems to be asking the question, "Why isn't God real to me?"

He thinks about a deer in the forest during the dry season, desperately searching for a living stream to quench its thirst. *That's how I feel,* he seems to say. *If only I could come to face with the living God! If only God would become real to me!* His exact words are, *When shall I come and behold the face of God?*

And that's why we have come to church this morning, isn't it? We want to see the face of God—figuratively speaking. *God* is a concept that is vague, and blurred, and out of focus. It's beyond the ability of our finite minds to grasp. How can we possibly see his face?

So . . . what does this Psalmist do when he feels that way? He goes to church!

Where else but in the Temple, the House of God, could he hope to come face to face with the living God? Here, of all places, God should become real to him. And so he goes to church with the others of his faith. He even leads the procession, eagerly taking his place in the church, and lifts his voice and his heart in glad shouts and songs of thanksgiving. But . . . *why are you cast down, O my soul? And why are you disquieted within me?*

I think I know exactly how this Psalmist feels, don't you? Even in church, when we are supposed to be closer to God than at any other time, we wonder if he is real. When you consider the vast gulf between the infinite God and little you, how can you possibly know anything about him? Is there any way that God can become real to us? Or as the Psalmist said, *When shall I come and behold the face of God?*

For the answer to the Psalmist—and our own question, for that matter—we must go to the New Testament, and our Christian doctrine. The answer to the problem of making God real to us—to "see his face"—is the theological doctrine of the Trinity.

What? The doctrine of the *Trinity?* How can that be?

If you know anything at all about the doctrine of the Triune God—the Father, Son and Holy Spirit—you know for sure that it is one of the most difficult doctrines of the Christian faith. The very word "Trinity" is confusing. It means "Tri-unity," or three in one. I don't know about you, but that bothers me. Is God three, or is he one?

One of the most fundamental tenants of Judeo-Christian doctrine is that God is one. From ancient times, our Hebrew ancestors have told us: *Shemai Israel! Adonai Elohim, Adonai echod!* Hear, O Israel, the Lord is God; the Lord is *One!*

Then Jesus sent his disciples out to make disciples of all nations, baptizing them in the name of the Father, *and* the Son, *and* the Holy Spirit. Three of them. Now tell me: is God three, or is he one?

This morning we ask ourselves the very serious question, *How shall I behold the face of God?* Why should we start with the doctrine of the Trinity? Doesn't that confuse more than it clarifies?

No.

The preposterous claim of the Christian faith is that the purpose of this doctrine is to *clarify,* not confuse. With this doctrine, we behold the face of God.

What helped clarify it for me was an illustration from the ancient Greek and Roman theater, which was about the time the Christian doctrine of the Trinity was formulated. They used the word *persona,* from which comes our word "persons." The *persona* was a mask used by an actor to portray a different character on the stage. Maybe they had a shortage of actors, but they used one actor to portray two or three different characters, and the audience knew that when he used a different mask, he was portraying that character. One actor, different *personas.*

Now, if I were God (and you should be grateful that I'm not),

I would ask myself, "Now how can I reveal myself to these stupid mortals in such a way that they can understand?" And so I—God—would answer myself this way: "Why, that's easy. I'll just explain myself to them in three *personas*. And that's what God proceeded to do.

First, God says, *I am your Father.*

God is our Father. Now we've got something. We may not know what "God" means, but we all know what "father" means.

Everybody has a father. I am a father myself. Maybe not a perfect father, but at least I have some grasp of the concept of fatherhood. I can see—to some extent, at least—the difference between human fatherhood and perfect fatherhood. And if I can try to understand God as the perfect Father, then I have at least a glimpse into what God is like.

And that's comforting to me. I like to think of God as my loving Father. Some wise person once told me, "God treats each one of us as though we were an only child." No earthly father can do that, but God can—and does. I find that very comforting, and so I call God "my Father."

Some people think of God like the old woman in the nursery rhyme:

> *There was an old lady who lived in a shoe.*
> *She had so many children, she didn't know what to do.*
> *So she gave them some broth without any bread,*
> *And spanked them all soundly and sent them to bed.*

That's not the concept of God Jesus taught us. He said, think of God as our Father. So when you ask the big question, How shall I come and behold the face of God? Think of him not as *God*—with all the vague, mysterious connotations that word implies—but as *Father*. Then his face will be focused for you.

Incidentally, I have no problem with the first *persona* of the Trinity being a Mother. It might even work better to try to catch a glimpse of the mystery of God by seeing *her* that way. But when the doctrine of the Trinity was formulated back in the early centuries of the Christian era, the culture of the times demanded that we see God as a Father, not a Mother. But either one works for me; it's just that all my life I have thought of God as my Father. It works for me, and I'll stick with the idea of beholding the face of God as my Father.

Behold the face of God. Think of him also as *Jesus*.

God—that mystery beyond our comprehension—was in the man called Jesus. *The Word became flesh, and dwelt among us.* When we look at that man who lived in the 1st Century, we behold the face of God.

We see the face of a real man, who walked the dusty roads of Palestine, who talked with Samaritans and adulterers, who played with children, who touched lepers and wept with those who mourned the dead. He put laughter into the heart of the depressed, and health into the body of the diseased, and hope into the soul of the despairing. As we look fully into the face of this man who loved, and suffered, and healed, and laughed, and cared for individuals, we begin to see a little more clearly what the face of God is like. Don't ask me how that's possible, because I don't know. But somehow, in that man called Jesus of Nazareth, we see the face of God.

And then, this man suffered and died on a cross. And in some mysterious way, in a way beyond our ability to understand, the face of God became focused for us more sharply than ever before. In that incomprehensible moment, when the sky darkened and all creation groaned, that man cried out from his cross, *"Eloi, Eloi, lama sabachthani!"* Was he really forsaken? Or . . . in that magical, mystical moment, were we enabled to look fully into the face of God, and see him as we were never able to see him before?

There are questions involved in the doctrine of the deity of Christ and the atonement that I can't answer. But I do know that when I look at Jesus, I see the face of God. And that face is focused for me in a way that is remarkable!

Behold the face of God! We see him also in the *Holy Spirit*.

Now, here is a doctrine that is most difficult. Scholars and theologians have debated it, and stupid preachers like me have tried to explain it. *The doctrine of the Holy Spirit.* Most of us don't even know whether to call the Holy Spirit an "it" or a "he"!

I want to ask you now to strip from this doctrine all that is difficult and confusing. Look at it this way. The Spirit of God is simply the presence of the living God in our lives. That's all. Don't make it any more difficult than that.

God is present in my life. And yours. Here, in the *(your church's name)* in *(your city)*. Now, on Sunday, *(this date)* at *(look at your watch and state the time)*.

Maybe you aren't aware of his presence, but that makes no difference. Your awareness of him is not a condition of his being with you. He's there anyway.

And he calls you by your name. He looks after you. Not as a disciplinarian, frowning on you when you do something wrong. But rather as a companion, a loving and very close friend, who is beside you in every moment, whether you know it or not. At those times when you feel that God is farthest from you, that's usually when he is closest.

So come, behold the face of God! Don't look for him in the theology books, or the confusing doctrines stated in grim theological terms. See him as your Father. See him in the man Jesus. And see him in the ever-present Spirit.

Behold, the face of God!

HEAVEN: EVERYONE IS JUST DYING TO FIND OUT WHAT IT'S LIKE

Scripture: *Matthew 22:23-30* The Sadducees ask Jesus what heaven is like, and Jesus gives a very mysterious answer.

The Preacher's Notes:

If you think I know what heaven will look like, you won't think so after you read this sermon. One of my illustrations describes it in the Latin words *"totaliter aliter,"* which means "totally different." Way beyond our experience, so how can we picture it? Well, that doesn't stop me from picturing it. Or trying to.

HEAVEN (EVERYONE IS JUST DYING TO FIND OUT WHAT IT'S LIKE)

Most of us at some time in our lives had the experience of standing beside an open grave, or attending a memorial service, for a loved one. It is one of the most difficult moments of our existence.

Death . . . the final mystery. What's it like? What happens beyond that moment when we pass from one life to another? What is the Christian doctrine of heaven? If we just knew something about it, it would turn sorrow into joy, and grief into celebration.

The older I get, the less I know about these things. You would think it would work the other way, wouldn't you? That the older I get, the more I should know. But it doesn't, as I'm sure many of you have discovered. I wish I knew as much now as I did many years ago when I graduated from the seminary. I knew *everything* then.

Wouldn't it be nice if heaven were on the Internet, and all you had to do was go to the heaven website, press "enter" and bring up heaven on your computer screen? Then we would know for sure. In the meantime, we don't know, so we guess. And any one of us may be right. Your view of heaven may be just as comforting for you as mine is for me.

I suppose at this point I *should* say that I know exactly what heaven is like, because I have read about it in the Bible. Well, I *have* read about it in the Bible, and I still don't know what it's like. And maybe that's as it should be. Our Christian faith is not filled with facts and clarifications, but rather mysteries and unknowns, leaving room for faith and hope and imagination, rather than final explanations.

There is a legend that tells of two monks in a monastery discussing what heaven would be like. One said it would be *taliter*, the Latin word meaning "like"—that is, very much like this present life only better. The other monk said it would *aliter*—meaning "unlike"—that is, just the opposite of this life. So they decided that whichever one died first would communicate with the other left on earth. According to the legend, one died and was buried, and a short time later the other had a dream in which he saw the dead monk speaking to him the words, *Non taliter, non aliter, sed totaliter aliter*. "Not like, nor unlike, but totally different."

I subscribe to the *totaliter aliter* viewpoint. We who live in this material world have no hope of ever conceiving what the next life will be like.

And so one Biblical writer used symbolism to describe heaven. In the book of Revelation, heaven is pictured as a holy city, the new Jerusalem, foursquare, with walls of jasper, studded with precious stones, gates of pearl, and streets of transparent gold. Well, why not? The Biblical writer lived in the 1st Century, when a city such as he describes was the ultimate in earthly living, a scene out of Arabian nights, a Utopia on earth. What better way to describe heaven, a spiritual concept, than in the grandest material terms the imagination can muster?

This idea of using the material to symbolically describe the spiritual is also used to describe hell. The word often translated "hell" in the New Testament is literally *Gehenna*. When Jesus spoke of Gehenna, the people to whom he spoke knew exactly what he meant. Gehenna was the name of the city dump just outside Jerusalem, and when he said "Gehenna" there arose in the mind of his hearers the picture of a horrible place, a place of garbage and filth, constantly burning, with an abominable stench. The only people who went there were the outcasts, the lepers, the crippled, the criminals, and they didn't live long because of the impure air. It was to the people of Jerusalem the worst place on earth. What better way to describe hell than to say "Gehenna?"

And so the Biblical writers used material concepts to describe the spiritual. So do we. We have to. We who live our lives bound by these material walls can do nothing else. How in the world can we describe heaven, a spiritual concept, when we live and think in a world that is totally material?

Ah, but it isn't totally material. There are spiritual things that we live with every day. Let me mention just a few of them: love, friendship, happiness, peace of mind, honor and respect—these are spiritual concepts; we might even say they're heavenly.

Let me give just one example. Beauty is a spiritual concept. What is beauty? Can you define it? The only way to define it is to give material examples: a mother, holding in her arms a little baby, is beautiful. Beauty is sunset on a clear day, or a rose in full bloom glistening in the morning sunlight. For someone who lives near the ocean, beauty is to stand on a mountain peak, absorbing the grandeur of the green flowing hills below, with snow cresting a distant peak. For someone who lives in the mountains, beauty is standing barefoot in the gentle surf, letting the sun-warmed water caress your feet as you look out across the ocean to a distant horizon. Beauty—a spiritual concept, described only in pictures that are specific and material.

On the other hand, there are some things that can make your life a hell on earth. And for the most part, they are spiritual concepts. What about pain? A toothache, a muscle cramp, a burn—these are material pains. But what about spiritual pains? Disappointment. Disillusionment. Frustration. Embarrassment. Rejection. And the greatest pain of all: the loss of a loved one. These can make for a hell on earth. I'd rather have a broken bone than a broken heart. A child would rather endure the pain of a spanking than the pain of being ignored. See what I mean? Spiritual pain hurts more than physical pain.

Heaven and hell—concepts we live with every day. Would it be fair to say that the joys we know are greater when they are spiritual, and the pain is worse when it is spiritual?

Let's put this on a chart. Use your imagination for a moment to picture a large graph. There is a line drawn across the middle of the chart separating the joys from the pain. Then the higher on the graph you go, the greater the joy. The lower on the graph you go, the worse the pain. Now, let's put some specific things on this graph.

I'm going to start with chocolate. Naturally, I put it above the line in the realm of joys. For some of us, it's a little higher on the graph than for others.

Go a little higher, putting other things on the graph. When you're hot and sweaty, and you come into an air-conditioned room. Or when you are shivering with cold, and you come into a warm place. Joy. You put these things wherever you want on the graph—high or low—depending on what brings you the most joy.

You don't have to work very long with this graph before you discover that the higher you go above the line, the more you get into the spiritual realm. The older I get, the higher up on the chart I put the concept of beauty. Or the love of family. Or peace of mind. Spiritual concepts. Joys. The best this life has to offer.

Now, draw a line across the top of this graph. Above that line is heaven. The life beyond this life.

I can't describe it to you, and even if someone could, we wouldn't understand it. It is *totaliter aliter*—totally different. But better. Infinitely better.

This is the Christian concept of heaven. And it is extremely comforting when a close loved one has passed on into that mysterious unknown realm. It is equally comforting when you face the fact of your own death.

Before I leave the subject of the Christian view of heaven, I should at least acknowledge the most asked question about it: Will we know our loved ones in heaven? It almost seems that heaven would be a pretty lonely place without them. And in this life one of the precious thoughts that sustains us in time of sorrow is the hope of reunion in the life to come. Is this really true, or is it just wishful thinking on our part?

For an answer, I will turn to something Jesus said. The Sadducees, who didn't believe in life beyond the grave, challenged him one day. They asked Jesus this little riddle: Suppose a man marries, then dies and goes to heaven. His brother, according to Jewish law, then marries his widow, and he dies. The next brother marries her, and this goes on until she has run through seven brothers. Boy, is she tough on husbands! Now the question: In heaven, whose wife will she be?

I want to quote Jesus' answer: *"You are wrong, because you know neither the Scripture not the power of God. For in the resurrection they neither marry nor are given in marriage, but are like angels in heaven."*

Now, you look at me and ask me to interpret exactly what Jesus meant. I wish I knew. He spoke of angels. I'm afraid I don't have any idea what an angel is. There are some people who do, but they are a lot smarter than I am. To me, an angel is a spiritual being, beyond my understanding. We can use material examples to try to explain, like a winged being flying around playing a harp, or Gabriel ready to blow his horn, or Clarence in that Jimmy Stewart movie, or those popular TV programs that are so sweet and mushy. But an angel is a spiritual being, and if we are honest, we come face to face once more with the concept of *totaliter aliter*—totally different.

The Apostle Paul offered a suggestion. In one of his epistles, he said that we would be given a "spiritual body" when that time comes. Now, what in the world is a spiritual body? An oxymoron if I ever heard one. *Totaliter aliter.* I really don't know, but I would like to think it implies some way to communicate with and relate to each other. It will be a totally different arrangement from the sight/sound/touch/taste/smell arrangements we have in this life. Once again, *totaliter aliter.* But it *will* be better. And that's about all we can honestly say.

I want to believe that. I don't need to understand it, but I very much want to believe it. Some may call this wishful thinking. Others call it faith. Whatever you call it, it's something I want very much to believe. Because believing this brings deep and abiding peace.

As we sit here today talking about heaven, we each think of a different name, and we picture in our mind a familiar face—someone who has already crossed that line, passed through the tunnel, entered the door—or whatever. Someone who has already gone to this heavenly home: a father or mother, brother or sister, son or daughter, a spouse, a grandparent, or a close friend. Each one of us tries in our imagination to picture what it's like over there, and how nice the reunion will be. For each one of us, that picture may be different, but we all say the same creed: *I believe in the communion of saints, the resurrection of the body, and the life everlasting.*

And while there are mysteries beyond which we will never penetrate during this life, we can hold fast to our hope, our faith, our unshakable convictions. Jesus, using a symbolism we do understand to prepare us for something we don't, said: *"In my Father's house are many rooms; I go to prepare a place for you."*

And that thought brings us incredible peace.

GOD'S NAME

Scripture: *Exodus 3:1-6, John 8:48-59* The Exodus Scripture tells about Moses' encounter with God at the burning bush, when he asks God what his name is. God tells him. The passage from John's Gospel describes Jesus arguing with the chief priests. The text focuses on verse 58, where Jesus said, "Before Abraham was, *I am!*"

The Preacher's Notes:

God's name in Hebrew is JHVH. (No vowels in Hebrew.) Some Bible translations call him Jehovah. Yahweh would be better. What does it mean? It is related to the Hebrew verb "to be," so it really means "I am." And then Jesus says that's his name! Blasphemy? Or a theological premise in our Christian faith?

Sure, this is a difficult sermon, but it tells us something about God that we might want to keep in mind.

GOD'S NAME

God! What's your name?

That is no idle question. When Moses asked it before the burning bush, he was deadly serious. His whole future and the future of the Hebrews depended on the answer.

To the people of Bible times, the name of a person was a lot more than just a convenient handle to call somebody, to keep from saying to him, "Hey, you!" The name described the person himself. If Moses could know God's name, he would know what God is like. If he were to go back to Egypt, stand before the pharaoh and say, " *"This says God, let my people go!"* then it would be important for him to know who this God was who was sponsoring him.

It's an important question for us, too. What is God like? Does he really exist? Is he a personal God; that is, does he know *my* name? Does he have anything to do with my life? These are some of the questions involved in *our* question: *"God, what's your name?"*

It's a question we ask when we are struggling with the decisions and perplexing problems of life. Sometimes life gets too heavy for us to handle. There are problems that won't go away. The future doesn't look good. The present looks worse. Nobody seems to understand or care. Does God care? Is there a God to care? *God . . . what is your name?*

There comes a time when we stand at the grave of a loved one and ask this question. Is this the end? Is the grave, with its lifeless body, all there is to what was once a beautiful life? Will we meet again in a place God has created for us? Is there even a God to create such a place? *Please, God . . . tell us your name.*

There also comes a time when each one of us must face the fact of our own death. Is this an end to life, or merely the beginning of a new adventure? There are promises given to us by God about this, and if they are true, then death has lost its sting and its victory. But are these promises true? Can we count on them? Is there a God to make them come true? *God . . . what is your name?*

So much depends on God's name. There are thousands of questions that would not bother us if only we knew God's name. Questions like, why does God allow someone to die young? Why does a certain person suffer, this person who is so close to God and has such a good and radiant life? Why is there so much injustice in the world, when innocent righteous people suffer, and strong evil people prevail? In our personal lives, why, if God is real, does he allow me to have the problems that I have? Why? Why? *Why? God . . . tell us your name!* Are you really a living God? Or is all this a delusion?

And so, like Moses, we stand in the presence of the burning bush, with our shoes off, and confront him with the all-important question: God, what is your name? Do you really exist, or have we bet our lives, our lifestyle, our hope for eternity, on nothing at all, a delusion? We too have to face our Egypts and our pharaohs, and we'd sure like to know who's sponsoring us. *God, are you for real? What is your name?*

And God answers. He answers us as well as Moses. Take off your shoes and stand quietly now, for Almighty God is about to tell you his name.

His name is: **YAHWEH.**

This is the Hebrew name for God. Some versions of the Bible translate this Jehovah, but most simply say "The Lord." We Christians have a name for God also, and we'll look at that in a moment. For now, let's take a look at this ancient and mysterious name that the Hebrews called their God.

Yahweh. My Hebrew professor, who was a recognized authority on the Hebrew language and history, said that nobody knows how they pronounced it 3300 years ago when God spoke to Moses. As it appeared in the ancient manuscripts written in Hebrew, it had no vowels, just four consonants, and two of the consonants were the Hebrew *aleph*, which is a letter we do not have in the English language. It is a guttural sound unfamiliar to us. As best he could figure, the name was probably pronounced something like this: *JECH-O-WECH*. It has a high and holy sound, doesn't it?

But it isn't the pronunciation that we want to know about. Remember that to the Hebrews the name describes the person. **Yahweh.** What does it mean?

Scholars are not in total agreement about this, but the consensus of scholarship seems to agree that somehow the word is related to the Hebrew verb: "I am."

It is as though God is saying to Moses, "I AM! *I really am!* I *do* exist! Go tell that to the pharaoh, and see if his gods can match *that*!"

And God says to us, I AM. Well ... of course we believe in God. At least we say we do, every Sunday, in church. We say and sing and affirm with our presence that we really do believe in God. But do we ... really? All the time? I don't believe I'm the only one who has had this small doubt in the back of my mind, this lingering reservation, this private very personal hesitation, which we keep in the closet and never display publicly. "I believe in God," we say, but way back in there, deep down in our minds where we really live, there is a small voice that whispers, "I wonder ... "

And then God speaks to us. We like Moses hear his name. It's something we need to hear. He says, "I am. I really am. You can count on that. And *that's* my name!"

God also said to Moses, "I am the God of your ancestors, Abraham, Isaac and Jacob." I don't know about you, but I find this a very comforting thought. This God who claims to be present and real in my life right now, the God who says his name is "I am", is not some new fad that has just appeared on the scene. Through the centuries others have asked the question which Moses asked, and which we ask too. Our parents asked it, and our grandparents, and all the people you knew years ago in your church back home, whose faith meant so much to them. Others before us have known him, and have felt his love and strength, have heard him say to them, "I am," and have found their lives enriched by his presence. Others have been this way before. We aren't the first to ask him, "What is your name? Are you real?" Others before us have asked this, and have been satisfactorily answered.

He is the great *I AM*. We can tell our children and our grandchildren who he is. We can go about our lives and lie down to rest at the end with the assurance that the faith, which means so much to us, will not die out when we die. It goes on, and on, and on. A thousand years from now, people will be asking the same question, and hearing the same answer.

All we have said—that God is the great I Am—is still not enough. We need one more Word, a Word that shall burn itself into our lives and never be extinguished. We need a Word that will speak to each one personally, as we stand with shoes off and ask our question, *"God, what is your name?"*

And he tells us. He speaks to us the one Word we need to hear. And that Word is . . . JESUS!

The religious leaders of Israel were asking Jesus the same question essentially that Moses directed to the burning bush: "*Who are you? What is your name?*" The tone of their question was more like, *"Just who do you think you are?"* But the substance of the question is the same one we ask when we stand before him. *What is your name? Just who are you . . . really?*

And Jesus said—and again, take off your shoes and stand quietly now—Jesus said, *"I am telling you the truth. Before Abraham was,* I AM!*"*

No wonder they picked up stones to throw at him! This was blasphemy! He was using the sacred name of the Hebrews, in effect saying, "*I am* **Yahweh,** *the great* **I AM!** *That's my name!"*

Is he really? The answer to that is an either/or. Either he is the greatest blasphemer of all time, in which case nothing he said can be believed, *or* he really is who he claims to be. Take your choice. Stand on one side of the line or the other. Either bet all your marbles on him, or turn your back and walk away.

If you accept his name, then relax. You've got it made. He really is the living God. He has told us his name!

And that's why we come to church, Sunday after Sunday. Like Moses, we climb the mountain, seeking the burning bush. Like Moses, we take off our shoes and stand quietly and respectfully, waiting and listening. And we hear again the voice we need to hear. He spoke to Moses through the burning bush. He speaks to each one of us in a different way. But he speaks.

And he says the Word we need to hear: Y*ahweh!* *JAHWEH!* I AM!

GOD IS OUR FATHER

Scripture: *Luke 15:11-24, Romans 8:14-17* In Luke's Gospel, Jesus tells the parable of the Prodigal Son. Then in the Epistle to the Romans, Paul talks about what it means to be a child of God.

The Preacher's Notes:

This is a rather simple sermon (simple-minded may be more like it) that merely makes the obvious point that God is our Father, and how nice it is to be one of his children. It does have a compelling illustration at the end.

GOD IS OUR FATHER

Each one of us has his or her own favorite way of thinking about God. For me, as for many of you, my favorite way is to think of him as my Heavenly Father. Over the years, that has come to me as the most satisfying and comfortable way to think of my relationship to him.

But pause for a moment this morning and look at it this way. You and I are *not* the natural, begotten children of God. We are *adopted!*

Several years ago, I was visiting in a home where there was an adopted boy about five years old. He was quite proud of the fact that he had been adopted. In fact, when his parents asked him to explain it to me, he proudly said, "I've been *chosen!*"

That's a good way of looking at it. Perhaps in his young mind, he carried the picture of his parents going to an adoption agency where there was a long line of children up for adoption, and out of all these kids, they chose only this one. What an honor! It almost implied that the rest of us had to take whatever we got, but *he* had been chosen!

This is a very good way to understand our relationship with God. He has specially chosen me—and you—to be adopted into his family. How about that? Quite an honor, isn't it?

Through the centuries, our Church doctrine has insisted that we think of Jesus as the only begotten Son of God. We are his adopted children.

Let me tell you the greatest thing about being adopted by God into his family. It's the cost of this adoption. I'm told that when a young couple wants to adopt a child, it costs a lot of money to do so. But that's nothing, compared to what it cost God to adopt you and me.

Suppose God would say this to you right now—this is *not* what he says, just a supposition for the sake of illustration—God says, "I hope you will get along all right, but there is nothing I can do to help you. You see, a long time ago, I passed some laws in this universe, and you have been breaking these laws. I am a God of justice, and when my laws are broken, you must be punished. There is nothing I can do to help you. Oh, there *is* something I *could* do. I could give up my only begotten Son to save you. But that would cost too much. He would have to become one of you, and he would have to die horribly on a cross, and I couldn't stand that. After all, he *is* my beloved Son. My *only* Son. You can understand that, can't you? No, I can't give him up, just to save you. The laws of justice demand that you are a law-breaker, and you must pay the punishment."

What if God had said that? I'm sure glad he didn't, aren't you? If he had said that, he may be God, the all-powerful Being who rules the universe... but he wouldn't be our *Father!* But because he didn't say that, because he did sacrifice his only begotten Son, he paid the awful price, and he has *chosen* us to be his adopted child.

In the story of the Prodigal Son, we have a vivid scene of this foolish boy coming to his senses, wanting to come home. There he was out in the field, without any money, so hungry that even the slop the pigs were eating looked good to him. That's a familiar story to us. We read the parable a moment ago in the Scripture lesson. We know how it turned out.

Now let me tell you a modern version of this same story.

A young man left home when he was young. He was restless, and he felt the need to get away from his father's house and be on his own. A few sharp words had been exchanged with his parents, and the boy walked out, vowing never to come back. He was on his own.

A couple of years passed. During that time, he had no communication with his parents. By this time, he had grown up a little. No longer did he have anger and resentment toward his father's overbearing attitude. He recalled instead those good moments, those treasured memories, when he found love and respect as a child of that home. He began to feel a longing, a deep unsatisfied ache within him, to go home.

But he couldn't go home. He had said some things he wished he had not said. He had cut the cords that bound him to his father. He had burned his bridges behind him.

But his need to see his family again overwhelmed him. It grew on him. He was fed up with the mistakes he had made that led him to such loneliness and suffering. He just wanted to go home.

One day he made up his mind. He would do it! He would go home.

If they didn't want him back, well . . . so be it. He would continue his life's journey alone. But the longing within him was so overpowering that he just had to try.

He wrote a brief note to his father, telling him what day he would be coming home. The train on which he would ride went right past the back yard of his house, just before pulling into the depot at his hometown. How was he to know if he would be welcome? In the note he asked his father to hang a white sheet on the line in the back yard if he would be welcome at home.

As the train approached his hometown, he became more and more apprehensive. What if they wouldn't take him back? They shouldn't, after what he had said and done. He didn't deserve a thing. There would probably be no sheet hanging on the line and no one to meet him at the station. And so he would have to go on, making his own way, an immature boy in a grown-up world.

As he rode those last few agonizing miles, he just couldn't look. So he covered his face and ducked his head.

Then he heard a buzzing among the passengers around him. "Look at that, will you?" somebody said. "I never saw anything like it in my life!" said another. And the boy opened his eyes and looked.

There was his home, his father's house. It wasn't hard to spot, because the back yard was covered with white. Every sheet in the house was on the line. Every sheet, every pillowcase, every white towel, every white shirt, every handkerchief—every piece of cloth in the house that was white was out there in the back yard. And in that moment, he wanted to go home more than anything else.

Any illustration is inadequate, but this may give us a glimpse into what it means to be chosen by God to be his adopted child. We are tremendously and voluminously *loved!* Far beyond anything our weak illustrations can imagine.

Just think of it! This is the Great God Almighty, ruler of the Universe, the all-powerful, infinite *God!* And you and I are his children. Can you believe that?

And then . . . we remember what it cost God to make it possible for us to call him "Our Father." *Amazing!*

THE JOY OF IGNORANCE:
Do We Have to Know Everything?

Scripture: *Proverbs 30: 18-18* Agur the Proverb writer has four things he cannot understand.

The Preacher's Notes:

So . . . Agur has four things he can't understand. All right, let's explain them to him. We can do that with our modern-day education in scientific matters. After we have done it, we discover that we are better off wondering—as Agur did—about the mysteries involved in these four things that have been totally destroyed by the scientific explanations.

What do we do with the idea that scientific explanations destroy our need for God? Tom, Dick and Harry have answers to that question. Which answer is the right one? I'm not sure . . . are you?

But maybe . . . all three answers are necessary in the complex society we live in.

THE JOY OF IGNORANCE: DO WE HAVE TO KNOW EVERYTHING?

Three things are too wonderful for me; four things I do not understand: The way of an eagle in the sky, the way of a serpent on a rock, the way of a ship on the high seas, and the way of a man with a maiden.

I feel a little sorry for Agur, son of Jakeh, the collector of proverbs in this particular chapter in the book of *Proverbs*, don't you? Poor fellow! He lived so long ago. He never heard of aero-dynamics, biological mutations, astral-physics, chromosomes and genes, DNA. He didn't even have access to the Internet! Everything was a mystery to him. It was "wonderful"—filled with wonder—because he didn't understand. But he lived almost three thousand years ago. If he had only lived in our time, he would know these things.

Wouldn't it be fun to meet with Agur the primitive Proverb writer, and explain his four mysteries to him? Why don't we do it?

Agur, listen to me.

First, you inquired about *the way of an eagle in the sky*.

All right. Here's how that happens. It's all a question of air displacement. Given the weight of the bird and the span of the wings, a little lateral motion of the wings to push air under the body, and the eagle flies! Speed, elevation and direction are achieved by appropriate muscular movements. As a primitive heavier-than-air mechanism, however, the eagle has long been out-classed in speed and efficiency by the jet airplane, the SST and the space shuttle—which I don't understand, but some people do, and so it takes the mystery out of it.

While Agur the primitive Proverb collector is recovering from this, let's hit him with another one.

You asked about *the way of a serpent on a rock*.

I see your difficulty. No legs, no wings! How does it move? Elementary zoology would soon explain that. Movement is made possible by a series of waves from the front of the body toward the back, each wave pressing against the rock and forcing the reptile forward. The microscope has shown that the underside of the snake's body is composed of tiny movable scales, which, when the snake moves in a rhythmic undulating movement, come forward in the air, press down on the rock, and then push backward against the rock, propelling the snake forward. Oh, you have a problem about the rock? How does it move on such a smooth surface without slipping? Well, those little scales are equipped with many very tiny suction cups, so that it can find traction on even the smoothest rock surface.

You see? There's nothing wonderful about the way of a serpent on a rock. Modern biology and the microscope have a perfectly good explanation.

Next question. Ah, yes: *The way of a ship on the high seas*.

I suppose, Agur, your problem is, how can a boat pick its way across the vast ocean to the desired harbor? Well, it's not so difficult. It's called the science of navigation. In your day, that science was very primitive. But now, there's no real mystery. We have the compass, the sextant, sonar, radar, satellites, and if you still need help, you can always call the Coast Guard.

Now, what was that last thing you mentioned? Ah, yes: *The way of a man with a maiden*.

You don't understand? Now really, if there is one area where we've made great strides in recent years, it's this business of sex. You primitive people made such a mystery of it, with your poems and music, your romantic tales. But our modern generation knows all about sex. I could show you one of our modern sex manuals, which explains everything, complete with illustrations and a scientific term for every part of the body. It would tell you that it's just a matter of testosterone and estrogen. We even have computers that can match the right man with the right maiden. We no longer hesitate to talk about it in our modern society, and if you want to know about it in black and white, read any novel; or in living color, see any movie. You don't need to wonder any more. There's no more mystery.

Agur, now that you know all about the eagle, the serpent, the ship and the man/maiden relationship, how do you feel about it? Perfectly satisfied? Or ... do you miss that sense of awe—finding that some everyday events, when you think about them, are *wonder-full?* Do you long for mystery, for the unexplained, the awe-inspiring?

I hope you won't think that, as a result of my little satire on explaining everything, I disapprove of our enlightened age. I think we are living in a marvelous time. It's great to be more advanced, more knowledgeable, better educated, less superstitious than ever before. I wouldn't want for a minute to return to the so-called "good old days," when there were so many unknowns. We have come too far, and we're going even further. The marvelous strides in medicine, communications, travel, computer technology, space exploration are much too valuable to wish away. This is an exciting time, and the excitement grows with every passing year.

But it is a time for adjustments in our thinking. In the age in which we live, what is the place of religious faith?

What Agur did when faced with things that he did not understand was say, "Look what God has done," and he would be filled with wonder and awe. What we do is say, "Look at what science and technology have explained to us." Does God have any place in our modern age?

When people try to adjust their thinking to our modern times, they usually go in one of three directions. Let's look at those three directions through the eyes of three people: Tom, Dick and Harry.

Let's listen to Tom first.

Tom says, "I don't believe in God any more. Oh, I used to, back in the days when I was young and naïve, before I began to learn that there are answers to the unknowns of the universe. Once there was a time when the only way you *could* explain the unknown was by saying *'God did it.'*

"And let's not knock our former age," Tom goes on. "After all, it was the only way our forefathers had of explaining things. It was very helpful for them.

"But times are different." (Still Tom speaking.) "We live in a different age. No reasonable educated person needs a God to explain the unknowns of our present age. It would be foolish to reject our advances in knowledge. Therefore the only thing left is to reject religion, which is based on superstition and ignorance. We don't need God as a way of explaining things any more."

That's Tom's answer. I respect his viewpoint, which he undoubtedly struggled with for a long time, finally reaching his decision to reject religion. And there are a lot of Toms today, and I'm sure many of you share his viewpoint.

Now let's listen to Dick.

Dick says, "My need for a meaningful faith is so deep, so basic, that I will believe in God no matter what. All the explanations in the world cannot shake my faith; it is much too meaningful to me. We humans are essentially religious creatures, and we can't get rid of God—or our need for him—by replacing him with science. Therefore if I am faced with a choice of believing in God or believing in scientific explanations, I must not reject God or my life has no meaning.

"And," Dick continues, "if my religion, to cite just one example out of many, tells me that God created mankind, and my science tells me that humans evolved from lower forms of animal life, I will reject the evolutionary theory and reaffirm my belief in God the Creator. I don't care how foolish and backward this makes me; I will not deny my faith. That's how much I need to believe in God."

That's Dick's answer, and he's not alone. There are many in the various religions who feel as he does.

I admire his faith, and I share his feeling of a need to believe in God. And if Dick's approach satisfies him, more power to him. But it does not satisfy me. But I will never ridicule his belief, because obviously it is meaningful to him and gives him peace of mind.

With respect, however, I must point out that Dick's explanation is just as narrow as Tom's. To Dick, as to Tom, belief in God is no more than an explanation of that which is not understood. If you don't understand something—it's easy: *God did it!* The only difference between them is that Tom rejects religion in favor of science, while Dick rejects science in favor of religion.

Now, let's listen to Harry.

Harry says, "I do not find religion and science incompatible and contradictory. I can accept them both. When science uncovers one of the secrets of the universe, my reaction is: *So that's how God did it! Praise God!* It is good to know that God is such an accomplished scientist! I'm glad I know more than Agur the Biblical collector of Proverbs, because my God is bigger than his!"

This is Harry's approach, and it's mine. It's an exciting age in which we live. It stimulates and enlarges my faith in God. And it enables me to live in a modern world, filled with education and knowledge and science, going beyond the superstitious approach to religion that Harry and I have long ago rejected.

And I insist that, whatever viewpoint you may subscribe to—Tom's, Dick's or Harry's—don't hold in distain the other two. Disagree with them, of course. But respectfully. And never, *never,* ridicule them, for they have found meaning in their world view, and maybe even that elusive, enigmatic, mysterious entity called peace of mind.

Another way of looking at it is that all three are right. Tom's approach is right—for him. Dick's is right also—for him. And Harry, even though it's my viewpoint, is right for me, but is it the final answer, the last, undeniably final answer that proves everybody else wrong? Or is it just the best we can do?

Which brings me to the point of this sermon: Do we have to know everything? Or just enough to enable is to be at peace with ourselves?

Let me quote to you from the Gospel According to Saint James the Shott: When I engage in a discussion of theology, some people say I'm arrogant. But I'm not arrogant. I'm just . . . always . . . right!

But whether you are a follower of Tom, Dick or Harry, perhaps you will agree with me that too much knowledge is a dangerous thing. It may place in danger something that all of us need: a sense of awe and wonder when we contemplate something mysterious, enigmatic, defying explanation, beyond our finite minds to explain adequately. We need to experience moments of humility, to be able to gasp in awe, to bow in reverence before something unexplained and unexplainable, a majestic mystery!

Once again, let's bring Agur the primitive Proverb collector into modern times, and paraphrase his small quest for knowledge. Agur, what do you think about bringing your collection up-to-date by putting these into your verses about what gives you a sense of awe:

> *There are three things that are wonderful; no, four, which fill me with awe.*
>
> *One, the Hubble telescope, pushing past the farthest planets in our solar system, transmitting back to our tiny planet new and startling secrets in the vast infinity of space, secrets that hint to us of the mysterious origin of our universe, and raising the startling possibility that there very likely may be other life forms out there.*
>
> *Two, the ability of the human race to survive in spite of itself, with its own self-destructive tendencies toward pollution, bad health habits, nuclear warfare technology, rampant terrorism, and our insatiable need for a war in every generation.*
>
> *Three, the diversity of human beings on our planet: the believers and the non-believers, the liberals and the conservatives, the hawks and the doves, the realists and the dreamers, the leaders and the followers, and especially the delicate balance that all this diversity creates in the ongoing drama of the human race.*
>
> *And four: in spite of our knowledge of the biological reproductive system, and the constant display of sex in books and movies . . . the wonder and joy of one of life's most delightful mysteries: the way of a man with a maiden.*
>
> *And five—aw, why not? The insatiable need within us to believe in Something bigger than ourselves. I call it God. What do you call it?*

INFINITY

Scripture: *Psalm 8* The Psalmist looks up at the sky at night and utters rhapsodic praises to God.

The Preacher's Notes:

The theme of this sermon is introduced by a rather spectacular poem called "The Mystic." It says something like Psalm 8, wondering about God in the universe. Then this ignorant preacher (me!) tries to define the word "infinity," and immediately shows his ignorance. Try to reconcile the concept of an infinite God with the undeniable fact that this God is personalized; that is, a Father to each one of us.

INFINITY

Abraham Lincoln once said, "I cannot conceive how a person can stand out under the stars at night and say there is no God."

That must have been how the Psalmist felt when he wrote the 8th Psalm. I have done what he has done, and I suspect you have too. The Psalmist stood outdoors on a clear night, looking up into the heavens. His mind was filled with the beauty and the grandeur that he saw displayed above him, and he very thoughtfully asked the question, *When I consider the heavens, the moon and the stars that you have created . . . what is man?*

When I was young—in college—I discovered a poem that very quickly became one of my favorites. The author is not a household name: Cale Young Rice. The title of the poem is "The Mystic." This poem appealed to me in those youthful days when I was struggling with my faith, and even today it has a resonance and depth that thrills me. Listen to this:

> *There is a quest that calls me*
>   *In nights when I am lone,*
> *The need to ride where the ways divide*
>   *The Known from the Unknown.*
> *I mount what thought is near me*
>   *And soon I reach the place,*
> *The tenuous rim where the Seen grows dim*
>   *And the Sightless hides its face.*
> *I have ridden the wind,*
> *I have ridden the sea,*
> *I have ridden the moon and stars,*
> *I have set my feet in the stirrup seat*
> *Of a comet coursing Mars.*

And everywhere, thro' the earth and air
My thought speeds, lightning-shod,
It comes to a place, where checking pace
It cries, "Beyond lies God!"

Can you imagine me as a young man, wondering who God is and what he means to me, mounting some thought like a horse and galloping all over the vastness of the universe asking questions about who God is and what he is to me? It sounds pretty silly now, but it didn't then. The Psalmist must have done the same thing, even without the benefits of this poem. Let me go on with the second verse of this poem:

It calls me out of the darkness
It calls me out of sleep,
"Ride, ride! For you must, to the end of Dust!"
It bids—and on I sweep
To the vast outposts of Being
Where there is Gulf alone—
And thro' a vast that was never passed
I listen for Life's tone.
I have ridden the wind,
I have ridden the night,
I have ridden the ghosts that flee
From the vaults of death like a chilling breath
Over eternity.
And everywhere is the earth laid bare—
Ether and star and clod—
Until I wind to its brink and find
But the cry, "Beyond lies God!"

Now as I did that in my youth, I had one distinct advantage over the Psalmist. I had taken a course in Astronomy 101. I knew a little bit more about this universe than that ancient Psalmist who saw only a thousand points of light up there in the sky. He never suspected what I knew, that each one of those stars was a sun, which might have its own solar system. He didn't know about distances, which I had just heard described in class and had carefully written down in my notebook.

I knew for example that light travels at 186,284 miles per second, or six trillion miles a year. The universe is so vast we have to measure distances in light years, rather than miles. The nearest star, not counting our own sun, is 25 trillion miles away, or 3 light years. In other words, what we see when we look at that star is what it was like three years ago.

Can you comprehend that distance? It's a little farther than from here to Orlando! But how far *is* it? A scientist once figured out a unique way of demonstrating how far it is from our earth to Alpha Centauri, the nearest star outside our solar system. He measured several feet of spider web and then proceeded to calculate that if a thread could be made from this spider's web long enough to encircle the earth, 25 thousand miles, it would weigh two pounds. But such a thread long enough to reach Alpha Centauri would weigh six . . . hundred . . . thousand . . . tons!

That Psalmist also didn't know how many stars there are out there. My textbook said that there are about six thousand stars visible to the naked eye, but the larger telescopes have revealed millions. Today that figure is in the billions, now that the Hubble telescope is up there and opening up for us vistas that constantly amaze us as to how big our universe really is.

Back in my youth, there was no Hubble telescope. Even so, I stood out there in the night and mounted a thought like a horse and rode out in search of the outer limits of the universe. I rode and rode and rode, and finally I came to the end. And as I pulled up on my exhausted steed, I had to ask myself, what's out there—beyond the end? How far out does it actually go?

There is a word to describe this: Infinity. It comes from the Latin meaning *without limits*. We who are earthbound cannot begin to understand what that means. Everything we have ever experienced when it comes to distances has a limit. But what does infinity mean? You go out there as far as you can go, and what is beyond that? When do you come to an end? And when you do, what is on the other side of the end?

Infinity.

It's a word that is resonant in its depth and breadth, sonorous in its majesty and meaning. It is a word of mystery. It is beyond our finite understanding. It's a shame that this impressive word has been used in our time to describe a Japanese car!

Back in my college days, one of my fellow students in that astronomy class said to me once: "I learn in class that the universe is so vast that a God who is big enough to explain it could not care whether I live or cheat or starve or . . . whatever." This was a question that I struggled with in those days.

This is the same question the Psalmist asked: *When I consider the universe, the moon and the stars that you have created, what is man, that you think of him? Mere man, that you care for him?*

Faced with a vast universe, we find it difficult not to believe that there is a Mastermind behind its creation and governance. But the bigger question is not, "Do you believe in God?" but rather, "Do you believe in a *personal* God?"

Actually, there aren't too many pure atheists around. Yes, there are some, but there are even more agnostics—people who say: There must be a God, that's undeniable; but how can we know anything about him? How can we know if he isn't just some distant Being in the universe, who doesn't have time to care about this tiny planet, let alone the vast population on it, and especially little old me?

That bothered me, back in those youthful days when I struggled with my faith. Sometimes I thought of God as being like the little old woman in the Mother Goose rhyme:

> *There was an old woman who lived in a shoe.*
> *She had so many children, she didn't know what to do.*

If God were like that flustered old woman, then he would probably find the same sort of solution she did:

She gave them some broth without any bread,
And spanked them all soundly and sent them to bed.

Wouldn't it be horrible to believe in a God like that? But we don't. Our Christian faith tells us that God is personalized.

Look at this pen and pencil set. Solid gold? Well . . . not exactly. But there is one thing about it that makes it different from any other pen and pencil: it has my name on it. It's personalized. So don't try to steal it; it won't write for anyone else but me!

Our Christian faith is like that. It's personalized. It has my name on it. And yours too.

How do we know that? That was the question I struggled with in my youthful days. And my answer led me to the cross of Christ. God may be the God of the universe—the God of infinity—but he has broken into human history in Jesus. He paid the price for this—a pretty terrible price—but because he did, we can have a personalized faith. We can know that this infinite God, creator of the infinite universe, is our Father, who knows our name, who loves each one of us as though we were the only child he has. All this is embodied in the meaning of the term "infinity." Our God is infinite, without limits. That's why he's big enough to be a Father to individuals.

Once in ancient Rome, there was a big parade, and the legions marched triumphantly into the city. In a chariot leading the procession was the emperor, the mighty Caesar. A little boy dashed out from the crowd and ran toward the chariot that held the emperor. He was stopped by a big burly Roman legionnaire who said to him, "You can't go there. Don't you know that's Caesar?" The boy replied, "Yes, but he's also my father." The boy was the emperor's son.

That's a pretty big thought for this morning. Think of the God who created, owns and rules this vast universe. He's the infinite God. But . . . he's also your Father. He personalized our faith, and because of what God has done for us on the cross, we can say, "Almighty God," but we can also say, "Our Father." So say it softly, reverently, and with awe as you think about infinity: *"Almighty God . . . our Father!"*

THE FLEECE TEST

Scripture: *Judges 6:36-40, John 20:24-29* The story in Judges is about Gideon, who wanted to be sure God was with him, so he gave God the "Fleece Test." The story in John's Gospel takes place after the resurrection of Jesus, focusing on the disciple Thomas, who doubted that Jesus had really risen.

The Preacher's Notes:

The "Fleece Test" is a test that we often try to prove that God really is with us. Almost always, it doesn't work. But many of us would like to see some kind of spectacular miracle; otherwise, can we be sure God is with us? We can, if we can just get rid of that "miracle mentality."

THE FLEECE TEST

Like most educated, intelligent adults, I am an avid reader of the comics. To me, they rank up there in value beside the editorial page and the sports page. I wouldn't miss my daily reading of the comics for anything.

This morning my sermon begins with a comic strip, this time B.C. In this strip, B.C. is standing on top of a hill, looking up. He says, "God, if you're up there, give me a sign."

The next picture shows B.C. walking down the hill, and there is a small rain shower coming down right on him. He is saying, "Well, we know two things: He's up there, and He's got a sense of humor."

B.C. was looking for a "Fleece Test." That's what I call it when you ask God to give you a sign.

It's not hard to understand where the term "Fleece Test" comes from. That was Gideon's test. First, the fleece was wet with dew, and the ground was dry. The next night the fleece was dry, and there was dew on the ground around it. Then Gideon knew God was with him. That's the Fleece Test.

I can tell you this, however: *Don't count on it!* It doesn't work. I've tried it. When I was a little boy, I tried it over and over again. It *never* worked.

For example, there was the time I said to God, "Lord, please give me an A on this history test. Then I'll know you're really with me." It didn't work. Maybe that had something to do with the fact that I didn't study very much for the test. But as a Fleece Test, it failed.

I used to try the Fleece Test a lot, and I can tell you, it *never* worked for me. And yet I kept hearing in Sunday School and from the sermons that it does work. The Bible, they told me, is filled with examples of miracles. Missionaries and people very close to God made it work occasionally. But it never worked for me.

Childish? Immature? Perhaps. But I wonder how many other children have encountered the same experience. Did you? Were you, like me, a sensitive super-religious kid who was concerned about whether God was with you? Is he really there? Is he, as the Psalm says, *a very present help in time of need?*

I really think my experience was shared with other children. We were bewildered, confused, unable even to put our problem into words. It wasn't until my mature years that I was finally able to articulate what the problem was. And that is what I now call the Fleece Test.

There are several responses that a person can make when the Fleece Test fails. Let me see if I can list them. I couldn't when I was a child. Maybe I can now.

Response Number One: There is no God up there. Or, if there is, he doesn't pay any attention to me.

I rejected that response. I have an idea that a lot of children didn't. That may be why a lot of young people leave the Church when mature. The failure of the Fleece Test proved to them that there is no God to help them in time of need.

The reason I—and a lot of others, perhaps you—rejected that response is that I really wanted to be a religious person. I wanted desperately to believe in God. If there was any way I could have a faith, I would, in spite of the consistent failure of the Fleece test. For some of us, belief doesn't come easy; we have to work at it.

Response Number Two: We don't have enough faith. That's why we think the Fleece Test doesn't work. It would work, if we just had more faith.

One Sunday afternoon when I was a child, I was playing in my back yard with my friend Jack. In Sunday School or church that morning, I had learned the text, *If you have faith, you can move mountains.* I was eager to put that statement to the Fleece Test.

"Jack," I said, "do you see that mountain over there?" I pointed to the mountain ridge across the River, visible from our house on Fourth Street. "If you have enough faith, you could move that mountain."

Jack turned and faced that mountain, his hands on his hips, staring. Finally, he turned back to me and said, "It ain't moving!"

"That's because you don't have enough faith," I said. "Here, let me try."

I stood there staring at that mountain, willing it to move. I asked God to move it for me. It didn't. I tried harder; it still didn't move. Finally I turned back to Jack and said, "Well, I guess neither one of us has enough faith."

That, I believe, is a common response, either for children or adults. Any time the Fleece Test fails, we think, it's because we didn't have enough faith. If we pray for a loved one to be healed, and that loved one dies, was it because we didn't have enough faith? Would he or she have lived if our faith were greater? And does that make you feel guilty? Is that why you grieve so much?

If we try to accomplish something, and we pray to God for success—and we fail—does our failure mean we don't have enough faith?

If we need something, desperately need it, and we pray to God for it—and don't get it—does that mean our faith was lacking?

Is that why our Fleece Tests fail, because we don't have enough faith?

If that is so, how do you go about getting more faith? Is it *fervency* that counts? If our faith were a little more fervent, would the Fleece Test work? All we have to do is pray harder, offer more prayers, wear out our knees, storm the gates of heaven with our prayers. Maybe that will convince God that we really mean it, that we have enough faith for him to answer that prayer.

That seems so silly when you look at it that way. Of course God's mind will not be changed by the fervency of our prayers—any more than a wise and caring parent will change his or her mind because of pressure from a child, by crying, tantrums, nagging, or anything else. God will answer a prayer because of what he knows is right, not by how badly we want it. His will, not ours, is what counts. The purpose of prayer is *not* to get God to do what we want.

And that's why the best prayer ever offered to God was said by Jesus in the Garden of Gethsemane. That prayer in itself was a kind of Fleece Test. He knew that suffering and death lay ahead of him, and he asked that the cup—the cup of suffering—be removed from him. We read that *he prayed more fervently, with sweat on his forehead like great drops of blood.* You can't get much more fervent than that. But still, his Fleece Test failed. The cup of suffering was not removed from him. But . . . what makes that prayer so great was his concluding statement: *Nevertheless, not my will, but thine be done."*

This leads me to *Response Number Three* when the Fleece Test fails: Revise your understanding of how God works. Forget the Fleece Test. It not only doesn't work, but it is based on an understanding of the nature of God that is totally false.

This misunderstanding is what I like to call a "miracle mentality." That is, many people think that the only way God works in this world is by miracles. That is the whole reason for the Fleece Test: to prove the existence of God in my life by a miracle. Miracles worked in Bible times. Miracles of faith healing or spectacular interventions by God have changed things around for some people. And so a lot of us expect it, believing that God only works that way.

And he doesn't. The Fleece Test almost always fails, because it is based on a misconception of the nature of God.

One of my favorite ways to picture that misconception is "The Old Genie-in-the-bottle Trick." God is like that genie who lives in a bottle. He has wonderful magical powers. If we want to make use of that power, all we have to do is rub the bottle (that's called "praying fervently") and God will come to us and give us whatever we want. He's got the power. He answers prayer. So . . . get him to do whatever you want.

The person who has that kind of picture of God has a miracle mentality, believing that God works only in miracles.

Every time in my life, and especially in my ministry, when I have made that statement, people think I'm a non-believer. If I don't believe in a miracle-working God, they say I don't believe in God. Not so. I believe in God. I just don't believe that the only way he works is by miracles.

That is why I was forced to find a new way of understanding God's presence in my life than trying to get the Fleece Test to work. Instead of looking for *proof*, I began to look for *faith*.

Faith is *not* believing in something proven by a miracle. Faith is believing in God when all the Fleece Tests fail.

I have one more thought on this concept of faith rather than proof.

After the resurrection of Jesus, when he was meeting with his disciples, there was a moment that I have found to be one of the most precious scenes in the New Testament. He met with his disciples when the Apostle Thomas was not present. Thomas, later, had some doubts about this preposterous notion that Jesus had come back to life. I don't blame him; I would too.

"Unless I see him," Thomas said, "and touch his wounds, I will not believe."

In other words, Thomas wanted a Fleece Test. He wanted proof. He wanted to see the miracle himself. It wasn't good enough for him to hear it from others. He wanted to be there and see for himself.

Wouldn't it have been great to have been there that day? To be with Thomas, to see for ourselves the risen living Jesus? To touch him, to make sure? It happened to Thomas; why doesn't it happen to me?

Not too many people have had an experience like Tomas. I wasn't there. Neither were you. So what should we do? Should we say, Unless I see . . . and touch . . . I will not believe? Unless I experience a miracle myself, I will not believe that God is with me?

The answer to that is the answer Jesus gave to Thomas. Or rather, it is the answer he gives to us. It is simply this: *"Ah, Thomas. You have seen, and you believe."* Then turning to us, Jesus says, *"Blessed are those who have not seen, yet believe."*

That's me. That's you. We have not seen, yet we believe. And nothing—including all the Fleece Tests we have ever devised—will get us to abandon our faith. As Jesus said, *"Blessed are **you**, who have not seen, yet believe.*

THE OTHER MARY

Scripture: *Matthew 27:57-61, 28:1-7* These two stories in Matthew describe the crucifixion scene and also the resurrection. It focuses on the women who were present, including the vague character simply called "the other Mary."

The Preacher's Notes:

How would you like to have been a witness to both the crucifixion and resurrection of Jesus, and simply be known in history as "the other Mary?" And isn't this what we feel sometimes? A nobody. Someone of no importance. Well . . . not in God's eyes. God knew that "other Mary," and she was important to him. Isn't that what counts?

THE OTHER MARY

When I was in the parish ministry, I preached a series of sermons on the women in the New Testament named Mary. Would you believe, there were seven of them? I heard recently that Mary was the most popular name for women in the culture of First Century Palestine, though I don't know why. The Hebrews gave names to their children that were meaningful, and the name Mary means "sorrow." And still it was the most popular name for a woman.

The seven Mary's in the New Testament:

1. **Mary, the mother of Jesus,** sometimes called "The Virgin Mary."
2. **Mary Magdalene.** I wrote a novel about her, and in my research I discovered that she was not the prostitute most people believe she was. But that's another story.
3. **Mary of Bethany,** the sister of Martha and Lazarus.
4. **Mary the mother of John Mark,** who may have been the owner of the big house in Jerusalem were the Last Supper took place in the Upper Room.
5. **Mary the wife of Alphaeus,** who was the mother of one of the disciples.
6. **Mary of Rome,** whom Paul commends in his epistle because she was a leader in the early church which in itself is remarkable, given the chauvinistic culture of the times and especially Paul's attitude toward women.

These are six Mary's in the New Testament. Who was the seventh? She is the subject of my sermon this morning. You'll hear about her as I read the New Testament lesson for today.

Read Matthew 27:57-61, 28:1-7

The Other Mary!
Who was she? Matthew twice refers to her. She's a very important person in Christian history, because she was a witness to both the crucifixion and resurrection of Jesus. But she is known throughout history simply as "the other Mary." She was lost in history because of her common name.

There are churches that have been named for Mary. But most of these churches are named for Mary the mother of Jesus. Some are called the Church of St. Mary Magdalene. I even heard of the Church of Mary and Martha. But I have never heard of a church called the Church of the Other Mary.

I feel sorry for that Other Mary, whoever she is. She was lost in the crowd, just because of her name.

I think I know how she feels, a little bit. Sometimes I feel like "the other Mary." When I go to Pennsylvania to visit relatives, I become just another one of the Shott boys. When I visit my wife's relatives, I am just another one of the in-laws. I usually attend church at the Presbyterian Church of the Good Shepherd because my wife is the organist, and there I am known as "Esther's husband."

I wonder if that was the story of the Other Mary. She was a nobody. Other people around her were more important and honored than she was. Mary Magdalene, for example. Both Mary's were the first to realize that Jesus had risen, but the Magdalene gets all the credit. And the Other Mary was just lost in the crowd.

Do you feel that way sometimes? That nobody knows you? That nobody cares? That other people get all the credit, and you are lost in the crowd? Just another Mary.

I think I know exactly what the Other Mary needs. She needs a Social Security number. Then she would be a real person, and have a sense of identity. I know who I am: I am 210-20-2297. Without that name, I couldn't drive a car, own property, vote, get a passport, charge purchases at the store. If the Other Mary just had a number, we would know exactly who she is.

Everybody has to have a number. The culture we live in is so big, and has so many people, that we have to have a number in order to be somebody. Some people resent the fact that we are becoming a faceless society, a world full of Other Mary's. This says something about our modern world, about humanity's growth, about the population explosion. We have to have numbers to keep it all straight. But it still makes us feel like the Other Mary.

It has to be done, of course. The alternative is chaos. There are too many Mary's in our society. If we went by names only, I might be confused with an Orlando man I heard about several years ago when I first moved to Palm Bay. His name was Jim Schott, and he was the Superintendent of Schools for Orange County. Now, which one of us is "the other Jim Shott?"

I heard of a man who was disgusted with the idea of just being a number, so to prove a point he sent himself a postcard addressed with nothing but numbers. In place of his name was his Social Security number. He had his box number and rural route number, and then his zip code. No words, just numbers. The card was delivered with no problem. But if he had addressed it to himself with no numbers—just his name, his street, his town, his state—the Post Office might have had a hard time finding him!

Does all this make you feel like the Other Mary? Nobody likes to be lost in the crowd, a faceless person, adrift in a sea of humanity. Just another Mary. We all want to be known for who we are. We want to be recognized as a person in our own right, someone with a name, a face, a personality, someone who hurts, someone who is sensitive and has deep feelings and cries out desperately to be understood.

Every person we meet is that way. If our society in the interests of efficiency is forced to treat people as a number, then it becomes even more important for each of us to treat each person we meet as a person. That's hard, isn't it, because all those people out there we meet every day are just another Mary to us, maybe because we are so wrapped up in ourselves. We want everybody else to see the real me—and . . . maybe . . . that leads us to treat everyone else as just another Mary.

I don't want to be just another Mary in God's eyes. I want him to see me as an individual, to understand me, to hear my prayers, not treat me as just another person on this crowded planet. And the marvelous thing about our Christian faith is that God knows the name of each one of us, and he has tailor-made a faith for you and me.

I have a little fantasy that I hope you will indulge me for a moment. What would it be like to have a tailor-made suit? I've never owned one. My fantasy is that some day I'll walk into a tailor shop and say to the tailor, "Make me a suit!"

"O.K." says the tailor. "Now tell me exactly what you want. What size? What materials? What style? What color?"

Now, if I'm smart, I will say, "I don't know. You're the expert, not me. You make one for me in whatever way you think will be comfortable and make me look good."

So he does. He very carefully takes my measurements, so that the suit will fit me just right. He selects the very best material, and he chooses a color to match my coloring. The cut of the suit will be so clever that it will cover up my pot belly, which is getting bigger and bigger as the years pass. Then there will come a day when I walk out of that tailor shop dressed in magnificent sartorial splendor, and I can strut around in front of all you "other Mary's" who bought your suits off the rack at J.C.Penney's and say, "See? Mine was tailor-made!"

After telling you that fantasy, I'll have to confess that owning a tailor-made suit is way, way down on my list of priorities. That was strictly a fantasy. But I also must tell you that having a comforting faith is high, high on my list of priorities. And this is no fantasy.

I can go to my God and say to him, "I want a tailor-made faith."

He will reply, "O.K. What kind of a faith do you want?"

Now, if I'm smart, I will say, "I really don't know. You're the expert. Suppose you make a faith for me that you think will be just right for me."

So God goes to work. He studies me very carefully, taking my measurements. He considers my family background, my personality, my temperament. He looks at my early life, the good things I have done, and also the bad, and the amount of guilt I carry around with me. He takes into account my intelligence quotient, my level of education, whether I think with my right brain or my left brain. He doesn't have to give me the Meyers-Briggs test for a personality profile, or the Rohrschacht Ink Blot test; he already knows what kind of a profile I have. He knows where I hurt. He knows my sensitivities. He knows what kind of worship is meaningful to me, whether it emotional or intellectual. And he knows my shortcomings and failures and inadequacies. He even takes into consideration my age, because my spiritual needs have changed through the years.

And he makes for me a tailor-made faith.

It's not like the faith he made for Billy Graham, or for Pope John Paul II, or Mother Teresa, or President Bush, or my pastor, or yours. It's not the same as the one he made my parents, or my brothers, or my friends, or my spouse, or any other member of my family. It's tailor-made just for me.

And do you know, it fits me perfectly! And, he also makes a faith for you, that fits you perfectly... just you and nobody else!

Now, when those evangelists come to your door—the Jehovah's Witnesses or young Morman missionaries or whoever—respect their faith because it's tailor made just for them. But don't feel guilty because it's not your faith, because yours fits you and you only.

When you stand before God, you are not just another Mary. You are you, and God knows exactly who you are, and he cares about you... just you! As some wise person said, "Our heavenly Father treats each one of us as though we were his only child!"

Mary, whoever you are, we are sorry we don't know very much about you. We shall forever know you by what Matthew called you: The Other Mary. But you must have been somebody in your own right. You may have been somebody's wife, and you knew what it means to love and be loved. You may have been a mother, with children to worry about and fuss over and be proud of as they grow. You had your own little set of hurts, and you experienced your own bouts of depression, and loneliness, and embarrassments and frustrations.

We do know that you had one very big traumatic moment in

your life, as you stood at a distance and watched your beloved Master be crucified. We admire your devotion as you followed to see where his tomb would be, and then as you prepared spices to lovingly anoint his body. And we can at least try to imagine your bewilderment as you found the tomb empty on that memorable Sunday morning, and your surprise and joy when you met the living risen Jesus.

Maybe you do have to be known in history as the Other Mary, but nothing can take away those precious moments from you. You really are somebody, even if we don't know who you are.

But Mary, God knows who you are. You are not just a number in God's celestial computer; nor are you known to him as the Other Mary. In God's eyes, you are you. You are a person whom God understands and loves. He knows how you feel about everything. He knows when you feel good, and when you hurt, and when you are afraid, and when you are lonely, and when you feel guilty. He understands. And he loves. He will never treat you as just another Mary.

And that's a moving thought for anyone who feels that he or she is walking through this world alone.

WHO REALLY IS MY NEIGHBOR?

Scripture: *Luke 10:25-37* The parable of the Good Samaritan is familiar, but this time focus on a question by the teacher of the Law who asked Jesus, "Who is my neighbor?" Jesus answered him with the familiar parable.

The Preacher's Notes:

This sermon might well have been included under the Fictional Sermons category, because a large part of it is retelling the parable fictionally in a modern setting. There is also a story about Clarence Jordan, who preached a controversial sermon on this parable in Atlanta, Georgia, during the volatile days of the 1960's. He put a fictional twist on the parable to reflect the equality of the races during our time.

WHO REALLY IS MY NEIGHBOR?

I've never been to Central Park in New York, but I have heard that it is one of the most beautiful—and dangerous—places in America. Maybe there was a time when a person could stroll safely through the park after dark, but no more. You would be in great danger.

One night, shortly after dark, an old man came shuffling through the park on his way home. He lived on a pension and couldn't afford the high cab fare in New York. He knew about Central Park, and he was afraid.

He was attacked very suddenly. He never knew what hit him. Skillfully the thief came up behind him, hit him over the head with a sap, and then began to expertly go through his clothes. He took the old man's wallet containing $17 and some credit cards, his wrist watch, and then almost as an afterthought he stripped off the old man's yellow windbreaker, and fled into the night.

About this time the Session meeting at the nearby Presbyterian Church was breaking up, and the minister began to walk home. Usually he drove his car because of the dangerous park, but his car was in the shop tonight. The manse was directly across Central Park, and it wasn't far, so he thought he would take a chance and walk it. Usually when he walked he was accompanied by one of the elders, but that elder was delayed by some business at the church, so he had to go alone.

As he hurried through the park, he noticed the still figure of the old man lying by the path.

Poor man, thought the minister. He's probably drunk. What a pathetic figure! So many like him!

The minister's heart filled with pity. He was a man of prayer compassion. Oh Lord, he mumbled, bless this poor man, one of your children. He needs your help. Give him your strength, your courage, your power. May he become well, and make something worthy of himself.

The minister felt pretty good about himself, for not long ago he had preached on the text, "Pray for those who despitefully use you," and he was glad he could practice what he preached. And so he hurried on home.

It wasn't very long after this that the elder who had been delayed at the church came hurrying by. By this time the old man on the ground was stirring, and the elder heard him moan. He noticed what the minister had not seen, the bloody cut on the back of his head. The elder also knew about Central Park, and he was afraid.

Maybe it's a trap, he thought. He had heard about mobs who use a decoy like this. I don't want to get involved. Besides, if he does need help, it's his own fault. An old man shouldn't be out after dark in a dangerous place like this. What is the world coming to, that you can't walk safely in the park any more? Anyway, I sure don't want to get involved; it's none of my business. And so he hurried on by.

The old man on the ground was beginning to regain consciousness. He was aware of a terrible pain in his head, and he felt weak and drained. He struggled to his knees, the effort bringing more pain and dizziness.

Then he heard footsteps approaching from behind him. Oh no! he thought, in a near-panic. I'm going to be attacked again! In my weakened condition, I'm helpless!

Then he smelled a slight odor of wine coming from the man, and he felt a hand on his shoulder. A wino, he thought.

Gentle hands lifted him to his feet. Supporting him, he led him to the street. The old man raised his head and looked into the black face of the man who held him up. Oh no! he thought. Not only a drunk, but probably from one of those vicious gangs!

A taxi came by, and the black man held up his hand. The taxi pulled over and they struggled into the back seat.

"I can't pay for a cab," the old man mumbled. "I don't have any money on me."

"Don't sweat it man," came the reply. "I got it covered."

A few minutes later they pulled up at the hospital. The black man paid the cabbie, and helped the old man into the emergency room. Capable nurses came forward and he was led off to a treatment room, where he received the medical attention he needed.

A few hours later, when he was discharged, he went to the front desk looking for his benefactor. But he was gone. The hospital bill had been completely paid for, but the unknown man who helped him had vanished into the night.

I'm sure you recognize this story as the Parable of the Good Samaritan updated to modern times. Do you like it when I took the story out of its First Century context and put it into a situation in real life . . . here and now?

Someone who was a master at bringing the First Century Gospel into our century was a man by the name of Clarence Jordan. He's been dead for thirty years, but recently a ceremony was held to honor and remember him. Let me tell you about him.

Clarence Jordan was half farmer and half preacher. He went to college at the University of Georgia and received a B.S. degree in agriculture. Then he went to the Southern Baptist Theological Seminary and received his Th.M. degree, and was ordained to the ministry. He also continued his education and received from his seminary a Ph.D. degree in New Testament Greek. A farmer and a preacher . . . an interesting combination! He's not the first person to start out in life with one career and end up in another.

But Clarence Jordan was a preacher who believed in bringing the First Century Gospel into the 20th Century. He preached in Atlanta during the 1960's. Many of us can remember vividly those turbulent years. The voice of Dr. Martin Luther King was heard in our land. It was a time of turmoil, when Rosa Parks rode a bus, black people were arrested for eating at white lunch counters, large crowds marched in southern cities like Selma, Alabama, and the Black Manifesto was read in certain selected churches. Troubled times for our country, especially in the South.

And Clarence Jordan preached a sermon on the parable of the Good Samaritan in his church in Atlanta, and the sermon was so radical and disturbing that they fired him! The congregation can't fire a preacher in the Presbyterian Church, but they can in the Baptist Church, and he was fired.

So Clarence Jordan, half farmer and half preacher, went to Americus, Georgia, and founded the Koinonia Farm. It was a true farm, but it was different. It was dedicated to ministries to people in need, and there were several ways they did that. Probably the way we are most familiar with is the Habitat for Humanity program, in which people come together to build a house for a family who can't afford to build it themselves.

There was something else that Clarence Jordan did, while he was at the Koinonia Farm. He translated the Bible. Don't forget, he had a Ph.D. in New Testament Greek, and translating the Bible was something he was academically qualified to do.

This was a time when there were many translations of the Bible coming out. But his translation was like no other. I was a young minister in the 1960's, and I fell in love with his translation. It was called "The Cotton Patch Version." What it did was bring the Gospel of the First Century into the Twentieth Century... with a bang!

His translation of Jesus' parable of the Good Samaritan, for example. This was very much like the sermon he had preached in the church in Atlanta that got him fired. I would like to read it to you now. It's not as radical and earth-shaking today as it was during the 1960's, but it is an excellent example of bringing the Gospel into our times.

READ LUKE 19:25-37 FROM COTTON PATCH

How are we doing as neighbors? The Cotton Patch version helps bring home to us what I think Jesus really wanted us to grasp: that we are the neighbor to the person who needs us. This neighbor may be someone in your neighborhood, but maybe not. He may be someone in the congregation, or in our community, or our country, or halfway around the world. Whoever they may be, we can be a neighbor to them.

Everybody needs our compassion, our neighborliness. Everybody... without exception. There isn't a person who walks the face of this earth who doesn't have some kind of burden, and who needs understanding and compassion from you and me. Walk softly. That person you meet today, or tomorrow, or sometime this week, needs a little neighborliness. And you may be the one who can give it to him.

So... be a neighbor. Bring the First Century Gospel of Jesus into the 21st Century... where it belongs!

TOLERATING INTOLERANCE

Scripture: Frankly, there is no Scripture for this sermon. It was preached at a Unitarian Universalist congregation, and they had "Readings" on the subject of "intolerance."

The Preacher's Notes:

This sermon is not about people who tolerate you. On the contrary, it is about tolerating people who do **not** tolerate you!

TOLERATING INTOLERANCE

I'd like to begin by reading to you a few lines from the Gospel According to Saint James the Shott:

> *I hate violence. People who practice violence ought to be lined up against the wall and shot!*
>
> *I am a very humble person, and I'm proud of my humility.*
>
> *People who lose their temper and cuss make me so damn mad....*
>
> *When I get into an argument, some people think I'm arrogant. But I'm not. I'm just always right!*

My text for today's message comes from this same Gospel According to Saint James the Shott: I can't tolerate intolerance. This might be an appropriate thought for Martin Luther King's birthday.

About thirty years ago, I was the parish minister at a Presbyterian church in Jacksonville, Florida, during those turbulent years of the 1960's.

I didn't get many Sundays off, but the few times I did, I liked to attend the Unitarian Church in Jacksonville, because I admired so much their minister, Dr. McGehee. Some of you may remember him. He was one of the most respected ministers in Jacksonville at the time.

In the bulletin one Sunday were the results of a poll taken in their fairly large congregation, asking the members to tell what religious or philosophical area of thought most appealed to them. I don't recall the results, but I vaguely remember that many of them were humanists, or agnostics, and some even atheists.

If I had been there the Sunday the poll was taken, there would have been one Christian. One lonely Christian! I can imagine them looking around furtively, wondering, *Who was that?*

I recall one rare occasion when both my wife Esther and I attended the Unitarian Church. One member of their congregation, who was a fellow teacher with my wife in the public schools, knew something about our being Presbyterians and even knew that I was a minister. When she saw us, her jaw dropped and she blurted out, "What are *you* doing *here?*"

The question implied that not too many Christians darkened the door of a Unitarian Church. I explained to her my high regard for Dr. McGehee, which seemed to satisfy her. But I suspect she wondered if there were more to it than that. And there is.

The Unitarian Church offers me something that is missing in my Presbyterian Church, or in any Christian Church for that matter. I get tired of hearing the same old platitudes, or shallow preaching, which is the hallmark of my denomination. I am drawn to the speakers of the Unitarian Churches who take a subject, no matter how controversial, and make it come alive. There is a mental stimulation, an intellectual depth, which I seem to crave. Not that I, a Christian, agree with everything I hear in the U.U. Church, but I certainly enjoy hearing it!

Your church has an umbrella that is very large. Under it are all kinds of approaches to the meaning of life: humanism, agnosticism, atheism, whatever. Although I am classified as a liberal Christian, here I am probably seen as a conservative. Incidentally, my favorite definition of a conservative is: "one who worships at the shrine of a dead liberal."

But I do feel comfortable here. It doesn't seem to matter to you that my beliefs are somewhat different than yours. It doesn't matter to me, either. I thoroughly enjoy hearing these views expressed in a thoughtful, reasonable way. You "welcome diversity of belief and lifestyle because everyone deserves the stimulation of an intellectually active, emotionally supportive, and socially conscious community." If that last statement sounds vaguely familiar to you, it's because I stole it off your bulletin. But it does express why I feel so comfortable in your church, although I may be the only professing Christian in this room today.

Let me tell you one of my beliefs that make me a very liberal Christian. I don't believe in evangelism. Talk about liberal! That, in the eyes of some of my fellow Christians, almost makes me a heretic!

I believe in respecting the viewpoint of others, even when I don't agree. I like to listen, to understand, to appreciate, to support. Evangelism, in which I would be compelled to persuade you to adopt my viewpoint because it is the only right one, is a little arrogant. That's why, much to the dismay of my Christian colleagues, I don't believe in evangelism. Let me assure you that there will be no altar call at the end of this service.

And that's why I like the large umbrella of the U.U. Churches. I feel very much at home here. You respect me; I respect you.

Well, that's the easy part. If that were the only message I have for you today, I would have to change my sermon topic to "Tolerating Tolerance." That's easy. That's comfortable. We could respect each other, and exchange sweet platitudes until this service is over. But no, I have to dabble into the hard subject: "Tolerating Intolerance."

When someone of a different belief respects my belief, listens to me courteously, expresses his own views, and then respects my views, I like that person. I feel comfortable and warm toward him or her. But when that person tells me I'm wrong, I'm unworthy, I'm going to hell because my view is different from his, then what do I do? Answer in kind? Oh, I would love to. Sometimes I do. Is that because I'm not strong enough to tolerate his intolerance? Is it my weakness when I snap back at him, put him down, yell at him, and turn up my nose at him? How can I tolerate intolerance?

Let me now quote from the words of Jesus, who spoke something very hard to listen to:

> *You have heard it said by men of old, "You shall love your neighbor and hate your enemy. But I say to you, Love your enemies and pray for those*

> *who persecute you* (One translation reads, *pray for those who despitefully use you.*) *For if you love those who love you, what reward have you? Do not even the tax collectors do the same? And if you salute only your brethren, what more are you doing than others? Do not even the Gentiles do the same?*

Ouch! Jesus sure makes it difficult for me to be one of his followers!

So today, let's think about tolerating the *in*tolerant. Those people who do not tolerate us, how can we tolerate them?

Let me give you a few examples, out of my own experience. Each one of you may have similar examples from your experience, but I'm the one doing the preaching, so I'm gonna give you my own stories of intolerance.

Many years ago, I got into an argument with a right-to-lifer, who had some very strong feelings about abortion. I lost that argument, because I couldn't talk fast enough or yell loud enough. That was the first time that has happened to me, and it was also the last. I know better now. This is an emotional subject. I was called a "baby killer" and was told I was not a Christian, and I could expect nothing but hellfire for eternity. Talk about intolerance and lack of respect for what I believe! How could I tolerate her viewpoint if she did not tolerate mine?

I'm a little older now, and maybe even a little wiser. Now, when I meet an adamant right-to-lifer (are there any other kind?), I listen respectfully, try to understand his or her viewpoint, and respect it. I don't have to agree with that person in order to respect him. And my new-found wisdom tells me that, even if she doesn't tolerate me, I can tolerate her.

One footnote to that approach: if that person with whom I respectfully disagree uses harassment and terrorist methods to force a young pregnant woman to abandon what was for her an agonizing decision, that's different. Somewhere I must draw the line, but I draw that line somewhere between my tolerating an intolerant viewpoint, and the use of force and terrorist methods to impose that viewpoint on others.

My second example from my experience. About a year ago, I had a discussion with a man on the subject of homosexuality. It didn't take me long to discover that this too is an emotional subject. I think this person had been listening too much to Rush Limbaugh, because he began to spout the party line on abortion. He quoted the Bible, saying that it clearly states that homosexuality is an abomination, condemned by God, and those who practice it will go to hell. That's not the kind of God I believe in, but I could not match his intensity or decibels.

My problem was that I had a hard time respecting his viewpoint, which I totally disagreed with. That was mainly because he did not respect mine. I find it very hard to tolerate the intolerant. But if I don't, then—as Jesus said—how am I different from him?

Another example: a fundamentalist Christian. A liberal Christian, such as myself, has just as much trouble tolerating a fundamentalist Christian as you who don't classify yourselves as Christian. Maybe more so, because he considers me a traitor for abandoning what he would call the basic fundamentals of our faith.

I have heard from this pulpit speakers say disparaging things about Fundamentalist Christians. Often it includes ridicule. I cringe a little when I hear that, and I wonder if this is not so much because the speaker disagrees with their viewpoint as it is because they are intolerant of his.

And that's the heart and core of our problem. Tolerating intolerance. When I meet up with an intolerant Fundamentalist, I want to call him a fellow Christian, a brother in the family of God. We have differing viewpoints, but we are both Christians. But he doesn't call me that. He has placed me outside the Christian sheepfold, disowned and abandoned by my Shepherd, on my way to hell, and in the same company as those heathen Unitarians! I find that pretty good company, even if he doesn't.

The point is, how can I tolerate him, if he doesn't tolerate me? But if I don't, how am I different from him?

As I have struggled with this agonizing problem of tolerating the intolerant, I have arrived at a few hard principles, which I try to follow. I'll share them with you.

First, I recognize a difference between agreeing with a person, and respecting him. If I honestly try to understand his viewpoint, where he's coming from, and appreciate and support that person in his approach to a subject, that doesn't mean that I have to agree with him. Even if he *disrespectfully* disagrees with me, I will try to *respectfully* disagree with him. And that ain't easy.

Second, if a person with whom I disagree takes action that is unlawful, or seeks by unacceptable methods to impose his viewpoint on others, I will take a stand against him. I will still try to understand and respect his viewpoint, but I will stand firm against his program. In other words, I will try to tolerate the intolerant, even if I can't tolerate his intolerable actions.

I have a closing thought to share with you, or rather a scene from the life of Jesus, which has burned itself into my life. On the day he was crucified, the first words he spoke after being nailed to the cross was a prayer. He looked down on his cruel executioners, and then said, "Father, forgive them, for they know not what they do."

That, I believe, is the ultimate example of tolerating the intolerant!

THE GAMALIEL PRINCIPLE

Scripture: *Acts 5:33-39* The story of how the disciples were arrested in Jerusalem for preaching that Jesus had risen, and were brought to trial before the Sanhedrin. A respected member of the Sanhedrin then spoke, urging them to let these men go free, for a surprising—and wise—reason.

The Preacher's Notes:

The "Gamaliel Principle" is what I call one of the wisest approaches ever offered to the problem of condemning troublemakers in the Church. The Principle was put forth by a respected Jewish rabbi. His message may be summarized this way: "Let them alone. If they are of God, you can't stop them. And if not, they'll die out anyway." Good advice, for our time.

THE GAMALIEL PRINCIPLE

Slowly and with great dignity, the old man rose to speak. All eyes were on him, and everyone listened closely . . . because this was Gamaliel.

"Gentlemen," he said calmly, "let the prisoners be taken out, for I have something to say."

While the prisoners were being removed, let's take a look at this man who could command such respect. This was Gamaliel. He was the best of the 1st Century rabbis. A member of the Council of the Sanhedrin. Only the most revered, the greatest scholars, the men of proven wisdom, were admitted to this honored Council. And Gamaliel was the best of the best.

The historian Josephus speaks of him. He was a descendent of Hillel, and had once been the president of the Council. He had been given the title Rabban, which was accorded to very few men in Jewish history. After he died, it was written, *Since Rabban Gamaliel the elder died, there has been no more reverence for the Law.* All the bright promising young men studied under him, among them the Pharisee from Tarsus named Saul, whom we know as the Apostle Paul.

Now the prisoners had been removed, and Gamaliel could address the Council. The prisoners were the Apostles: Peter and John and the others, who had been preaching about Jesus. Their message was that Jesus was not only the Messiah, but he had risen from the dead. Some of the members of the Council were angry with them, and if they had their way, these blasphemers would be imprisoned and even executed. But . . . well . . . let's listen to what Rabban Gamaliel had to say.

He spoke gently, moderately, and with obvious wisdom. He proposed what I like to call The Gamaliel Principle.

"Let them alone," he said. "If they are of God, you can't stop them, and you'll be in the awkward position of opposing God. If they are not of God, they'll die out anyway."

He gave two examples: Theudas and Judas the Galilean. The members of the Council knew them, because they had lived only a few years before. The historian Josephus wrote about both these men.

Theudas led a revolt against the Romans in Jerusalem. The Roman army went out after Theudas and his men, and chased them to the Jordan River. There they were trapped, with the Jordan River in flood in front and the Roman army behind. "No problem," Theudas told his men. "I'll just part the waters like Moses did." He tried, they didn't part, and the Romans killed them all. So much for Theudas.

The same sort of thing happened to Judas the Galilean. He didn't like the idea of the Romans taking a census for taxation purposes, so he led a revolt against Rome. The Romans didn't take too kindly to this; you know what happens when you defy the Internal Revenue Service. The revolt was put down and Judas executed. So much for Judas the Galilean.

Those were Gamaliel's examples. Now, some of mine.

About fifty years ago, a man by the name of Thomas J. Altizer made the news. Do any of you remember him?

Dr. Altizer was a professor at Emery University School of Theology. He caused quite a stir throughout the Church when he proclaimed "God is dead!" I recall clearly the fuss he caused, and the Church was deeply disturbed. He borrowed the phrase from the German philosopher Nietchze, whose philosophy had some influence on Adolph Hitler. Now, half a century later, take a look: Nietchze is dead. Hitler is dead. Dr. Altizer is dead. But God is alive and well, as evidenced by his living healthy Church.

So much for the "God is dead" movement.

Some other examples. I can recall within my lifetime several horrible threats to the Christian Church. There was Angela Davis, the Communist, who accepted a small gift from one branch of the Presbyterian Church. That really shook the Church. I recall when

James Foreman, a young black activist, marched into the fashionable Riverside Church in New York City and read what he called "The Black Manifesto," demanding $4 million for "reparations" for injustices against black people in the past. I can remember when Senator McCarthy began his investigation of Communists and "fellow travelers" in America. He said that many of them were ministers, and the Church was infested with secret agents. I recall Madeline Murray O'Hare, the Atheist, who fought against prayer in the public schools, the motto In God we trust on our coins, and many other causes. All of these shook the Church to its foundations.

But the Church survived. And grew stronger. And just about every decade, some big upheaval or shattering issue comes along, such as abortion, homosexuality, or prayer in the public schools, or the "under God" phrase in the Pledge of Allegiance. The prophets of doom begin crying, "The sky is falling down!" But somehow, the Church survives. And grows stronger. And all these terrible, massive blows strike the Church, and then fade, just another fad like the hoola hoop.

Here's my favorite example.

While I was still in the parish ministry, a book was published called The Passover Plot. When it came to the city near my parish, I went to see it. The movie was just as dumb as the book. It said that Jesus didn't really die on the cross; he survived and appeared to his disciples and claimed that he had risen from the dead. I was almost alone in the movie theater that day; it ran for about a week and that was it. Nobody cared.

Then six months later, the same movie came back to that city and was shown in the same theater. But this time, the Bible Baptist Church heard about it and mounted a campaign to stop it. They picketed the theater, deluged the newspaper with letters to the editors, they telephoned the radio talk shows, they made the television news just about every evening urging people to boycott the theater. They did everything they could to prevent this blasphemous movie from being shown. The movie ran for many weeks and played to a full house every night. The theater owners made a lot of money.

The Bible Baptist Church should have listened to Rabban Gamaliel. The Gamaliel Principle works. "Let them alone," said Gamaliel. "If they are of God, don't oppose them. If they are not, they'll die a natural death anyway."

Always, there seems to be a crisis facing the Church, something that shakes the Church to its very foundation. Always, there seems to be a Chicken Little who cries in despair, "The sky is falling down!" And always, the Church survives. Ah, Gamaliel, where are you when we need you the most?

There's an old story about the country philosopher who ambles into the Blacksmith Shop and looks around. He notices all the worn-out hammers on the floor, and in the center of the shop, the ancient anvil. He asks about this, and the blacksmith drawls, "Yeah . . . well . . . the anvil always wears the hammers out, you know."

This old Church has been around for a long time, and it has worn out a lot of hammers.

It always puzzles me why there is so much concern. Will whatever new blasphemy that comes along destroy the Church? Will it put bad ideas into the minds of our young people? Is God so weak that the Church must come to his rescue with a big defense?

No. The Church has survived Thomas J. Altizer, Neitchze, Angela Davis, Madeline Murray O'Hare, gays and lesbians, atheists, and bad movies. But always, without fail, the anvil wears out all the hammers that strike against it. Stay tuned; there's more to come.

These are fads, which, like the hula hoop, arise for a time and then fade. But the Church goes on forever. So sit back and relax. Watch with interest and amusement the fuss and furor over whatever happens next: movie, book, a controversial issue such as the Pledge of Allegiance . . . whatever. See if the Gamaliel Principle works again. When all the dust settles, and the Chicken Littles calm down until the next great crisis arises, just watch. The Church will still be alive, and healthy. God lives!

The opening words of the 90th Psalm will help put all this into perspective:

Lord, thou hast been our dwelling place in all generations.
Before the mountains were brought forth,
    Or ever thou hadst formed the earth and the world,
From everlasting to everlasting,
Thou art God!

THE GOSPEL ACCORDING TO SAINT VINCENT OF LOMBARDI

Scripture: *Deuteronomy 34:1-7* The story of the last days of Moses. On the mountaintop, dying, with only a brief glimpse of the Promised Land, Moses appeared to be a loser. But he wasn't.

The Preacher's Notes:

Vince Lombardi, the legendary football coach, is often quoted: "Winning isn't everything; it's the only thing." This sermon is on winning and losing. The odd conclusion is that maybe mediocrity isn't so bad after all. Look at Moses. And look at that biggest "loser" of all time: Jesus. They were actually winners, but you have to look at winning and losing a different way.

THE GOSPEL ACCORDING TO SAINT VINCENT OF LOMBARDI

Do you remember Vince Lombardi? He was one of professional football's greatest legends. He coached the Green Bay Packers to three straight Superbowl victories. To football fans, he has attained sainthood, and so he was "canonized," that is, he was enshrined for all eternity in the Pro Football Hall of Fame in Canton, Ohion.

Vince Lombardi is best known for his immortal statement: "Winning isn't everything; it's the only thing." And that's the Gospel According to Saint Vincent of Lombardi.

I'm not trying to say that we shouldn't teach our kids how to win. Competition is healthy. The problem comes when we don't teach our young people how to lose.

Do you know what I think is the most fascinating sport in our American sports culture? You'd never guess.

It's T-ball.

Maybe I like it so much because I was introduced to it several years ago when one of my granddaughters played in a T-ball league. This is played by youngsters who are four or five or six years old. When they bat, the ball is not pitched to them, but rather placed on a tee on home plate, about waist high, and they swing at the stationary ball. Other than that, it's like any other baseball game . . . except for one thing: winning is not the most important thing in the game.

Grandma and I watched a few of these games one summer, and they were fascinating! Of course, that's partly because our granddaughter played second base.

In one game, the bases were loaded, and a young batter stepped up to the plate and very seriously eyed the ball on the tee in front of him. He swung with all his might. Splat! The ball popped off the tee and dropped a few feet in front of the plate.

"Run! Run!" shouted the coach, and the boy took off toward first base.

The catcher ran out and picked up the ball. Then she looked around wondering what to do with it. Remember, the bases were loaded. Parents were screaming. The coaches were shouting. Finally, a coach's instructions got through to her, and he yelled, "Step on home plate!"

Obediently, she put the ball down on the ground where she found it, and went and stepped on home plate.

Can you see why this is a fascinating game? It doesn't matter who wins. They enjoy the ice cream cones at Dairy Queen after the game, whether they won or lost.

The kids who play T-ball graduate to a higher league. As they move up, they soon learn the first rule of athletic competition: you gotta win! Win! WIN! That's the only thing that counts. Gone are the carefree days when just playing was fun. Now the only thing that's fun is to win!

The boys say, "We don't want to play with girls any more. They keep us from winning!" The girls say the same thing about the boys. So they separate into sexist leagues, because it's so important to win.

I recall a game in a youth league when the coach called a team meeting after the game. The girls had played hard, but they lost a close one to a very good team. The coach bawled them out for it, calling them a bunch of losers, gave them no credit for their effort, criticized them individually for their mistakes, and sent them home feeling miserable.

Fortunately, most coaches are not that way. They instill in their players a sense of self-worth, who can make them feel proud of themselves, inspire them to another good effort in the next game, and in general teach them that winning is good, but losing is okay, too.

But too often in our American sports culture, they are taught the Gospel According to Saint Vincent of Lombardi: Winning isn't everything; it's the only thing.

Win at any cost has become a way of life for many people. When that is taught on the field or court or track, the lesson is learned and carried on in life. Nobody wants to be a loser. Do whatever you can to win, whether it's take steroids, or recruit athletes without following the rules, or whatever it takes... just win! And to be successful in life, a person must win, must rise to the top, must make a lot of money, no matter what he does to other people, or his family, or his own integrity. *Just win!*

Nobody likes a loser. There is a word in the American vocabulary that has become a dirty word. That word is... MEDIOCRITY. A mediocre person is a loser, and nobody likes a loser.

The strange thing about being a loser is that there are usually more losers than winners. Now, that's a startling thought.

Take the National Basketball Association (NBA) for example. There are thirteen players to a team, and twenty-eight teams in the NBA. But only one winner. That means only thirteen players are winners. Do you know how many losers there are? Six hundred thirty-one! The same is true in every sport, including the Olympics. So many losers. So few winners. And the losers are nobody.

Yes, it's important to teach our young people how to win. But it's equally important to teach them how to lose.

I look forward to the Olympic Games held every four years. At this quadrennial athletic event, all the best athletes of the world will gather to compete. They work hard to meet this goal, and they arrive in top physical condition and with high hopes. And the majority of them—almost all of them—go home losers.

I have an especially vivid memory of one Olympic event in the past. In Munich, Germany, the basketball finals came down to a young collegiate USA team against an older, professional team from the Soviet Union. The United States had never lost an Olympic final in basketball before, but they had a rough time in this game. We watched on TV as the close game got tense in the closing seconds, when the U.S. team sank a basket and won the game by one point. And then, for some strange reason, the officials put a few more seconds on the time clock, and gave the ball to the Soviets. The US team was caught off guard, and the Soviets scored a basket to win the game.

The United States team protested, but when the Olympic Board, composed mostly of Communist sympathizers, would not recognize the protest, the U.S. team refused to stay for the medal awards and closing ceremonies, but went home in disgust.

They didn't know how to lose. They acted like little boys who say, "You cheat!" and take their marbles and go home. What if, instead, they had congratulated the Soviet team, accepted their silver medal, and went home with their heads held high, with never a bitter word about what had happened? Yes, they were cheated; the whole world saw that on television. But if they had acted with maturity and good will, what a message it would have sent to young people in America. Instead, they proclaimed the Gospel According to Saint Vincent of Lombardi: *Winning isn't everything; it's the only thing!*

Maybe you think I'm overdoing it a little in my diatribe against our over-emphasis on winning in our American culture. So let me take a slightly different tack.

In our Scripture lesson, we heard the final chapter in the life story of Moses. All his life, he had struggled and worked and sacrificed to get to the Promised Land. He had led his people for forty years in the wilderness, through many difficulties, striving to attain the ultimate goal: the Promised Land. It was just ahead. And the people were ready.

But Moses couldn't go.

I have pictured with the mind of a fiction writer the final days of Moses. He stood there on the top of the mountain, looking over the Promised Land. What were his thoughts as he stood there?

So close. He almost made it, but not quite. I'm not sure why God told him he couldn't go there; that part is vague and unclear. After a lifetime of struggle, he couldn't make it to his final goal.

He was a loser.

But as he stood there, watching the long line of the people of Israel cross the Jordan River and blow their trumpets bravely against the walls of Jericho, maybe he realized that he wasn't a loser after all. Maybe he discovered in that moment of awareness that there was something more important than winning. And that was that his people would win.

Maybe he couldn't reach the Promised Land himself. But his people could, and he had enabled them to do it. And he discovered that this was far more important than getting there himself.

If ever you feel that your life is unfulfilled, that you haven't done anything outstanding or significant with the life you have been given for just a few short precious years, that you are a loser in the game of life, consider this: Have you ever enabled someone else to reach that Promised Land? Some son or daughter, or other family member, or close friend, or nameless faceless people whom you have helped from behind the scenes? You have become a loser, because you have helped others become winners.

That's what Moses taught us. That's the Gospel According to Moses, that winning isn't everything. Enabling others to win is even more important. Maybe there comes a moment in your life when you stand on your own mountain, watching someone else enter the Promised Land, and realize that this is far more important to you than the Gospel According to Saint Vincent of Lombardi.

I have one final thought on this subject of winning and losing. Let me tell you about the one person in history who was the greatest loser of all time.

His name was Jesus.

He was born in a barn, of peasant parents. In the early years of his life he was a fugitive, a refugee. His father was a common laborer. He became an itinerant rabbi. He never made any money; he never became a powerful leader, and although he was popular with the common people, he never made it with the rich, the influential people who count, the politicians. They framed him, and he was tried in a kangaroo court, convicted on false testimony, sentenced under pressure by a mob, and executed as a common criminal. His only possession was one suit of clothing, his seamless robe. One of the soldiers won that in a lottery. So at the time of his death, he owned nothing. Nothing. He was the biggest loser of all time. This loser was the one who said, "Greater love has no man than this: that he lay down his life for a friend. You are my friends." Jesus, like Moses, was a loser. But . . . because he lost, we win! And that's the Gospel According to Jesus. Compare that to the Gospel According to Saint Vincent of Lombardi!

THE MEANING IS MORE IMPORTANT THAN THE METHOD

Scripture: *I Corinthians 11:17-29* In Paul's epistle to the church in Corinth, he gives them some instructions on how to celebrate the Sacrament of Communion. This passage includes the familiar words of the Institution of the Sacrament.

The Preacher's Notes:

Actually, this sermon is about both Sacraments: Baptism and Communion. The title summarizes the message of this sermon. Included here is one of my favorite stories of an experience in my ministry. I hope you enjoy it as much as I enjoy this memory.

THE MEANING IS MORE IMPORTANT THAN THE METHOD

During my thirty years in the parish ministry, many unusual and fascinating adventures happened to me. This morning I want to tell you about one of my most memorable experiences.

In 1955, I was called to be the minister of a small community church in a little coal-mining town in southern West Virginia. This was a non-denominational church, and before me, all their ministers were Baptists.

So... before they called me to be their pastor, they had one question: "How do you feel about the Sacrament of Baptism?"

I knew exactly what they wanted to know: not the meaning of Baptism, but the method. They were Southern Baptists, and they had all been baptized by immersion.

And so I told them, and this was an honest answer. I said, "The meaning is more important than the method."

I went on to explain that it didn't really matter how much water was used, whether a few drops on a person's head, or a whole lot of water all over him. What really counted was not the symbol, but rather what was symbolized. The person's faith in the cleansing power of Christ and his belief that God had touched his life was more important than how much water was used. Of course, I also explained that I believe that baptism of infants was equally important, but they weren't much interested in that. All they wanted to know was how I felt about baptizing adults by immersion.

My answer seemed to satisfy them, but it sure got me into hot water after I became their pastor. Did I say hot water? I really meant cold water. Let me explain.

One of my first duties was to instruct a Communicants Class of young people who wanted to join the Church. There were thirteen of them. One of the lessons in this class was on the meaning of the Sacrament of Baptism, and, after carefully explaining to them, among other things, that the meaning is more important than the method, I asked them how they wanted to be baptized. All thirteen said, "By immersion."

Well . . . I had to do it. After my ranting and raving about the meaning being more important than the method, I couldn't very well back out. Even though I made sure they understood the meaning of the Sacrament, it was the method that worried me. I had never even seen an immersion.

The church building was a beautiful red brick structure of Colonial architecture. The Baptists who built it had placed a small baptistery in the front of the sanctuary. That's where I would do it, during a Sunday evening service. And, of course, I had to do it properly, without drowning anybody.

Now, this was wintertime, and it was cold in West Virginia. At least it was in a baptistery and not in a creek. All I had to do was fill the baptismal tank with warm water. But . . . I didn't know how to turn on the hot water tank. So . . . the tank was filled with cold water.

But I was smart in those youthful days, and I knew exactly what I would do. In that congregation there was a man who did a lot of hunting and fishing, and I knew he owned a large pair of waterproof boots. I borrowed them. They came up to my chest, and the water in the tank was only waist deep. Those young people were gonna freeze, but I would be snug and dry!

The baptism came at the end of the service. I waded into the water with those rubberized boots, and everything was fine. The first young person came into the water, and I felt sorry for her. She was a pretty young girl named Marcia, and her teeth began to chatter as soon as she stepped in. But she bravely came on, since this was a big occasion for her: she was about to be baptized!

I held her in the proper position, just as I had been instructed: one arm behind her shoulders and the other in front of her for her to hang on to. I pronounced the words of baptism and plunged her into the water. As I did so, I had to bend over, and the water came over the top of those boots. Ice water! And once in those boots, there was no way for it to get out. I did that thirteen times, and by the time I was finished, I looked and felt like the Goodyear Blimp!

Through chattering teeth, I pronounced the benediction, and then tried to climb out of the tank. It took me a good fifteen minutes to do that, in my loaded boots. Then I had to go down the steps on the other side, out the back door, down the steps into the basement. Finally, I took off those boots, and I almost flooded the basement of the church.

After that, I learned how to turn on the hot water for the baptistery. I also pressed home the point that the meaning is more important than the method, and before I left that church several years later, almost all my baptisms were by sprinkling. I heard in later years that the Presbyterian ministers who followed me never once had to baptize by immersion. I guess it took my ministry to—if you'll pardon the expression—break the ice.

This is not merely a sermon about baptism; it is on the Sacraments. There are two Sacraments that we Protestants observe: Baptism and Communion. The point that I want to make applies just as much to the Sacrament of Communion as it does to Baptism: the meaning is important; the method is not. The emphasis should not be on the symbol, but rather what is symbolized. The bread and the wine are not central in this worship service; the body and blood of Christ are.

Different methods appeal to different people, and no method is actually wrong if it is meaningful. In some churches, the Sacrament of Communion is celebrated by the people coming forward and kneeling at the altar rail, while the minister or priest administers the Sacrament. In some churches, the people gather around tables and pass the bread and wine to each other. Many churches, including ours, have elders or others designated by the officers pass the elements to the congregation. For some churches there is high liturgy and formal ceremony; for others there is simplicity and informality. All these methods are proper, and it is up to the individual worshipper which method is the most meaningful.

In the Corinthian Church, which we read about in our Scripture reading, there was bickering and nit-picking about little things in the service that caused division. The Apostle Paul had to call their attention to what was really important in that service.

A long time ago, we used to say, "This is the Presbyterian way," or "This is the Methodist way," or "This is the Baptist way." But these labels don't mean that much to us any more. This is the ecumenical age. We are no longer bound by rigid denominational rules and customs. We might say that we are all one Church, united not by our customs and methods, but by the meaning of our common Baptism and what we do at this Table.

My wife and I attended a church a few years ago where they observed "closed communion." The minister explained to us before the service that only members of that denomination could partake. I'll never forget that morning. We felt left out, as though they were saying to us, "You are not part of our Christian family." That hurt.

As a part of each Communion service, we have an Invitation, a few words that precede the serving of the Sacrament. The minister issues this invitation to anyone who finds meaning in the Sacrament to join us. Anyone. If you consider yourself a member of the family of God, come break bread with us. We are all united into one family, a family that crosses lines of denomination and theology and customs. We are all one, in the family of Christ, and we are united at this Table.

Children, too. We don't hesitate to serve children who have not yet made their Profession of Faith and become members of the Church. They too are part of the family. But it would be helpful— for the children most of all—if the parents would teach the child the meaning of the Sacrament, so that he or she will not consider it just a break for refreshments.

So when that piece of bread or cup of wine is passed to you—by whatever method—consider the meaning. Pause a few seconds before you eat or drink it. Think about what it means—to you. And that's what is important in this service.

Pause, and think: This symbol, so common and ordinary, has profound meaning. It reminds us that many years ago, a man's body was broken and his blood was shed. For you. For me. And for a reason. *May the words of our mouths and the meditations of our hearts be acceptable in the sight of God, our strength and our Redeemer.*

CONFESSION: I STOLE A GIDEON BIBLE

Scripture: *2 Timothy 3:14-17* In Paul's epistle to the young minister Timothy, he says some meaningful things about the Bible, and how important it is for his ministry.

The Preacher's Notes:

The basic idea of this sermon was taken from a pamphlet published by the Gideon Association, telling the story of a Bible that organization had placed in a hotel room. It looks at the five most read passages of Scripture in that Bible. Maybe this sermon will lead you to think a little bit about how important the Bible is to you.

CONFESSION: I STOLE A GIDEON BIBLE

I have a confession to make. I stole a Gideon Bible.

Several years ago, I came home from vacation and was unpacking my suitcase when I discovered to my horror a Gideon Bible in among my clothes. I have no idea how it got there. Ever since then I have felt guilty, and I have made several healthy contributions to the Gideons through the years to atone for my sin.

Now, you know what happens when you contribute to a charitable organization. You get a lot of mail from them, wanting more money. But they also send a lot of information about themselves. Among these was a pamphlet that started a train of thought that led to this sermon.

The pamphlet described a retired Gideon Bible that had been placed in a hotel room in Jackson, Tennessee, in 1920. Because it was worn out, they replaced it about thirty years later with a new one. The Gideon pamphlet then told the story of this particular Bible, because it was probably typical of all Gideon Bibles placed in hotel rooms.

For many years, this Bible was available to travelers who occupied that room. Its cover had spots and rings on it. The pages were worn and patched with scotch tape. How many people read it? What passages did they turn to? How much good did that Bible do? There are no answers to these questions, but examination of the old, well-worn Bible gave some clues to the passages that were most popular.

There were five well-worn sections. Let's look at them, because they may give us a clue to what parts of the Bible are most meaningful to the average Bible reader.

The first was at the very beginning. The opening pages of Genesis were torn, dog-eared and thumb-printed. I suspect the reason for this—although the Gideons did not admit it, of course—was that the weary traveler wanted something to read that would put him to sleep, and so he just started at the beginning of the Bible and read until he dropped off to sleep. Remember, this was in the days before TV and swimming pools, and perhaps the traveler was bored.

However, there is undoubtedly more to it than that. Curiosity could explain it. Perhaps the traveler was completely unfamiliar with the Bible, and he opened it up just to see what it was all about. Naturally he would start at the beginning.

The opening chapter would tell him about the Creation: *In the beginning, God created the heavens and the earth, and the earth was without form, and void, and darkness was upon the face of the deep, and the Spirit of God brooded upon the face of the deep. And God said, "Let there be light!" and there was light. And God saw that it was good.*

This is the majestic first chapter on the creative energy of God, followed by the intriguing second chapter on the creation of the man and the woman. Then comes the mysterious third chapter, including the temptation in the Garden, and the fall of the man and the woman into sin. What are the thoughts of the traveler as he reads these three chapters? Is he skeptical? Does he think of this as ancient Hebrew folklore, and nothing more? Or does he see here the beautiful story of the basic problem of the human race—the problem of you and me—a problem that the Bible calls sin. Psychology has another name for it, and so does sociology, but it all adds up to the same thing. This human creature created by God is now on his own. He has decided to live his life apart from God.

In its own simple and charming way, the Bible begins with the problem of the human race. The man and the woman were created by God for eternal fellowship with their Maker. And then they turned aside from their true destiny to go it alone. The path they chose would lead them to eternal death. What should God do about it? Thus the story begins, and the rest of the Bible is the dramatic and compelling story of what God did about it.

The second most used section of the Gideon Bible was the Psalms. The whole book of Psalms was well worn, but surprisingly the most used Psalm was not the familiar 23rd Psalm that begins *The Lord is my Shepherd, I shall not want*, but rather Psalm 119, an unfamiliar Psalm beginning with these cryptic words: *Blessed are the undefiled in the way, who walk in the Law of the Lord.*

This Psalm had been patched with scotch tape twice. Maybe the reason for this was that the 119th Psalm is the longest Psalm—in fact, the longest chapter in the Bible—with 179 verses, compared with only six in the 23rd Psalm.

The 119th Psalm is an acrostic, and each section begins with a different letter in the Hebrew alphabet, but of course the reader wouldn't know that.

What the reader would discover in this Psalm is instruction for a person that the best way of life is to follow the ways of God, as stated in such verses as: *Oh, how I love thy Law! It is my meditation all the day . . . Thy Word is a lamp unto my feet and a light to my path . . . Thy Word have I hid in my heart that I might not sin against thee.*

The other Psalms in the Gideon Bible were pretty well worn also. Can you imagine the thoughts of a weary traveler, tired at the end of a days work or travel, perhaps lonely, sitting in his room and reading such words as these: *Hear my prayer, O Lord; let my cry come to thee! Do not hide thy face from me in the day of my distress! Incline thine ear to me; answer me speedily in the day when I call!"*

Or this passage: *As for man, his days are like grass; he flourishes like a flower in the field. For the wind passes over it, and it is gone, and its place knows it no more. But the steadfast love of the Lord is from everlasting to everlasting upon those who fear him, and his righteousness to children's children, to those who keep his Covenant and remember to do his commandments.* What would the traveler think of that?

The third most used place in the old Gideon Bible was the Sermon on the Mount. These words of Jesus are found in Matthew's Gospel in chapters 5 through 7. Right at the very beginning was the most used; in fact the page was almost too far-gone to read. These are the Beatitudes.

Blessed are the poor in spirit, for theirs is the kingdom of heaven. Blessed are they that mourn, for they shall be comforted. Blessed are the merciful, for they shall obtain mercy. Blessed are the pure in heart, for they shall see God.

Here is the blessed life outlined by Jesus. Here the hardened businessman, at the end of a fast day in the world of commerce where it's every man for himself, reads about an entirely different set of values. Is there any blessedness in making money, getting the best of a business deal, or the hard soul-sacrificing road that leads to success? Perhaps the reader in the hotel room realized that here is the reason he could not find peace and happiness in his fast empty life. The life of blessedness is outlined before him. Here is the secret of the contentment in life. Blessed are the poor in spirit . . . the meek . . . the merciful . . . those who hunger and thirst after righteousness . . . the pure in heart . . . the peacemakers. These are the people who will inherit the earth, be comforted, and see God.

The traveler reads on in this remarkable sermon preached so many years ago. He reads what Jesus said about loving your enemies, about hypocrisy, about prayer, about putting first things first. And finally, he reads the story of the two men who built their houses, one on the sand and the other on solid rock. And perhaps, as he puts the old Bible down and turns out the light, he wonders what kind of a foundation has he built his house on?

The fourth section of the Gideon Bible that showed the most use was Matthew's story of the crucifixion of Jesus. Actually several pages preceding this story and leading up to it were pretty well worn. Obviously many travelers have read the ancient story of the events leading up to the greatest event of all. They read about our Lord's triumphal entry, when the people waved their palm branches and shouted "Hosanna!" They read about the Last Supper, and the prayer of Jesus in the Garden of Gethsemane. They read about the elaborate plot of the chief priests, and then of Judas' betrayal, Jesus' trial and finally his crucifixion. Who read this? Salesmen, buyers, lawyers, executives, vacationers? Devout Christians or curious unbelievers? What kind of responsive note did this strike in their minds as they read through this fascinating and moving account of a man's death at the hands of his enemies? Did they merely feel sorry for an innocent man, or did they see in him someone who could give meaning to life?

Oddly enough, the pages following the crucifixion story were intact. The resurrection chapter was untorn, fairly clean, and obviously little read. Why? Did they feel that the story, like most tragedies—like life itself—ends dramatically in Jesus' death? Did they find the story of treachery and cruelty and pain and death believable, but the resurrection with its happy ending a fairy tale? Why was not the resurrection story as popular with readers as the crucifixion story? I don't know the answer. Do you?

And finally, the fifth part of the old Gideon Bible that was well worn was the last four chapters of the book of Revelation. Why so fascinating to the traveler? Was it his curiosity—like the reader of a mystery novel—to find out how the book turned out in the end? Or did he find fascination in the fast-moving text that speaks of great mysteries in symbolic terms? Here he reads of the final end of Satan, who is thrown into a lake of fire. Here he finds the intriguing description of the New Jerusalem, the beautiful city symbolic of heaven, where God himself is with his people, where *he will wipe away every tear from their eyes, and death shall be no more, neither shall there be mourning nor crying nor pain any more, for the former things have passed away.* The reader hears Jesus saying, *"I am the Alpha and the Omega, the beginning and the end. To the thirsty I will give water without price from the fountain of the water of life."* What are his thoughts as he reads these majestic concluding words of the Bible? Comfort? Skepticism? Or bewilderment? Who knows?

And so the old Gideon Bible is retired from active service, having done its job, having been read by hundreds of people who spent the night in that room over a period of many years. How many read it? Did they find faith or doubt? Comfort or skepticism? Wisdom for life, or just a substitute for a sleeping pill?

These are questions we'll never know the answer to. How much good was done by that Bible? Who knows? But God is at work, quietly, unobtrusively, and things are happening that we know nothing about.

I wonder what the reader of that Gideon Bible would think if he came upon that obscure verse in the Old Testament book of the prophet Habakkuk, which reads: *Look among the nations and see; wonder and be astounded. For I am doing a work in your days that you would not believe if told!*

HOW GOD SPEAKS

Scripture: *Hebrews 1:1* The text reads, *In many and various ways God spoke of old to our fathers by the prophets, but in these latter days he has spoken to us by a Son.* If further Scriptures are needed, use one or more of the following: *Exodus 3:1-6* (Moses and the burning bush), *I Samuel 3:1-10* (how God spoke to young Samuel one night), *II Samuel 12:1-7a* (David's sin, and the prophet Nathan's parable accusing him), *Hosea 1:1-9* (the prophet Hosea tells how God spoke to him by events in his personal life).

The Preacher's Notes:

Using four illustrations from the Old Testament (listed above in the alternate Scripture readings), this sermon points out how God spoke "in many and various ways to our fathers by the prophets." The sermon goes on to point out how God also speaks to us "in many and various ways" today.

HOW GOD SPEAKS

Does God speak to us today?

Of course, we recognize that there is a God. But who is he? What is he like? And most important: is he a personal God? Does he speak to you and me?

The writer of the Epistle to the Hebrews answers this question in the very first verse of the Epistle. And the answer is yes, God does speak to us. *In many and various ways God spoke of old to our fathers by the prophets, but in these latter days, he has spoken to us by a Son.*

The first part of our text is concerned with the Old Testament: In many and various ways God spoke of old to our fathers by the prophets. God would choose someone from this century or that part of the country and commission him a prophet, and through him speak to the people.

Consider for example the way God spoke to Moses.

Moses was a shepherd taking care of a small flock of sheep in the desolate wilderness we now call the Sinai Peninsula. His journeys took him to the foot of Mount Sinai.

One day, as he led his flock, he saw a light on the slopes of the mountain. Strange. It looked like a fire, but nothing in that part of the country could burn. What could it be? Curiosity overcame his fear of the impressive mountain, and he said to himself, "I will turn aside and see this remarkable sight."

As he approached, he saw that it indeed was a fire, and furthermore, the bush on fire was not being consumed by the flames. Then suddenly, he was halted by a voice coming out of the bush, calling his name: "Moses! Moses!"

Can you imagine the feeling of awe that came upon Moses as he realized that he was standing in the presence of God?

"Moses," the voice continued. "Take off your shoes, because you are standing in the presence of God. I am the God of your fathers, Abraham, Isaac and Jacob." Then followed the commission to Moses to return to Egypt where the people of Israel were enslaved. Go before the pharaoh and say, Thus says God, "Let my people go!"

A strange way for God to speak to a prophet, wasn't it? By a voice in a burning bush!

In many and various ways God spoke of old to our fathers.

Consider for example the way God spoke to Samuel. As a boy, Samuel was dedicated to the service of God in the Temple, and he lived there with the high priest Eli.

One night as Samuel lay sleeping, he was suddenly awakened by a voice calling his name: "Samuel! Samuel!"

Thinking it was Eli calling him, the boy got up and went to Eli's room. "Did you call me, sir?" he asked.

"No, my son," replied Eli. "Go back to sleep."

Samuel returned to his room and once again was awakened by the voice calling his name. Again Samuel went to Eli and asked, "Did you call me, sir?" And again, Eli told him no, go back to sleep.

But this time, I can imagine old Eli, the priest of Israel, lying awake in his bed thinking about what was happening. So when for the third time Samuel came to him asking if he called, Eli replied, "No, my son. But this time when you hear the voice, say, 'Here I am, Lord. I'm listening.'"

Samuel did so, and the voice of God spoke to him in the night. God spoke often to Samuel after that, and he became one of Israel's greatest prophets. But isn't that a strange way for God to speak to a prophet, by a voice in the night to a little child?

In many and various ways God spoke of old through his prophets. Consider, for example, the way God spoke to David.

David was king of Israel. He was a great and powerful king, and had built up the kingdom so that it was one of the greatest in the world. But David was human, too. One day he saw a beautiful woman, and he fell in love with her immediately. The fact that she was married and her husband was a captain in the army presented some problems. But wasn't he king of Israel? Couldn't he have anything he wanted? So he made arrangements for the captain to be killed in battle. When the news was brought to the king that the captain had been killed, he took the woman into his home and she became one of his wives.

One day, sometime later, the prophet Nathan appeared in David's court. Nathan was not well liked, not only because he wore rags for clothing and seemed always dirty and his beard untrimmed, but also because he always spoke the truth, and the truth often hurt. But because he was God's prophet, he was respected, and David listened to him.

Nathan spoke in a parable. He told the story of a poor man who had one ewe lamb. The poor man lived near a rich man who had a large flock of sheep. The rich man saw the poor man's lamb and wanted it for himself. So he made arrangements for the poor man to be killed, and the lamb taken into his large flock. Nathan concluded with the question, "What shall be done about this, O King?"

David was proud of his reputation as a just king, and he rose in anger and said, "That man shall die!"

Then Nathan, with a dramatic gesture, pointed to David and said, "You are that man!" Immediately David realized the significance of the parable, and knew that he had sinned in God's sight.

Isn't that a strange way for God to speak, through the lips of another person?

In many and various ways God spoke of old to our fathers through the prophets. Consider for example the way God spoke to the prophet Hosea.

Hosea was a farmer living comfortably in the northern kingdom of Israel with his wife and child. Then tragedy entered his life. His wife and child left him. Hosea loved them greatly, and his sorrow over his loss was deep and genuine. As the years went by, his grief became greater.

Then one day he found them ... in the slave market. But his

wife had not just one child, but three, and Hosea knew that two of these children were not his own. But so great was his love for his wife that he paid the purchase price of a slave for her, and returned her to a place of honor in his home and even adopted the other two children.

But that isn't the end of the story. As the years went by, Hosea thought a great deal about his tragic experience, and came to realize that God was speaking to him through it. And this in substance is the message that God gave to him: "I love Israel as you love your wife. And just as your wife left you, so has Israel turned away from me. But because I love Israel as you love your wife, I will some day buy her back to me."

It was a message of God's love to a sinful nation, a message that Hosea preached to his people. Now that message has survived and come down to us in the Bible in the book of the prophet Hosea.

But isn't that an unusual way for God to speak to a person, through a tragic experience in his own personal life?

Isn't it true that in many and various ways God spoke of old to our fathers through the prophets? But those four examples, Moses, Samuel, David and Hosea, are stories from the Bible. Of course we realize that God spoke to people in Bible times, but does he speak to us today?

The second part of the text, Hebrews 1:1, answers this: *but in these latter days he has spoken to us by his Son.*

In Old Testament times God chose certain people called prophets, through whom he spoke to his people. But with the redemptive act of Christ on the cross, each one of us has the opportunity and privilege of coming into God's presence. Formerly God spoke only through chosen prophets; he now speaks personally to everyone who turns to him through Christ.

But it is also true that God speaks to us today—as he did in Old Testament times—*in many and various ways.*

God speaks to us today, as he spoke to Moses, through an act of nature.

Maybe God speaks to you in the beauty of the countryside, as you sit in silence and think of the Master Artist who created the beauty around you.

Maybe he speaks to you as you stand out under the stars at night, and gaze at the celestial panorama above you, in which you see no disorder, no chaos. Everything is perfectly coordinated, and your mind is led to the Master Hand behind it.

Maybe God speaks to you as you look at the simplicity of a flower. As you hold the little miracle of beauty in front of you, you are amazed at the complex simplicity of all nature, how everything large and small fits so perfectly and delicately in the master plan of nature, and you are impressed with the thoughtfulness and thoroughness of the intelligent mind who created it.

Or maybe God speaks to you through a dramatic and spectacular act of nature. Perhaps through an earthquake, or hurricane, or tornado, or some other event of nature—sensational or ordinary—God enters your life.

In many and various ways, God speaks to us today through his Son. Maybe, for you, God speaks as he spoke to the prophet Samuel, as a child.

Perhaps your experience has been like this: You were born in a Christian home. All your life you attended Sunday School and Church. Christian faith was practiced in your home. At a young age you became a member of the Church, and sincerely accepted your parents' faith as your own. As you grew older your faith deepened as with your family you attended church regularly and attempted to put into practice in your life your Christian faith. This faith means a lot to you now, even though you can't point to any particular point in your life and say, "That was when I was converted. That was when I accepted Christ as my Savior." God came into your life sometime when you were a child, and through the years you have grown closer to him. Your experience with God is just as real and valid as the person's who was converted in an unusual and dramatic way.

In many and various ways God speaks to us through his Son. Maybe he spoke to you, as he spoke to David through Nathan the prophet, by the voice of another person.

Perhaps in a revival service, God spoke to you through the message of the evangelist. Maybe God spoke to you sometime through a conversation with a friend, as he seeks to tell you of the joys of his own faith. Perhaps God speaks to you through the lips of your minister, as he preaches to you on Sunday or converses with you in your home. God may even be speaking to you right now, through the words coming from my lips. At some time in your life, as you listen to another person, maybe you became aware of the reality of God in your life. You may not have been aware of God's voice at the time, but now, as you look back, you know that in some precious moment, God spoke to you through another person.

In many and various ways God speaks to us through his Son. Maybe God speaks to you, as he spoke to the prophet Hosea, through an experience in your personal life.

As you lie in bed with an illness, your patience exhausted, your hope almost gone, your strength fading, you turn to the Great Physician, and are amazed at the courage and strength he gives you. You can look back now and see that God spoke to you through that illness and touched your life.

As you bow your head while sitting beside the bed of a loved one who is seriously ill, and realize how weak you are in such circumstances, there comes into your life an awareness of One who is always by your side.

Or, sometime when you are in the agony of grief because someone whom you love has been taken from you in death, there comes into your life a divine Comforter who enriches your life and gives you the courage to lift your head and smile. God has spoken to you.

Maybe there comes a time in your life when you are in physical danger, something threatens your life, and you are terrified. You turn to God for help, and he does not fail you. Fear is replaced by faith, weakness by strength. God has spoken.

It's true, isn't it, that in many and various ways God speaks to us today through his Son?

Out of all this that we have been talking about concerning how God speaks to us today, let us draw three conclusions:

One: God speaks to each one of us differently.

After all, we are individuals, and God respects that individuality. He does not speak to us *en masse*, but speaks to us as individuals. Since each one of us is different, God speaks to each one of us in a different way. Don't expect God to speak to you the same way he speaks to me, because he speaks to each one of us differently.

Two: Perhaps God has already spoken to you, but at the time you didn't recognize the voice of God in your life. But now, as you look back, you can point to one event in your life that completely changed your life, and you can now say, "That was when God spoke to me, even though I didn't recognize it at the time."

Three: God is speaking, has spoken, or will speak to each one of us.

He makes no exceptions. If you have never heard the voice of God in your life, it isn't because God does not choose to speak to you, but rather because you choose not to listen to him.

This is how God speaks to each one of us: through the daily experiences of life. This experience may be common or unusual, ordinary or spectacular, sudden or gradual. God's hand may touch your life once, or several times, or even daily. The difference between a religious experience and just an experience is the interpretation that you place upon that event.

Do you have the spiritual insight to see the hand of God in the experiences of your life?

ISAAC'S NAME

Scripture: *Genesis 18:1-15* (RSV), *Genesis 21:1-13* (NEB) These two passages of Scripture tell the story of Abraham and Sarah and the birth of their son Isaac. The reason for the use of different translations is to bring out the nuances of the word "laughter."

The Preacher's Notes:

Isaac's name means, "He laughed." The question is, who laughed? Abraham? Sarah? Ishmael? Isaac? Or . . . could it have been God? It really doesn't matter who laughed. Isaac is a delightful name.

ISAAC'S NAME

Isaac is a delightful name. It means "He laughs." It isn't a very common name today. I don't know why. Maybe it's because it's too hard to spell with its double A in the middle. Or maybe the nickname, "Ike," is a little too hackneyed, although it was the name of a popular president. Maybe Isaac sounds countryish, hayseed, ludicrous. For some reason, Isaac is an ugly name in the minds of many people. It shouldn't be, with its beautiful meaning, "He laughs."

In the ancient Hebrew culture, no name was given without a great deal of thought. The name was supposed to describe the person's character. Maybe the ancient Hebrews put into practice something that we already know: that if you name a child something, and tell him or her every day of his childhood that this is the kind of person he is, he will grow into that character. What would happen to the child if his name or nickname were something like "Joy," or "Happy," or "Sunny" (spelled with a u)? Would that child grow into the name?

So when Abraham and Sarah named their child "Isaac," meaning "He laughs," did they intend for this child to be full of joy and cheerfulness, enjoying life and constantly filling a room with laughter?

Maybe so. But several things happened before his birth that led up to the naming of this child. Several people laughed.

Abraham laughed. When God came to Abraham and told him he would establish a covenant with him and renew the Messianic Promise, he told Abraham that as a part of the Promise, a son should be born to him and Sarah his wife. Now, Abraham was 99 years old at the time, and his wife Sarah was 90. He laughed. Well, wouldn't you?

When the Bible says that Abraham laughed, we miss something in the English translation. This is a pun, a play on words. It really says, Abraham *isaaced*. And thus, the Genesis story carefully introduces the word to prepare us for the naming of the child later.

Abraham's laughter, when he was told he would father a child at age 99, was normal. It was a nervous reaction. He couldn't believe it. Well, it is kind of funny. Ridiculous. Abraham didn't mean to laugh at God . . . just at the absurdity of the situation. He didn't believe it would happen.

Well, I know just how Abraham felt. I wouldn't believe it either. I just can't believe anything that comes along. I want a lot of assurance that this is worth believing.

That's called skepticism. And I'm a skeptic, and proud of it. I don't accept anything quickly . . . any religious belief that someone tries to pressure me into accepting. It has taken me a lifetime to establish what I now believe, and it would take another lifetime to take it away and replace it with something else. I'm a skeptic about believing something.

For example, if someone says to me, "It's a miracle," I say, "Prove it," and then I begin to look for a natural explanation of the so-called "miracle." If someone tells me, "Renounce your theology and accept what I believe," I say, "Forget it. I respect your view, and I even support you in your belief, but I cannot accept it as mine." It took me a long time to accept such unbelievable doctrines as Incarnation, that God became a man; or that the crucifixion of Jesus had mysterious theological overtones relating to my relationship with God; or the resurrection of a man who died and came back to life within three days—these things came hard to me. I have accepted them as truth (otherwise I wouldn't have much faith) but believe me, accepting them was not easy.

I am by nature a skeptic. I suspect many of you are that way too, with our modern education and science and culture. We do believe in the basics of our Christian faith, but if you are like me, this belief didn't come easily.

So I can understand Abraham, when God told him that he

and Sarah would have a baby while they were in their nineties. He laughed. He was skeptical. You just don't believe that sort of thing easily.

And so Abraham laughed. And so did Sarah laugh.

Isn't that a delightful story? Sarah stood just inside the tent where she could hear the conversation between Abraham and these mysterious messengers from God. When she heard the promise of a son, she silently laughed to herself. She too *isaaced*, as the Hebrew would say.

Then to her horror she heard one of the men say, "Why did Sarah laugh?"

She was afraid, and embarrassed, and so when confronted she said, "No, I didn't laugh."

"You did so laugh," said the man, and then he repeated word for word her thoughts. Sarah was caught in her lie.

She was embarrassed. Have you ever been embarrassed? Of course you have. So have I. We know just how Sarah feels. She was caught in a lie, and she was so embarrassed she couldn't admit it and say, "I'm sorry." The hardest words in the English to say are, "I was wrong; I'm sorry."

But why does this have to be, knowing what we know about God? He is a loving and forgiving Father. He has shown us this forgiving nature by sending his Son to die for us. He warmly accepts the person who comes before him and says those most difficult words, "It was my fault; I'm sorry." And he forgives, and loves, and accepts. Isn't it great that we have that kind of a Heavenly Father?

Abraham laughed; Sarah laughed; and also, Ishmael laughed.

Ishmael was the half-brother of Isaac. When Ishmael was about twelve and Isaac was just a little toddler, Ishmael teased the child and made fun of him. In other words, he *isaaced* Isaac.

Children can be like that sometimes: cruel, insensitive, thoughtless. When they dislike another person, they sometimes shun him, or tease him, or ridicule him. Many a child has been reduced to tears because of another child's thoughtlessness, or cruelty. But this is immaturity. We can understand that, and forgive it, although at the time we try to teach the child something about respecting the feelings of others. Most children grow up, and learn to treat other people with respect, even though they may dislike that person. Right? Well . . . not always. Sometimes we adults can be insensitive and thoughtless and even vicious in our dealings with people we don't like. Have you ever laughed at someone? I have, and I'm ashamed of it. I'll try to be more thoughtful and sensitive in the future. Will you?

Abraham laughed, Sarah laughed, and Ishmael laughed. But there is no indication in the Scriptures that Isaac himself ever laughed. The closest he comes is Sarah's comment shortly after Isaac was born. "God has given me a good reason to laugh. Now everyone will laugh with me." And of course, in the Hebrew, this reads, "God has *isaaced* me and now everyone will *isaac* with me."

I can just picture the context in which Sarah would make such a statement. She was holding the baby on her knees, and she coaxed a smile out of him. She herself responded to this, and with a little further coaxing he was laughing. Something beautiful passed between them at that time. It was a precious moment, a moment of bonding, when mother and child are cemented together with an eternal bond of love. Every parent has experienced this, and it is an essential part of each child's infancy. I'm sure that in such a moment, Sarah could say, "God has i*saaced* me, and now everyone will *isaac* with me.

That picture came out of my imagination. Nowhere in the Bible does it give any indication that Isaac was a cheerful, happy, laughing person. Of course it doesn't say he wasn't. But I can't help but think that with a name meaning "He laughs," and surrounded with love and laughter, he would grow up into his name.

I hope so. We like the cheerful person. He or she is always saying something bright, and his hearty laugh fills the room and warms everyone in it. A cheerful disposition and a pleasant outlook on life . . . isn't that something lovable in a person? God bless all laughers, and may their tribe increase.

They laughed. Abraham, Sarah, Ishmael, Isaac (I hope!)—they all laughed. But in one Commentary, I read that it would be more reasonable to assume that the name "He laughs" refers to the fact that God laughed. The Commentary went on to say that this was in keeping with most of the names given during that time in history; they were as much about God as they were about the person. If this is so, then the name Isaac could mean "God laughs."

This has a very pleasant sound to me. Perhaps it should not be taken literally, but it would mean more like "God smiles," or "God looks benevolently and with favor upon this child." Wouldn't that be something great to say about little Isaac? Or about the child or children in your home, or your grandchildren? Or about any small child? Think of that the next time we have a baptism. It is very much in keeping with what the Bible teaches, that in every case God *isaacs* this child.

That is a good thought for each one of us, who consider ourselves to be a child of God. God loves each one of his children. He smiles on each one of us individually, with favor, with good thoughts. We're talking about God, not a finite human being, so it wouldn't be too out of line to say that each person—you, me, or those children whom we love—each person, each individual, is God's favorite! His personal pet. God *isaacs* us all.

For some people, God is a forbidding judge, who frowns on all the sins going on in the world. He hates sin. And his punishment to sinners is swift and terrible—and eternal. Fear him!

But this is not the God I read about in the Bible. The God I see is the father of Jesus. He loves. He smiles. He laughs. He is the kind of Father I like to have around all the time. We don't ever need to be afraid of him. Not the way he *isaacs* us!

I like God. Don't you?

THE WORLD'S GREATEST PRAYER

Scripture: *Luke 22:39-46* This is Jesus' prayer in the Garden of Gethsemane on the evening before his crucifixion. There are two parts to this prayer: *Let this cup pass from me,* and *Not my will, but thine, be done.*

The Preacher's Notes:

This is my nomination for the greatest prayer ever offered. As mentioned above, the two elements in this prayer are:

1. Let this cup pass from me. In other words, get me out of this mess. How human! Don't we all pray like that, asking God to use his powers to do something for us?
2. Not my will, but thine, be done. That's what makes this prayer great.

If we could say the second part with every prayer we offer, we would find peace.

The illustration at the end is one of my favorites.

THE WORLD'S GREATEST PRAYER

What is the greatest prayer ever offered?

That, of course, is a subjective question. One person's greatest prayer may be number two to someone else. Or what appeals to me may not appeal to you.

Many people would say The Lord's Prayer, because it is the best known. The Lord's Prayer is an outline, containing the elements of good prayer, and thus it is worthy of being put forward as the world's greatest prayer.

My nomination for the world's greatest prayer is the one in today's Scripture reading:

Read: Luke 22:39-46

In contrast to this, let me ask this question: What is the world's worst prayer? I would like to nominate the attitude toward prayer by Huckleberry Finn. Mark Twain, in his classic novel, uses his wit and wisdom to describe Huck's attitude to prayer, and now I quote from the book:

> *Miss Watson, she took me in the closet and we prayed, but nothing ever came of it. She told me to pray every day, and whatever I asked for I would get it. But it weren't so. I tried it. Once I got a fishline but no hooks. I tried to get the hooks three or four times, but somehow I couldn't make it work. By and by, one day, I asked Miss Watson to try for me, but she said I was a fool. She never told me why, and I couldn't make it out no way. I sat down one time back in the woods, and had a long think*

about it. I says to myself, if a body can get anything they pray for, why don't Deacon Winn get back the money he lost on pork? Why can't the widow get pack her silver snuffbox that was stole? Why can't Miss Watson fat up? No, says I to myself, there ain't nothing in it."

We can smile at this, and you might even agree with my nomination of Huck Finn's attitude as the worst kind of prayer. It's so selfish! He wants something, and so he says to God, "Give me this! Give me that!" He has God confused with that little fat man in the red suit who lives at the North Pole.

This kind of prayer is offered not only for material things, but for favors. "Lord, get me through this difficult time in my life" may be a prayer we offer occasionally. And how about, "Lord, heal me?" Or "Lord, heal this person whom I care about?" Are they selfish prayers to a Santa Claus type God? Are they Huck Finn type prayers?

Now, just a minute. Maybe that's going too far. Of course we turn to God for help. We ask him for things, for wisdom, for assistance in time of need. Is that selfish? Is that unhealthy prayer, like Huck Finn's?

If it is, then the prayer I nominated a few minutes ago as the world's greatest prayer would fall under that same category. Jesus in his prayer asked God for something for himself. Listen to his words: *"Father, if it be possible, let this cup pass from me."* Was this a selfish prayer?

The next day, Jesus would be crucified, and he knew it. He knew what lay ahead: betrayal, denial, loneliness, suffering, agony, and death. That was the cup he asked God to remove from him. How very human of him!

Let's never lose sight of the fact that Jesus was human. Sometimes we emphasize the doctrine of the divinity of Jesus to the exclusion of his humanity. The Christian doctrine through the centuries has firmly stated that Jesus was fully human and fully God. Sometimes we make the mistake of thinking that Jesus did not undergo the same kind of suffering any of us would experience because he was the Son of God. Not so. Jesus was fully human. He was afraid. He dreaded the next day. The sweat on his forehead was very real. When he asked that the cup be removed from him, he meant it!

And if Jesus could do it, so can we. Only let's be aware of the difference between honest prayer for God's help, and the selfish Huck Finn prayer, which only seeks to use God's power for our own gain.

And don't you find it fascinating that when Jesus came to God in prayer asking something for himself, God said "No!" God did not remove the cup of suffering from him. Jesus had to drink that cup to the bitter dregs.

Why? Why did God not grant him what he asked for? Was his prayer answered no because he didn't pray fervently enough? But we read that he prayed more earnestly, the sweat appearing on his forehead looking like great drops of blood. How much more fervent can you get?

Sometimes we make the mistake of thinking that all we need to do to get a favorable answer to prayer from God is to pray more fervently. And more often. I have known some who organize groups of people to pray for something, urging them to spend hours and hours in urgent prayer, as though by the very quantity of their prayer—by assaulting the gates of heaven with intensity—they can get God to change his mind and grant their request. As though God were like a weak human parent, whose child believes he can manipulate mom and dad by badgering him until in desperation the parent will say, "All right! I'll grant your request if you will just shut up!" When we look at it that way, we know God isn't like that. It isn't fervency that counts with God.

What does? Is it the amount of faith we have? If we just have enough faith, can we move mountains? Is that the secret of successful prayer—to have enough faith?

No. Certainly no one had more faith than Jesus, and God answered his prayer with a no.

Then why? How do we explain it when God says no to our prayer? I have been asked that many times when I was a pastor.

Why did God allow my baby to die? We prayed. You prayed for us also. Then why did he die?

Why does our Sunday School teacher, an outstanding Christian, have such a terrible physical affliction which cannot be healed?

Why did my husband, the father of our two children, have to die in the prime of his life?

Why was this promising youth killed so tragically in an auto accident?

When these questions were asked of me, I had to say, "I don't know." It's a terribly inadequate answer, but it's the truth. I felt inadequate often during the years of my ministry, because I didn't have answers to the hard questions they asked.

But I think I can see why God said no to Jesus' request that the cup be removed from him. God in his wisdom could see the greater good that would come from Jesus' suffering. Or, as one of Jesus' enemies so aptly expressed it, "It is expedient that one man should die for the good of many."

But the fact remains: Jesus asked for something for himself, and God in his wisdom said no. But that's not what makes this prayer my nomination for the greatest prayer ever offered.

Right in the middle of his prayer comes the word "Nevertheless." And it's the part after the "nevertheless" that makes this prayer so great.

Now listen to his whole prayer, which I place in nomination for the greatest prayer ever offered: *"Father, if it be possible, let this cup be removed from me. Nevertheless, not my will, but thine be done."*

The best kind of praying is not getting God to do our will, but rather to put us in the proper spirit to accept God's will. And that's not easy.

Wouldn't it be better if we could just get God to do our will? Wouldn't it be better if we knew how to get at God's great powers, perhaps by flattery, or by pressure, or by bargaining, or by hard work? Wouldn't it be better if we could just get God to do whatever we ask?

No, it wouldn't. It wouldn't, because God is wiser than we are, and God loves us. God's will is infinitely better than our will. God sees the total situation, which we don't. And God in his love knows what is best for us in this situation.

If you really want to find peace in your prayer, be sure to put in that part that follows the "Nevertheless." Put yourself into God's hands, and accept whatever way he wants to answer. Of course, you can tell God what you would like to have him do, but then add the part that you are willing to accept whatever he decides. For that way lies peace.

I have one closing thought. The best analogy I ever heard to describe a person's prayer life is to compare it to the relationship between a father and his son. And remember, in this illustration, we are talking about prayer.

When the boy is young, he comes to his father often, wanting love and assurance, and often asking his father to give him things. The more he grows up, the more he asks. As he moves from one age to another in childhood, he still wants things, but he also turns to his father for help when he gets into trouble.

His father always welcomes his son's requests. Sometimes he says yes, but just as often he says no. When he says no, it is because he loves his son, and he is also wiser. Occasionally when his son asks for help, his father says, "No. Get yourself out of this mess." And that too is a response of love.

Through the teenage years, the son sometimes despises his father, thinking he knows nothing. But he still turns to him when he needs something—like money. The father tolerates this immaturity, waiting patiently for his son to grow up.

His son does grow up, and gradually finds more and more respect for his father. Through the years of career building and raising a family, the son turns to his father often, with respect and growing admiration.

His requests for things, and for help, grow less and less. Now he occasionally asks his father for advice, which he respects and follows. Then as the son becomes old, the son often visits his father. They just talk. Maybe the son doesn't ask his father for anything. Often they just sit in silence, enjoying each other's company.

There comes a day when the son tries in his halting way to say thanks to his father for all the love and wisdom and understanding and patience during his life. And when night comes, it is time to go to bed.

"Good night, Father," says the son.

And the father replies, "Good night, son. I'll see you in the morning."

DOWN-TO-EARTH PRAYERS

Scripture: *Luke 11:1-4* When the disciples asked Jesus to teach them to pray, he answered with the familiar Lord's Prayer. This is Luke's version of it.

The Preacher's Notes:

What is a "down-to-earth prayer?" Isn't that an oxymoron?

This sermon explores the way you pray. Except it is the way **you** pray, not the way you are expected to pray like everybody else. Several examples are given, and I hope you agree with me that they are truly down-to-earth in the best sense of that phrase.

DOWN TO EARTH PRAYERS

When I graduated from the seminary and was ordained to the ministry, I was a brash young preacher who was going to set the world on fire. At a youth conference once, I was asked to say the blessing at one of the meals. And so I offered this prayer: "O Lord, we are grateful for this food. But you'll excuse us if we cut this prayer short; we're hungry. Amen."

A moment later, someone came up to me and said, "That was the most down-to-earth prayer I have ever heard."

A down-to-earth prayer?

Many years ago, in Boston, Massachusetts, a minister was asked to offer an invocation at a public meeting in Boston. This eventually became one of the most famous prayers of history. Listen to a part of that prayer:

> "We thank thee for the new life which comes tingling in the boughs of every great or little tree, which is green in the new-ascended grass, and transfigures itself in the flowers to greater righteousness than Solomon ever put on. We thank thee for the seed that the farmer has cradled in the ground, or which thence lifts up its happy face of multitudinous prophecy, telling us of harvests that are to come. We thank thee also for the garment of prophecy with which thou girdest the forests and adornest every tree all around our northern lands. We bless thee for the fresh life which teems in the waters that are about us, and in the little brooks which run among the hills, which warbles in the branches of the trees and hums with new-born insects throughout the peopled land."

How's that for a prayer? The next day, a Boston newspaper reported on that meeting, and it described this prayer as " . . . the finest prayer ever addressed to a Boston audience." Addressed to a Boston audience?

I have always enjoyed the prayer offered by a minister who said, "O Lord Jesus Christ, thou art the ne plus ultra of our desires, the sine qua non of our faith, and the ultima thule of our hopes." It's a good thing God understands Latin!

Are these "down-to-earth" prayers?

Perhaps I am a little bit out of line when I poke fun at people who offer prayers in their own way. Just because they aren't my way of praying doesn't mean they aren't valid. People are different. That means that we pray differently. If someone prays in a way that is different from the way I would say it, is God listening? Of course he is. We're all his children, no matter how we talk to him.

In Marjorie Kinnan Rawlings' delightful book *The Yearling*, a group of backwoods people gathered together at the graveside of a little boy, who had been crippled in mind and body. Penny Baxter then offered this prayer: *O Lord, Almighty God. Was ary one of us to be a-doin' of it, we'd not of brung this pore boy into the world a cripple, and his mind teched. But Lord, you done made it up to him. You made him knowin' and gentle. The birds come to him, and the varmints moved free about him. Lord, hit pleasures us to think that now you've done straightened out them legs and that pore bent back. And Lord, give him a few birds and mebbe a squirrel and a 'coon to keep him comp'ny if it ain't askin' too much to put a few varmints in heaven. Amen.*

That, to me, is prayer at its best. It's not my way of praying, but it was Penny Baxter's, and that's what counts. Each one of us must work out our own approach, our own way of holding conversation with God that is most natural for us.

Several years ago, when our children were growing up, we took turns offering the prayer at meal times. At lunch one day, it was our oldest daughter's turn to pray, and this was her prayer: "Dear God, we thank you for this soup. It's Campbell's Chicken Noodle soup, like they advertise on television. Is it as good as they say it is? We'll know your answer when we taste it. Amen."

How's that for a down-to-earth prayer?

Another example is taken from Malcolm Boyd's book of his own prayers. Malcolm Boyd is an Episcopal priest, and his book contains prayers that he jotted down in the course of his busy ministry. The title of the book is taken from the first prayer in the book: *Are You Running With Me, Jesus?* The prayer goes like this: "*It's morning, Jesus. It's morning, and here's that light and sound all over again. I've got to move fast . . . get into the bathroom, wash up, grab a bite to eat, and run some more. I just don't feel like it, Lord. What I really want to do is get back into bed, pull up the covers, and sleep. All I seem to want today is the big sleep, and here I've got to run all over again. Where am I running? You know these things I can't understand. It's not that I need to have you tell me. What counts most is just that somebody knows, and it's you. That helps a lot. So I'll follow along, okay? But lead, Lord. Now I've got to run. Are you running with me, Jesus?*"

These are down-to-earth prayers . . . different for each one of us.

One day, the disciples came to Jesus and said, "Lord, teach us to pray." Now, these were Jewish men, steeped in the ancient tradition of the Hebrew religion in which prayer was very real. They were men who were living in the presence of Jesus, who walked with him every day. And yet . . . they felt an inadequacy when it came to prayer. And—like us—they would say to Jesus, "Lord, teach us to pray."

Jesus answered them with an outline. This outline, which we know as "The Lord's Prayer," is more familiar to us in the Matthew version than in the Luke version that we read in our Scripture Lesson. But it contains elements of prayer that ought to be included in all of our prayers: praising God, asking for daily bread, seeking forgiveness and help in time of temptation. But it's an outline. How a person prays for these things is an individual matter, and each one of us must do it in our own way.

Sometimes, I must confess, when I pray, I wonder if I'm being heard. The only reason I have enough courage to make this confession is that I suspect that many of you feel that way sometimes. Is anybody really listening? Or is this—literally—a down-to-earth prayer?

Think about this God we are talking to. *Almighty God!* He's way out there somewhere, managing the vast universe. Maybe there are other planets with life forms in distant galaxies that demand his attention. Even if he were interested in this particular tiny planet, with its millions of people, how could he possibly be interested in little old me? Who do I think I am?

In still another book of prayers, now out of print, I came across a prayer that meant something to me. Listen to this prayer, which reflects this frustration, this sense of wondering if there really is somebody out there listening:

> *"Lord, I feel such a fool, talking to you, trying to believe. I'm not sure if you're listening... or laughing... or sleeping... or if you're there at all!*
>
> *"If I can't be honest with you, Lord, I can't be honest with anyone. You are the only person I know who can take it, no matter what I say.*
>
> *"People are offended if I'm honest. They want to hear nice things, sweet words of happiness, gentle hymns to a gentle God smiling somewhere on a red velvet throne.*
>
> *"Well, I'm sick of being phony and I don't like to act as if there's nothing wrong with me, or my friends, or the world, or you.*
>
> *"Sometimes I want to scream at you and let it all out. I have a million unanswered prayers stuck in my craw.*
>
> *"If only I could be positive and really believe! I don't have faith like that, something solid and certain.*
>
> *"I want you to listen when I yell at the sky, pound my pillow, kick the ground, throw stones at the stars, slam doors, or swear at the world.*
>
> *"Perhaps that's not giving all glory to God, as others do,*

with folded hands and frozen face, but for me it means I'm paying you the highest respect there is.
"It means I trust you with the truth—all the truth!"

How's that for an honest prayer? Would you call it "down-to-earth," or did it reach the ears of a God who bends down to listen carefully to each one of his children as they say their honest prayers in their own way?

So when you talk to God, do it your own way. Don't pray like your preacher prays, or use trite expressions. Be yourself. Tell God what's on your mind. Honestly and frankly, talk to him. If you're mad at him, tell him so. If you feel good about something, thank him. If you need help, ask for it. But do it in your own way. And God will listen to you, if you talk to him in your own voice.

THE HARP ON THE WILLOW TREE

Scripture: *Psalms 137 and 139* There couldn't possibly be two more dissimilar Psalms in the Psalter. In the first one, the Psalmist bitterly denounces his captors in Babylon. In the second, the Psalmists sings the praises of the God who is with him even in Exile.

The Preacher's Notes:

These two Psalms reflect different attitudes of prayer: the negative and the positive, or the "how not to do it" verses the "how to do it" prayers. In the world of uncertainty we live in, we could easily say the negative prayer. Let's say the positive one instead.

THE HARP ON THE WILLOW TREE

I find this 137th Psalm fascinating.

The writer of Psalm 137 was a Hebrew who was captured by the Babylonians and taken into exile, far away from his beloved homeland. There, "by the waters of Babylon," he sat down and wept, as he remembered the glories of Zion (Jerusalem). He wouldn't sing; instead he hung his harp on the willow tree, and sat sulking and brooding.

His captors, the Babylonians, taunted him, saying, "Sing us one of your folk songs of Jerusalem," but he wouldn't. He had hung his harp on the willow tree, and there it stayed. In the privacy of his thoughts, he cursed his captors. "How shall I sing the Lord's song in a strange land?" And inside him, his soul began to shrivel and curl up and die.

What if, instead of hanging his harp on the willow tree in sullen resentment, he had actually begun to sing? What if he had run his fingers over the melodious strings of his harp, and began to sing that most comforting of all the songs of Israel:

> *The Lord's my Shepherd, I'll not want.*
> *He makes me down to lie*
> *In pastures green; he leadeth me*
> *The quiet waters by.*

Who can say how much a song like that would have strengthened him? Who knows what courage and peace this might have given to his own family and friends? Who knows what effect this might have had on the Babylonians? Instead, there came out of this period of the Exile this weird song, Psalm 137, beautiful in its haunting way, yet so unlike the other Psalms of the Bible. Somehow, with great feeling and honesty, the writer expresses the homesickness and suffering of his people in exile.

There is something about this song that echoes in our time. Bob Dylon used to sing a song that expressed the same thought:

> *It ain't my day and it ain't my time.*
> *My songs won't sing and my words don't rhyme.*
> *It ain't my day and it ain't my way.*
> *I must be a man of yesterday.*

It is here, I think, that we can identify with the Psalmist. The message of the ancient Hebrew folk song and the modern Bob Dylon folk song seem to say much the same thing: how the singer dislikes life as it is now, and how he longs for life as it used to be . . . the "good ole days."

Of course, there are some good things in our modern life and if we are thoughtful, we would never want to go back to the so-called "good ole days." I can't imagine living here in Florida in the days before air conditioning. Do you remember what it was like before polyester and wrinkle-free clothing? Or cook on a wood stove rather than a gas or electric range, or a microwave. When you had to go to the doctor, there was no penicillin, and surgery was rather primitive. Or travel around the country by horse or train, rather than an air-conditioned car or airplane. Do you remember when you had to write a letter with a pen in hand, or even with that old-fashioned typewriter, rather than a word processor or computer? Do you remember when ice cream was loaded with fat and calories, before the days of fat-free frozen yogurt? And worst of all, before the days of television, you actually had to sit around and talk to each other in the evenings! Good grief!

But having said that, and having paid homage to the god of change, we still cringe a little when we remember fondly the good old days. Progress is good and even indispensable, but when it comes too fast, it brings with it some things that we don't like.

And it could easily lead us to hang our harps on the willow tree and wish for the way things used to be.

The drug culture has grown rampant, thanks to pushers without conscience who prey on innocent young people. Because of this, there is more crime than ever before. When I was a little boy, we never locked our house. You can't do that any more.

Probably the greatest change in our lives came on September 11, 2001, when terrorists struck the World Trade Center, and changed our way of life. So many things have changed since that terrible day, and we now know what it's like to live in a world that threatens us.

Sometimes we feel like we want to sit down by the rivers of Babylon and weep, as we remember Zion. *How shall we sing the Lord's song in a strange land?*

One answer to that is to follow the example of the writer of the 137th Psalm. And many do. We yearn for the good old days, when life was simpler, and we loudly condemn the present. How we wish we could stop this mad rush into the future, and go back, go back, go back. But we can't. And so many of us do what the Psalmist did; he hung his harp on the willow tree and sat down by the waters of Babylon and cursed his captors.

Notice what happens to the Psalmist as he develops his song. Slowly the mood of the song begins to shift from one of melancholy and wistfulness to a bitter curse on Babylon. This Psalm, more than any other place in the Bible, expresses such brutal hatred and desire for revenge that we wonder why it is even in the Bible!

Remember how the song ends?

> *O Babylon, Babylon, you destroyer!*
> *Happy is the man who repays you*
> *For all you did to us!*
> *Happy is he who shall seize your children*
> *And dash them against the rock!*

Now, these charming sentiments were not the utterances of the Jewish hoodlum element, the Hebrew mafia. This was an exclamation of an upstanding gentleman, a loyal patriotic citizen, an average, middle-class, church-going religious person.

How easily it can happen to any of us. When we hang our harps on the willow tree, we can very easily slide into the trap of bitterness, of cursing our captors. We can attack the terrible moral situation of our times, when sex and vulgarity and blasphemy and immorality are held up in public with no sense of shame or proper conduct. What used to be a sin is now acceptable and popular. How easy to slide into a negative approach to life, hang our harps on the willow tree, and be happy if all the pot-pushers, the pornographers, the terrorists, the rapists, the criminals, and everybody else who does such horrible things in our time, would be dashed against a rock!

That's one way to sing the Lord's song in a strange land. Take a negative approach to life, hang your harp on the willow tree, and denounce, bemoan, complain, and curse your captors.

But somewhere in that foreign land of Babylon, so far from their beloved homeland, someone else was singing a different song, singing and composing what has become one of the most beautiful of all the Psalms of the Bible. I hope it will become one of your favorites after contrasting it with the 137th Psalm. I'm talking about Psalm 139, just two Psalms away from the 137th, but what a contrast! It sings a song of praise to God, an expression of faith that even here in Babylon, God is in charge!

> *Whither shall I go from thy Spirit?*
> *Or whither shall I flee from thy presence?*
> *If I ascend to heaven, thou art there!*
> *If I make my bed in Sheol, thou art there!*
> *If I take the wings of the morning*
> *And dwell in the uttermost parts of the sea,*
> *Even there thy hand shall lead me,*
> *And thy right hand shall hold me.*

Here was a person who found serenity and peace in the Babylonian exile. While the other Psalmist hung his harp on the willow tree, this one was singing! From one Psalmist came negative thoughts and curses, from the other positive thoughts and praises. One Psalmist turned in upon himself, and began to shrivel up and die, while the other was able to feel at ease and live his life with poise and cheerfulness, even in the worst of days.

I see nothing in the 139th Psalm that tells us that the Psalmist approved of his situation. He was not saying, "Isn't it nice to be a Babylonian captive, and you know what they say, While in Babylonia, do as the Babylonians do." No. He missed Jerusalem just as much as the other Psalmist, but he was singing! He had accepted his situation, and had learned to live with it, live with it positively and cheerfully!

So . . . how can we sing the Lord's song in a strange land? How can we maintain a cheerful and serene outlook, rather than the bitterness and gloom of that other Psalmist? What was the secret of the positive Psalmist?

It's obvious. The 139th Psalmist had a bedrock faith in God. God never changes, even though the circumstances do. This is a God who towers o'er the wrecks of time. This was his secret: although what he saw around him would lead to pessimism, he took a very optimistic view of God. God is still in charge. He is not 'way back there in Jerusalem; he is here, in Babylon. And so he sings:

> *Even here thy hand shall lead me;*
> *Thy right hand shall hold me.*

So no matter how much you disapprove of the terrible things that happen in our century, don't hang your harp on the willow tree and curse your captors. Instead, sing! Sing the beautiful songs of Zion. Sing about God, who is alive and well even here in Babylon!

Now let's listen again to the lilting melody and lyric poetry of his song, as it is phrased for us so beautifully in the Living Bible:

> *O Lord, you have examined my heart and know everything*
> *about me. You know when I sit or stand. When far away you*
> *know my every thought. You chart the path ahead of me, and tell*

me where to stop and rest. Every moment you know where I am. You both precede and follow me, and place your hand of blessing on my head.

This is too glorious, too wonderful, to believe! I can never be lost to your Spirit! If I go up to heaven, you are there; if I go down to the place of the dead, you are there. If I ride the morning winds to the farthest oceans, even there your hand will guide me, your strength will support me!

How precious it is, Lord, to realize that you are thinking about me constantly! I can't even count how many times a day your thoughts turn toward me. And when I wake in the morning, you are still thinking of me!

Search me, O God, and know my heart; test my thoughts. Point out anything you find in me that makes you sad, and lead me along the path of everlasting life.

And that's the way to sing the Lord's song in a foreign land!

KING DAVID'S SWEETEST SONG

Scripture: *Psalm 23* contains the basic text. *I Samuel 23:10-13a* and *I Chronicles 29:10-15,18* tell stories illustrating the way David prayed. The first story is set in his youth, when he was a fugitive. The second is in his old age, when he was not far from death.

The Preacher's Notes:

When was the 23rd Psalm written? When David was young or old? My guess is when he was old, because it is the prayer of a very mature man of wisdom. The other two prayers in the Scripture readings reflect the changes in David's life as he grew older . . . and changes in our prayer life also.

KING DAVID'S SWEETEST SONG

David the king was known as the "Sweet Singer of Israel." No one knows how many of the Psalms attributed to him he really wrote, but most scholars agree that he wrote the 23rd Psalm. That, everyone agrees, was his sweetest song.

When did David write the 23rd Psalm? Was it when he was a boy, a young shepherd with a flock of sheep? Perhaps. You can picture him in the Judean wilderness, seated on a rock, his lyre on his lap, watching the sheep, and singing his songs to the sheep to help pass the lonely hours. His active mind may well have produced many of his Psalms during those long lonely days. Maybe he did write the 23rd Psalm when he was a boy.

Or maybe not. All the Bible commentaries that I consulted, along with the scholars who dig deeply into this sort of thing— there is a consensus of opinion that this Psalm was written in the later years of his life, or at least, the poem composed as a boy was rewritten and revised as an adult. The Shepherd Psalm is the work of a mature man, not a boy. Only a lifetime of experience could produce a Psalm like that.

I can picture David in his old age, death approaching, his body worn out and giving him all kinds of problems. But there's nothing wrong with his mind. It is sharper and more alert than it ever was in his whole life. He sees things clearly now, things he didn't have time to think about in his active youth. He recalls those beautiful casual days of youth when all he had to do was care for a flock of sheep. Picture him on the rooftop of his palace in Jerusalem, alone, thinking about his long life, perhaps comparing his carefree youthful days with his present situation.

He was still a shepherd. He had exchanged the flock of sheep for the nation of Israel. He had unified that nation, established its borders, fought wars to maintain its existence, struggled with rebellion, rebellion even in his own family, dealt with treachery, and established the line of succession through his son Solomon. These are his thoughts as he sits on the roof of his palace, thinking back, looking at his life in perspective. And with the wisdom of maturity, the shepherd of Israel puts it into words: *"The Lord is my Shepherd; I shall not want."*

I first read these stories of King David when I was a young man going to school. I loved them. They were adventure stories, stories of an ambitious young man who gained a kingdom. Stories as entertaining to read as any novel. A few years ago, those stories found their way into two of my books about King David. As I struggled with these stories and thought about King David in his old age, I tried to look at life through David's perspective.

Over the course of his life, David changed. This was a normal change, which happens to all of us over the years. I can see that now, because many of the changes in my own life were the same as David's.

There was no turning point in David's life, but there were certain milestones that he passed, milestones that were more of a symbol of the gradual change that was occurring. Like the time when King David led his troops into battle, and at the height of the action, David was hard pressed to defend himself. He became weak, and was in danger of losing his life. One of his officers moved in and rescued him, brought him safely out of the battle. They told him then that he was too old to fight battles now. They tactfully said, "Why should we risk snuffing out the light of Israel?" Let the younger men do the fighting; David should stay in Jerusalem and manage the affairs of the nation, rather than fight battles.

I wonder how David felt about passing this milestone in his life? Did he miss being the active young adventurer, who would wildly fling himself into battle, face danger, endure hardships, enjoy the company of brave companions and beautiful women—a young man, with the joy and exhilaration of youth? Now that was gone. Things had changed; he was getting old. Did he learn to accept that? Did he shed a tear over his lost youth? Did he make a fool of himself by trying to somehow recapture his lost youth, trying to prove to himself and everybody else that he was still young? Or . . . did he accept those changes gracefully—even gratefully—and look forward to the quiet years ahead?

Jack Benny used to say that life begins at 40. Before I was 40, I used to think Jack Benny was just whistling in the dark, making the best of things when he really was sorry he wasn't young any more. I don't think that any more.

Remember that song that goes: "Those were the days, my friends; those were the days." Change that: "*These* are the days, my friends; *these* are the days!" I often quote Robert Browning, who said, "Grow old along with me; the best is yet to be; the last of life, for which the first was made!"

You've heard the old saying: "Youth is a wonderful time of life; too bad it has to be wasted on young people." I'd like to paraphrase that this way: "Old age is a wonderful time of life; it's a good thing it isn't wasted on young people, who would never be able to appreciate it like we do."

This is what I see in King David, as he grows older. He has changed. His priorities are different. His values are different. His whole perspective on life is different.

When he was young, he was the dashing adventurer, who rode into battle singing. Now he is old . . . and thoughtful. He has time to pause and look around. He sees life in all its beauty. He sees a misty mountain scene, or the gentle lapping of waves on a peaceful shore, or the perfection of one small flower, or the flight of a graceful bird, or he listens to a bird sing on a quiet evening. And he smiles, for these things bring him peace.

Probably the biggest change in King David's life was his faith. His understanding of his relationship with God was completely different from his youth. It was fun to compare two of his prayers recorded in the Bible. The first one he prayed in the wilderness when he was fleeing from King Saul . . . his youth. The other was one of the last prayers before his death. What a change! The first was breathless, exciting, calling on God to help him in battle and confound his enemies. He prayed for strength and courage, for guidance in the course of the battle. The other prayer was much different: thoughtful, aware of life, aware of his family, asking God to bless those who would take his responsibilities after he was gone. The youthful prayer was, "Lord, help me to do these things." The mature prayer was, "Lord, thank you for what you have done." These two prayers exemplify the change that had taken place in David's religious life through the years.

That's why it makes sense that the 23rd Psalm was written when David was old. This sounds like a mature person's poem of praise. In this Psalm, he is not the ambitious, energetic young warrior going into battle. He is rather the thoughtful, peaceful old man, who has been there—and back, who knows who he is and where he is going, and knows what is important.

When David was young, his faith was a challenge. God was urging him to go, go, go. He was up and doing great things, and God was with him. His faith was a spur, a goad, to greater and greater achievements.

But no longer. He walks slowly and serenely with God now, There is a confidence in this walk, a security, knowing that all is well between him and the heavenly deity. He is at ease. Comfortable. And it's a good feeling.

And when the time came for David to face that last great adventure, he smiled and embraced it. Death was a friend, waiting for him at the end of a long journey.

And he smiled, unafraid.

GRASSHOPPER BURDENS

Scripture: *Ecclesiastes 11:19-12:8* This is a very gloomy picture of old age, using the metaphor of people inside an old house waiting for a storm. You might want to balance this with the joyful admonition of Paul in *Philippians 4:4-9*.

The Preacher's Notes:

This is the picture of old age, presented by "Gloomy Gus," the author of that enigmatic Book of Ecclesiastes. This sermon makes the argument that Gloomy Gus was really not an old man, but a young man who thought he knew what it is like to be old. How wrong he was.

If an old man had written this description of people in an old house waiting for the storm, it would have been much different. It would be positive, peaceful and unafraid. And filled with joy.

GRASSHOPPER BURDENS

Have you heard any of those jokes lately that begin, "You know you're getting old when . . . . " There are hundreds of them going around now. Every time I hear a new one, it seems to replace the favorite I had last week. This week my favorite goes like this: You know you're getting old when you look down and see that your sox are wrinkled. But when you bend down to straighten them out, you realize that you aren't even wearing sox.

The writer of the book of Ecclesiastes might have started his last chapter with the words, "You know you're getting old when . . . . " He described life as an old person with a metaphor of an old house with a big storm blowing up.

Growing old is very unpopular in our society. It shouldn't be. Actually, it is a privilege. Think of the people who die young, who never have the chance to experience old age. If you're old, don't be ashamed of it. Let's quit worshipping the god of Youth. Being old is fun.

However, let's not abuse this privilege. I think the writer of the book of Ecclesiastes did. He was certainly a Gloomy Gus. He told us how awful it is to grow old. Like everything else, he says, growing old is vanity and useless and striving after wind.

Well, it probably would be, if you looked at it like Ecclesiastes does. He's like the person who wrote that old prayer:

> *Lord, thou knowest better than I know myself that I am getting older . . . . Seal my lips, O Lord, on the aches and pains. They are increasing, and the love of rehearsing them is becoming sweeter as the years go by.*

One of the cardinal rules to follow as you grow older is: When someone says to you, "How are you?" . . . *don't tell them!*

The writer of Ecclesiastes was like that. His description of old age is rather tedious. He tells us that being old is like a large house just as a big storm is blowing up. *The keepers of the house tremble,* he says, referring to the way your hands shake when you grow old. No, that's not necessarily Parkinson's disease, just old age. *The strong men are bent*—calcium deficiency, osteoporosis, and your shoulders slump and your legs are bowed. *The grinders cease . . .* when you put them in a jar in the bathroom at night. *Your work is put away for the night* to get ready for that final storm, as you sit in your recliner and do little else but watch television all day. *You look dimly through the windows,* using bifocals and concerned about those creeping cataracts. *The front doors that overlook the street are shut,* because you are more and more afraid that someone will harm you, so you keep your doors locked. *The sound of the grinding is low,* and you are constantly saying to someone, "What did you say?" *All the daughters of music are brought low,* and your voice squeaks a little when you sing. The people in the house are *afraid of high places,* because falling and breaking one of those brittle bones is one of your greatest fears. *The almond tree is in blossom.* The blossoms are white, the color of your hair.

The grasshopper becomes a burden. That's one of my favorite expressions now-a-days. When I have trouble doing something that a few years ago was easy and no problem at all, I call it a "grasshopper burden." And there are a lot more of them now than there used to be.

And so you sit there in the house looking out. It's getting darker and darker outside. You just sit and wait—wait for the storm. The storm is death, and it's coming . . . coming . . . .

And then the storm strikes the old house! You look out in the courtyard where the well is, and you see the destruction the tempest brings. *The silver cord that holds the bucket is snapped, the golden bowl* (or bucket) *is broken, the pitcher* (that you keep at the well for water) *is shattered, and even the big wheel over the well is smashed.*

You . . . are . . . *dead!*

This is the last storm for this old house, and *the mourners go about in the streets, and the body is laid to rest, for the breath of life has gone from it, gone to God who gave it.*

Old age is awful, says Ecclesiastes, with its miseries, its aches and pains, its boredom, its uselessness, its waiting for death. Like everything else in his book, old age is vanity, useless, like chasing the wind. What a sour old man he must have been! I'll bet the old curmudgeon had acid indigestion when he wrote this.

What kind of a dried-up old prune was this so-called "preacher" who wrote this Old Testament book? This was not King Solomon. Every commentary, every responsible Bible scholar, agrees with that. It was written about seven or eight hundred years after the time of Solomon, and ascribed to him as the custom was. But it was like putting into Solomon's mouth the author's own ideas of what life is like when you grow old.

You know what I think? I'll bet my bi-focals against your hearing aid that he wasn't old at all. I think he must have been a young person, not an old man. There are several hints and clues along the way in the twelve chapters of this book, but nowhere is it more obvious than in the twelfth chapter. This was a youth trying to tell us what old age is like, and he didn't know what he was talking about. This is a pretty shallow view of old age. All he can see is what is on the outside. To an outsider—that is, someone who is not old himself—it may look like old age consists of decrepitude and miseries, creaky bones and rheumy joints, bent shoulders, grouchiness and depression—Curmudgeon time!—wretchedness beyond recounting, although some of us seem to be pretty good at recounting them. That's all this young man sees, and it's a very bleak picture. No wonder a young person says to himself, "Boy! I never want to get old!"

But there's more, much more. That young writer of Ecclesiastes sees only what is on the outside. He has no idea of what it's like on the inside. Old age has its compensations for the physical failings. And that's what prompted Robert Browning to say:

Grow old along with me,
The best is yet to be . . .
The last of life, for which the first was made.

There's more to that poem, and I'll quote you the rest of it in a moment.

The problem with the author of Ecclesiastes, besides being young, was that he was sour. To him, everything was vanity, useless, like chasing the wind. He reminds me of the professional "aginner" who is agin this, and agin that, who has a wall-to-wall grouch built into the little room he lives in.

What would happen if that writer of Ecclesiastes would suddenly come face to face with Jesus Christ? What if he could see life as an adventure, a challenge, a victory, rather than striving after the wind? What if he were to discover the joy of life that a cheerful Christian knows? What if he, when he reached old age himself, took this optimistic mental attitude and turned it on during his retirement years?

Well, I predict that he would find Robert Browning was right: The best is yet to be. Instead of dwelling on the physical aches and pains, he would look for the good things of old age. And he would find plenty, if only he would look.

There's freedom. Someone said that the definition of freedom is when the last kid leaves home and the last dog dies. Now you're doing what you want to do. Now, at last, you're free.

There's beauty. When you were young, you may have been too busy to look at and appreciate beauty. Now, as you grow older, beauty surrounds you and enthralls you. There comes a realization God is a God of beauty, who fathers forth in creative splendor in the land, and to see his handiwork is to see the Creator himself. You see so many things when you're older that you missed when you were young.

There are opportunities now to do things for others. When you were young, you were busy with your job, your family, your own little sphere of responsibility. Now you have time to look around, and you see so much that needs to be done, so many people who need you. You can pick your own way of expressing your love for others, and this meets a very deep need in your life that you never recognized before.

And of course there are grandchildren. You young parents think it's nice to have children; wait till you have grandchildren! There's nothing like it. One of my favorite cartoons shows Momma holding her grandson on her lap. She says, "Grandma loves Chuckie." The child responds, "Chuckie wuvs Gamma." Then Momma turns to us the readers and says, "Grandchildren are wonderful! No trauma, no aggravation, it's all fun. The secret of life is to skip having children and go directly to grandchildren!"

That's not entirely true, because it's a real joy to have children. But as a grandparent, when the kid gets weepy on one end and wet on the other, you can just hand him back to his parents. "All the privileges and none of the responsibilities," they always say about grandparenting.

Something especially nice happened to my wife and me a few years ago. We went to visit our granddaughter and her husband. She was halfway through her first pregnancy, and she took us with her to the doctor's office to see the ultra sound, when the nurse held a little tool on the enlarged stomach and we could see inside the tummy. And there was the baby, right up there on the monitor. We could see the head, with its eye sockets, its nose, its mouth, and the little hands opening and closing, and the feet kicking against its mother. What a lively little child! And then we heard the nurse say those magic words, "Everything looks normal." She told us that it was a girl, and I saw my grandson-in-law wipe the tears from his eyes. It was a precious moment for all of us, as my wife and I were introduced to our first great-grandchild. What an unexpected bonus of old age that was for us!

There are so many unexpected bonuses of old age, which you never expected when you were young. Probably one of the best surprises of old age is how much more your faith means to you, how much peace of mind it gives you.

There is something a little bit different about the faith of an older person. He has changed. His religious perception is not the same as it was when he was young. Different, yes, but not worse. Like many other things about growing old, you don't just get older, you get better!

But it was different. It isn't the exciting, adventurous faith of the youth, spurring you into action and leading you into new and thrilling adventures. It is rather a quiet faith, deeply personal, and very meaningful. God is a companion, an old friend. This is comforting, in its own way. And it brings immeasurable peace.

It brings security. When you were young, your faith was a frenzied quest, struggling with doubts, striving with all your powers to know the meaning of God in your life, and trying to understand some of the implications of your Christian faith as it applies to your job, your family, your social life, your life style. Now, when you are older, there is no feeling of urgency. These things have been settled for you. You now feel secure in your faith. You can lean back and relax and enjoy your faith. You know where you have been, and you know where you are going. And God is going with you, amiably leading you, not pushing and challenging you. So relax. You have a comfortable relationship with your Heavenly Father, and it is very, very pleasant.

Now listen to the rest of Robert Browning's poem:

> *Grow old along with me!*
> *The best is yet to be,*
> *The last of life, for which the first was made.*
> *Our times are in his hand*
> *Who says, "A whole I planned.*
> *Youth shows but half; trust God, see all, nor be afraid!"*

So when the storm comes, you're ready. It's not like the old house in Ecclesiastes, with doubts and fears beating upon the old structure, and nothing to do but wait and dwell upon the horrors of the storm. On the contrary, it is more like looking forward to the dawn after a night storm, when everything will be fresh and new, washed clean, with complete joy in the morning. In the face of death, there is peace.

It has been said often enough that the Old Testament is incomplete without the New Testament. This is nowhere more evident than in the final chapter of Ecclesiastes. This is a negative, pessimistic book, and its advice to both old and young is shallow and incomplete.

So let's add a new dimension to the metaphor of the old house waiting for the storm. Let's look inside. Do you see gloom and doom in there? No. You see smiles, laughter, happiness, even people telling jokes that begin with, "You know you're getting old when . . . . " And best of all, you see peace.

Now, look again into that old house. You see someone else in there with the occupants of the house. You know who that someone is. The writer of Ecclesiastes didn't know him. But you do. And he makes all the difference in the world.

What storm? There's nothing but sunshine in this old house!

OLD HUNDREDTH

Scripture: *Psalm 100* This is one of the more familiar Psalms of the Bible, beginning with *Make a joyful noise to the Lord, all the lands!*

The Preacher's Notes:

This Psalm, as it appears in the Bible, should be a song of joy. But when we sing "Old Hundredth," the paraphrase of this Psalm in the Presbyterian Church's hymnal, it becomes a dirge. This song, to be true to the spirit of the Psalm, should be loud and exuberant and expressively happy.

The sermon is broken up into a study of the four parts of the Psalm, which I suppose is a homiletics professor's idea of an expository sermon. It tells us why the Psalmist was so joyful.

I never did think this sermon was among my best, but maybe you will agree with that stuffy judge who awarded it first place in the Expository Sermons category.

OLD HUNDREDTH

In your imagination, come back with me into time, back about twenty-five hundred years. The date is approximately 500 B.C. The place is Jerusalem. The exile is over, and the people have come home to Jerusalem after about a century of captivity in a foreign country. The city is new. The Temple is new. There is that new feeling, that starting-over feeling, when the nation feels young and fresh. Here we are in Jerusalem on a festival day, and it's time to worship God.

Look there! What a magnificent sight!

Winding through the streets of Jerusalem is a body of Hebrew men, led by a group of Levite singers. They approach the Temple. As they march, they sing, and their voices are loud and triumphant. Do you feel it? There is a vibrant joy, a thrill of excitement, in their song!

In keeping with the spirit of Hebrew music, we hear a kind of chant, but it is certainly joyful! The Levites and others are walking slowly, but with a spring in their step and a smile on their faces. The music is bold and cheerful. Let's listen carefully to it, and we can hear the ancient Hebrew words translated for us by the Living Bible into English:

> *Shout with joy before the Lord, O earth!*
> *Obey him gladly; come before him, singing with joy!*
> *Try to realize what this means: the Lord is God!*
> *He made us; we are his people,*
> > *The sheep of his pasture!*

And there is the Temple before them, in its entire splendor. And there, at the Temple gates, in the inner court, another group of Hebrews waits for them. Another Levite choir! And they are all primed and rehearsed with a response to the approaching choir:

> *Go through his open gates with great thansgiving!*
> *Enter his courts with praise!*
> *Give thanks to him and bless his name!*
> *For the Lord is always good,*
> *He is always loving and kind,*
> *And his faithfulness goes on and on*
> > *to each succeeding generation!*

The choirs meet, the singing merges, and the worship at the Temple has begun.

What strikes me more than anything else about this experience that we saw in our imagination is the joy of the occasion. The tenor of the Hundredth Psalm is obviously happy. This is particularly true of the first verse. Any time this psalm is sun by any worshipping congregation, it *must* be sung with great joy!

My earliest recollections of church include the singing of "Old Hundredth." In the dignified reserved congregation in which I grew up, this was the opening hymn Sunday after Sunday, going back to the time Adam and Eve founded that church. It was a very old-fashioned, straight-laced congregation, and every Sunday the magnificent pipe organ brought everyone to their feet and they sang the Sixteenth Century paraphrase of Psalm 100*:

> *All people that on earth do dwell,*
> *Sing to the Lord with cheerful voice.*
> *Him serve with mirth, his praise forth tell*
> *Come ye before him and rejoice.*

... and if anyone so much as smiled, I'm sure they would have thrown him out!

---

*To be spoken slowly and somberly, with a deep frown!

The tune of Old Hundredth is a little too solemn to express the jubilant excitement of this psalm. The words of that old Geneva paraphrase don't catch the feeling of joy that is there. But if you think the Presbyterians botched it up, you should see what the Methodists did to it! This hymn, paraphrased by Isaac Watts, with the first stanza altered by John Wesley, reads like this:

Before Jehovah's awesome throne,
Ye nations, bow with sacred joy;
Know that the Lord is God alone,
He can create, and he destroy;
He can create, and he destroy!

That is a very powerful hymn, expressing the greatness of God over all the nations, but that isn't the 100th Psalm! Any paraphrase that omits the note of joyous exaltation from this psalm is missing the point.

The best paraphrase I have found is this one:

O shout for joy unto the Lord,
Earth's people far and near!
With gladness serve the Lord, O come
To him with songs of cheer!

Now, *that's* the way the 100th Psalm should be sung! It captures the true spirit of this song of praise and joy.

I found that paraphrase in a songbook of the Reformed Presbyterian Church, and in that small conservative denomination, they sing nothing but psalms. The only clue to its origin was the title, which was "Glasgow," so I assume it has a Scottish origin. No wonder Queen Elizabeth I scornfully referred to the Scottish Psalter as "those Geneva jigs!"

How appropriate that we approach the Lord in worship with joy! The second verse of the psalm tells us why, as translated by the New English Bible:

> *Know that the Lord is God!*
> *He made us, and we are his own, his people,*
> *the flock which he shepherds.*

This is a very good reason to be so joyous: because God is God, and we are his!

The Hebrews particularly were very much aware of this strong tie to their Covenant-making and Covenant-keeping God. This was the God who made and kept his ancient agreements with his chosen people. These Covenants were sealed in the blood of the paschal lamb that night when they left Egypt, as described in the book of Exodus, and they were aware of the Covenant-keeping God through the wilderness, in the Promised Land, through the Exile and the Return. No wonder when they came to the Temple to worship, they came with joy! They had a lot to be joyful about. They felt very secure with the God who established their nation, redeemed them, and nurtured them. They belonged to him; they were his people, his flock.

We can say the same thing about our Covenant-making and Covenant-keeping God. Our New Covenant was sealed by the blood of the Lamb also, with the New Testament meaning of that phrase. The early Church found much to celebrate each Sunday. In fact, they changed the worship time from the Hebrew Sabbath (that's Saturday) to the Lord's Day (Sunday) to celebrate every week the day Jesus rose from the dead. Each Sunday, then, was an Easter celebration. No wonder they celebrated with triumphant joy, because *he lives!*

Even their funerals reflected this note of joy. Why not? They firmly believed (and we still do) that for the Christian, death is not an end but a beginning. It is a time to celebrate the resurrection, to rejoice that death has been conquered, and eternal life awaits us beyond the grave. Even in the valley of the shadow of death, rejoice!

All worship should be characterized by this note of joy. Our Covenant God is present, to welcome us to his Temple and to call our attention to him. *He made us, and we are his!* He bought us with an exorbitant price, and so we are doubly his. We are his people; he is our God. We are his flock, he is our Shepherd. We are his children; he is our Father.

Therefore, *make a joyful noise, serve him with gladness, come into his presence with singing* . . . and rejoice! For we are his people, and he shepherds us.

The third verse calls on us to worship God with thanksgiving, as translated by the Jerusalem Bible:

> *Walk through his gates giving thanks,*
> *enter his courts praising him,*
> *give thanks to him, bless his name!*

The title above the 100th Psalm reads, "A Psalm for the Thank Offering." Evidently it was one of many psalms they used when they brought a thank offering to the Temple. We in our time have an annual Thanksgiving service, but there ought to be thanksgiving offered at every service of worship.

And we do. In our bulletin there is a prayer of thanksgiving. Do you see where it is? In connection with the offering! Because thanksgiving and thank offering go together. How appropriate it is to say thanks to God with our lips and with our money!

Psalm 96 says:

> *Ascribe to the Lord the glory due his Name!*
> *Bring an offering, and come into his courts!* (RSV)

This is one of the best ways to praise God: by giving him a gift as a part of the worship service.

I hope none of you thinks an offering is just a collection. A collection implies gathering up some money so we can pay our bills. An offering is more: it is an act of worship in which we give something to God. And the prayer with which we dedicate it should always contain a note of thanksgiving. With these gifts we say thanks to God.

But there is something more involved in this act of thank offering. The best way to worship God is to give ourselves to him, as symbolized in the giving of money. Notice that it comes at the end of our worship service. A climax. Our final act of dedication before we leave the worship service.

Therefore, *enter his gates with thanksgiving . . . bring an offering, and come into his courts!*

Why? That's in the last verse of the Hundredth Psalm. Because . . .

> *The Lord is always good!*
> *He is always loving and kind,*
> *and his faithfulness goes on and on*
> *to each succeeding generation.*

I'm sure those Hebrews as they approached the Temple that day singing their psalm of joy, each one had his own burdens. Look at them again, in your imagination. One of them has health problems; you can tell by his stumbling step, the way he's hunched over, and his shortness of breath. Another has a wife at home who is sick, and he is worried about her. Still another has recently lost a loved one, and the sorrow weighs heavily upon him. And another has financial problems that worry him. And another hangs his head in shame, troubled by a past sin. And another . . . and another . . . and another . . . each one of them walking in that procession to the Temple has his own needs and burdens and worries.

But look closely at this group of worshippers.

Something is happening in the singing of that joyous song. They are giving thanks! Their attention is focused not on their problems, but on God! And God is good! His steadfast love is not something that comes and goes, but it endures forever. And his constancy goes on and on, from one generation to another.

As they sing their song of joy and thanksgiving, their steps become lighter, and their burden—while it doesn't go away—is not quite so heavy. Some unseen presence walks beside them, sharing that burden. Look at them! Their step is a little stronger, their shoulders straighten, and they are smiling! And listen! There's that vibrant note of joy and thanksgiving in their song!

We too sing that song of joy. We sing it with gladness, as a celebration, a thanksgiving. We sing it with smiles, with head lifted high, with hearts rejoicing! The burden that each one of us carries is not quite so heavy now, because we have lifted our voices and our hearts in praise to God. Therefore, *Give thanks to God, bless his name, for he is always good, he is always loving and kind, and his faithfulness goes on and on to each succeeding generation!*

What a magnificent Psalm is Old Hundredth! *Come into God's presence with joy,"* it sings, *for God is God, and we are his. Give thanks, because God is good, constantly loving us, and this is forever!*

Let's respond to the Psalmists invitation to worship God with joy!

BVG